Empirical Studies of the Therapeutic Hour

Empirical Studies of the
Therapeutic Hour

Edited by Robert F. Bornstein and Joseph M. Masling

American Psychological Association • Washington, DC

Published by
American Psychological Association
750 First Street, NE
Washington, DC 20002

Copies may be ordered from
APA Order Department
P.O. Box 92984
Washington, DC 20090-2984

In the United Kingdom, Europe, Africa, and the Middle East, copies may be ordered from
American Psychological Association
3 Henrietta Street
Covent Garden
London WC2E 8LU
England

Typeset in Palatino by EPS Group Inc., Easton, MD

Printer: Braun-Brumfield, Inc., Ann Arbor, MI
Jacket designer: Berg Design, Albany, NY
Technical/production editor: Valerie Montenegro

Volumes 1, 2, and 3 of the series Empirical Studies of Psychoanalytic Theories, edited by Joseph Masling, were published by The Analytic Press, Hillsdale, NJ.

Library of Congress Cataloging-in-Publication Data
Empirical studies of the therapeutic hour / edited by Robert F. Bornstein
    and Joseph M. Masling.—1st ed.
        p.   cm.—(Empirical studies of psychoanalytic theories; vol. 8)
    Includes bibliographical references and indexes.
    ISBN 1-55798-526-X (cloth : acid-free paper)
    1. Psychoanalysis—Research.   2. Psychoanalysis—
Evaluation.   3. Psychodynamic psychotherapy—
Research.   4. Psychodynamic psychotherapy—Evaluation.   I. Bornstein,
Robert F.   II. Masling, Joseph M.   III. Series.
RC506.E457   1998
616.89'17—dc21   98-36423
                                                                              CIP

British Library Cataloguing-in-Publication Data
A CIP record is available from the British Library.

Printed in the United States of America
First edition

To Mary and Annette,
whose support, patience, and insight have
enhanced these volumes in countless ways

Contents

Contributors

Mosen Aryan, PhD, is Assistant Professor and Co-Director of Biostatistics and Information Management at the Mount Sinai Medical Center, Division of Psychiatry. Dr. Aryan's current research interest is outcome measures in disease management programs.

John S. Auerbach, PhD, is a staff psychologist and Coordinator of the Post-Traumatic Stress Program at the Mountain Home Veterans Affairs Medical Center. He is also a Clinical Associate Professor in the Department of Psychiatry and Behavioral Sciences at the James H. Quillen College of Medicine at East Tennessee State University and a Research Affiliate in the Department of Psychiatry at the Yale University School of Medicine. His research interests include borderline disorders, narcissism, and the relationships among representational processes, intersubjectivity, and the development of the self.

Sidney J. Blatt, PhD, is Professor in the Departments of Psychiatry and Psychology at Yale University and Chief of the Psychology Section of the Department of Psychiatry. He is a graduate of the Western New England Psychoanalytic Institute and a member of its faculty. His primary interest is in mental representations— their development, their differential impairment in various forms of psychopathology, and their change during treatment. He has been a visiting scholar at the Hampstead Child Therapy Centre in London (now the Anna Freud Centre), the Tavistock Centre and the Warburg Institute for Renaissance Studies, and the Hebrew University of Jerusalem, where he was a Fulbright Senior Research Fellow. Dr. Blatt is the author or coauthor of four books and coeditor of two others, and has published widely in psychoanalysis and clinical psychology. He has received awards for distinguished contributions to research from the Society for Personality Assessment and from the Association of Medical School Professors of Psychology.

Robert F. Bornstein, PhD, is Professor of Psychology at Gettysburg College. He has written numerous articles on perception without awareness and has published widely on the dynamics of dependent personality traits. Bornstein wrote *The Dependent Personality* (1993); coedited (with Thane Pittman) *Perception Without Awareness: Cognitive, Clinical and Social Perspectives* (1992); coedited (with Joseph Masling) Volumes 4 through 7 in the Empirical Studies of Psychoanalytic Theories series (1993, 1994, 1996, 1998); and received the Society for Personality Assessment's 1995 Walter Klopfer Award for Distinguished Contribution to the Literature on Personality Assessment.

Marshall Bush, PhD, is a training and supervising analyst at the San Francisco Psychoanalytic Institute, and an Assistant Clinical Professor in the Department of Psychiatry at the University of California, San Francisco. He is a member of the San Francisco Psychotherapy Research Group.

Mary Beth Connolly, PhD, is an Assistant Professor in the Center for Psychotherapy Research in the Department of Psychiatry at the University of Pennsylvania. Dr. Connolly received her PhD from Vanderbilt University in 1996. She has published 16 articles and chapters on psychotherapy research.

Paul Crits-Christoph, PhD, is Associate Professor in Psychiatry and Director of the Center for Psychotherapy Research at the Department of Psychiatry, University of Pennsylvania, where he has been since receiving his PhD in 1984 from Yale University. He has published more than 100 articles and chapters on psychotherapy research and has coauthored or edited several books, including *Understanding Transference: The CCRT Method* (1990; with Lester Luborsky); *Who Will Benefit From Psychotherapy? Predicting Therapeutic Outcomes* (1988; with Lester Luborsky, Jim Mintz, and Arthur Auerbach); *Handbook of Short-Term Dynamic Therapy* (1991; with Jacques Barber); and *Dynamic Therapies for Psychiatric Disorders* (1995; with Jacques Barber).

Hartvig Dahl, MD, is an Emeritus Professor in the Department of Psychiatry at the State University of New York Health Science Center at Brooklyn. He is still doing full-time psychoanalytic research, as he has been for most of the past 33 years.

Suzanne M. Gassner, PhD, is a training and supervising analyst of the San Francisco Psychoanalytic Institute and an adjunct faculty member of the Department of Psychology at the University of California, Berkeley. She has a private practice in Berkeley, California and is a member of the San Francisco Psychotherapy Research Group.

Stephen J. Holland, PhD, is a clinical psychologist in full-time private practice in Columbia, Maryland. He has taught in doctoral programs at Columbia University and the American School of Professional Psychology, and he has published articles and chapters on psychodynamic process research, cognitive–behavioral treatment, and psychotherapy integration.

Enrico E. Jones, PhD, is Professor of Psychology at the University of California at Berkeley, and past Director of its Clinical Psychology Program. In addition to conducting an ongoing psychotherapy research program, he is a member of the faculty of the San Francisco Psychoanalytic Institute and has a private practice in Berkeley.

Joseph M. Masling, PhD, is Emeritus Professor of Psychology at the State University of New York at Buffalo. He has written numerous articles on interpersonal and situational variables influencing projective tests, and he has published widely on the empirical study of psychoanalytic concepts. Masling edited the first three volumes of the Empirical Studies of Psychoanalytic Theories series (1983, 1986, 1990); coedited (with Robert F. Bornstein) *Psychoanalytic Perspectives on Psychopathology* (1993), *Empirical Perspectives on Object Relations Theory* (1994), *Psychoanalytic Perspectives on Developmental Psychology* (1996), and *Empirical Perspectives on the Psychoanalytic Unconscious* (1998); and received the Society for Personality Assessment's 1997 Bruno Klopfer Award for Lifetime Achievement in Personality Assessment.

Stanley B. Messer, PhD, is Professor and Chair of the Department of Clinical Psychology, Graduate School of Applied and Professional Psychology at Rutgers University. He is coauthor (with C. Seth Warren) of *Models of Brief Psychodynamic Therapy: A Comparative Approach* and coeditor (with Paul L. Wachtel) of *Theories of Psychotherapy: Origins and Evolution.*

Pauline B. Price, MA, is in the clinical psychology doctoral program at the University of California, Berkeley. Her research interests include psychodynamic psychotherapy, therapeutic alliance, and treatment of depression.

Donald P. Spence, PhD, is Clinical Professor of Psychiatry at the Robert Wood Johnson Medical School, University of Medicine and

Dentistry in New Jersey, Piscataway, New Jersey. He had previously been Professor of Psychology at New York University, and he has been a visiting professor at Stanford University, Princeton University, Louvain-le-Neuve, and the William Alanson White Institute. He graduated from Harvard in 1949, received his PhD at Teachers College–Columbia in 1955, and graduated from the New York Psychoanalytic Institute in 1966. He is the author of *Narrative Truth and Historical Truth* (1982), *The Freudian Metaphor* (1987), and *The Rhetorical Voice of Psychoanalysis* (1994). He was President of the American Psychological Association's Division of Theoretical and Philosophical Psychology during 1992–1993.

Hans H. Strupp, PhD, is Distinguished Professor of Psychology, Emeritus at Vanderbilt University. He has been an active contributor to psychotherapy research for more than 40 years, and he has authored or coauthored more than 300 articles and books.

Introduction:
Empirical Investigations of Events Within the Psychoanalytic Hour

Robert F. Bornstein and Joseph M. Masling

Few ideas have influenced Western thought as strongly as psychoanalytic theory, even in the absence of empirically confirmatory evidence. At one point, psychoanalysis dominated American psychiatry and was the preferred theory of a great many psychologists. Its impact on the general intellectual community cannot be exaggerated, influencing not only the several mental health disciplines but also anthropology, sociology, criminology, the cinema, philosophy, literary and art criticism, and even the physical sciences (Grunbaum, 1984; Holland, 1984). In his newspaper column, "Talking to Each Other," William Buckley, Jr. once noted that an examination of the Social Sciences Citation Index confirmed that Freud was the most frequently cited author, with 12,391 citations —almost twice as many as the next more frequently cited author, Karl Marx (6,807 citations). Even today, Freud remains the sixth most quoted authority in the world, following Lenin, Shakespeare, Aristotle, the Bible, and Plato (Friman, Allen, Kerwin, & Larzelere, 1993). Psychoanalytic classics are cited more frequently than classic contributions in behavioral and cognitive psychology (Friman et al., 1993).

That situation is changing, however. Psychoanalysis no longer dominates training in psychiatry, and citations of psychoanalytic literature have been declining since 1984 (Friman et al., 1993). The number of clinical psychologists whose primary theoretical orientation is psychodynamic has fallen from 35% in 1960 to half that number, 18%, in 1995. At the same time, cognitive therapy—unknown in 1960—was the primary orientation of 24% of clinical psychologists in 1995 (Norcross, Karg, & Prochaska, 1997).

The reasons for this decline are not difficult to find: the advent of drug and cognitive–behavioral therapies, the documented efficacy of these treatment methods, the resistance within psychoanalysis to empirical tests of its propositions or its therapeutic effectiveness, and the rise to power of the managed health care industry with its refusal to reimburse policyholders for long-term psychotherapy of statistically unproven merit.

This decline in popularity was predictable and probably avoidable. No other serious form of intellectual inquiry or treatment method has denied access to its primary data to anyone outside the system, all the while asking to be considered a science. Psychoanalysis took the unique position of publishing only selected data (case histories or portions of them) by an agent who helped generate those data. In contrast, for 50 years, nonpsychoanalytic psychotherapists, beginning with Rogers (1942), have made available to serious investigators the primary data of the psychotherapeutic session. It is incredible that so considerable an enterprise as psychoanalytic treatment could have remained so secret, so unavailable for public scrutiny, for so many years.

Its antiresearch stance prompted many psychologists to turn away from psychoanalysis without first becoming familiar with its propositions, tenets, and supporting empirical base. Consequently, in many academic settings today, psychoanalytic theory tends to be viewed as a mildly interesting piece of ancient history—an all but extinct species that briefly dominated the psychological world and then vanished due to its inability, or perhaps unwillingness,

to adapt to changing conditions. In many undergraduate departments (and even in many graduate training programs), psychoanalysis often is mentioned only as an example of what a personality theory should *not* be (i.e., tautological, sexist, refractory to
operational definitions, largely untested, and uncritically accepted
by its adherents).

Arguments from critics who do not have psychoanalytic training
and experience can be dismissed on several grounds, including the
resistance to psychoanalytic ideas that Freud discussed, but it is
not as easy to dismiss criticism that comes from within the psychoanalytic establishment. In his remarkably prescient presidential
address to the American Psychoanalytic Association, delivered
long before the advent of managed health care, Cooper (1984)
warned that "our exciting debates will become arid if they are not
sprinkled with new data. Even if we do not feel impelled by our
scientific and theoretical curiosity, we might respond to the demands of a society that will not forever allow us to practice clinical
psychoanalysis without evidence of its efficacy" (p. 259). Holt
(1992) was even more explicit, arguing that "American psychoanalysis is in a state of crisis in virtually every aspect . . . its status
as a science is shaky at best and its prospects for improvement
poor" (p. 375). Spence's (1994) position is similar: "This troubling
lack of progress can be laid to two factors: reliance on an outmoded
method of scientific data collection and a preference for fanciful
argument over hard fact. . . . Most disturbing of all is the absence
of data. Argument by authority stands directly in the way of the
benefits, zealously guarded since the Renaissance, of an adversar-
ial, critical, and dialectical tradition of investigation" (pp. 1–3).

The psychoanalytic treatment session has rarely been subjected
to public scrutiny, both because most psychoanalysts until recently
have been reluctant to allow others to inspect the psychoanalytic
hour and because research on psychoanalytic transactions is ex-
traordinarily difficult, labor-intensive, and expensive, requiring
competence in both psychoanalytic treatment and research design.
Nevertheless, as the chapters in this volume demonstrate, a few
researchers have managed to gain access to treatment protocols
and have examined empirically the transactions that occur within
the psychoanalytic session. Enormous credit is due these investigators for their commitment to empirical study and their willing-

ness to engage in the exquisitely difficult, costly task of preparing typescripts of analytic sessions and subjecting these protocols to minute, painstaking quantitative analysis. It must be acknowledged, however, that given the many years of psychoanalytic treatment, these few investigations do not constitute a glorious record of empirical study.

The situation is made even worse by the almost total disregard of these few studies by most psychoanalytic clinicians. Indeed, Wolitzky (1990) noted that of 200 references in a recent book by 16 analysts on treatment, only 6 referred to empirical work, and of these 6 citations, 5 were made by one author. In dramatic contrast, the literature on cognitive and behavioral therapies is filled with reports demonstrating the close interplay between treatment methods and research findings. The situation is so bad that Luborsky has commented that psychoanalysts who use experimental data in their presentations may actually forfeit their clinical status.

As Spence (1994) has so carefully delineated, Freud turned away from the careful empirical methods he used in the laboratory toward generalizations without presenting raw data. As a result, "the psychoanalytic literature tends to minimize evidence at the expense of conclusion and maximize argument at the expense of evidence, and these tendencies can be laid directly at Freud's door" (Spence, 1994, p. 30). His followers believed they had discovered a timeless truth that might need some tinkering here and there but otherwise represented some universal truth. Eissler's comment, reported by Dahl in this volume (see chap. 6) says it all: There was little to be changed in psychoanalytic theory.

This stasis, this paralysis, has kept psychoanalysis relatively immobilized since its inception. In contrast, think of the enormous changes in the various sciences since 1900, the publication date of *The Interpretation of Dreams* (Freud, 1900/1953). The chemistry, physics, astronomy, biology, and genetics of 1900 have given rise to information and theories not dreamed of then, and entirely new fields—quantum physics, cognitive psychology, molecular biology, neuroscience, electronics, to name only a few—have been created. In almost every field of knowledge but psychoanalysis, old theories have been tested and abandoned and newer, more accurate ideas have replaced them. A geneticist of 1900 could not sustain a conversation with a contemporary geneticist, but Freud would have no trouble recognizing the psychoanalysis of 1997 or reading a modern psychoanalytic journal.

Even the arts have undergone numerous transformations since 1900: the ideas and works of Schönberg, Bartok, Picasso, Kandinsky, Pollock, Brancusi, Phillip Glass, John Cage, James Joyce, and Allen Ginsberg are radical departures from the art forms that existed in Freud's day. Yet psychoanalysis, like some dowager presiding regally in her decaying mansion, has been content to shrug off the need to come to terms with the present. But time does not deal kindly with statues of explorers peering into the distance, and pigeons do visit the statue with some frequency, producing an image more famous for its historical value than its present beauty.

However, the criticisms of Cooper and others are egregiously incorrect in a larger sense in that psychoanalytic theories of personality have proven to be robustly heuristic. When Silverman (1976) declared that reports of the death of psychoanalysis "have been greatly exaggerated" (p. 621), he had in mind the health and vigor of efforts to study psychoanalytic theories of personality. There have probably been more well-designed empirical studies testing and extending psychoanalytic concepts during the past two decades than at any other time in the history of the discipline (Bornstein & Masling, 1998; Fisher & Greenberg, 1978, 1985, 1996; Masling, 1983, 1986, 1990; Masling & Bornstein, 1993, 1994, 1996; Shapiro & Emde, 1995). Indeed, it is quite likely that psychoanalytic theory has inspired more empirical research than any other theory of personality. Fisher and Greenberg (1996), for example, estimated that more than 2,500 research articles have been inspired by psychoanalytic theory, an estimate that is probably quite conservative. Furthermore, contrary to the assertions of many skeptics, many psychoanalytic propositions have been found to be consistent with empirical results. There is much more scientific merit in psychoanalytic theories of personality than critics have been willing to grant.

Thus, contrary to the predictions (and perhaps desires) of some critics, psychoanalysis is not disappearing. Psychoanalytic ideas have influenced research programs in clinical, social, developmental, and cognitive psychology (see, e.g., Aronson, 1992; Bornstein, 1992; Bornstein & Pittman, 1992; Bowers & Meichenbaum, 1984; Erdelyi, 1985; Horowitz, 1988, 1991; Singer, 1990; Stern, 1985; Tabin,

1985; Uleman & Bargh, 1989). As Emde (1992) observed, many recent (and not so recent) stage theories of social and personality
development are rooted in Freud's (1905/1953) psychosexual stage
model. The same is true of recent theories regarding the development of the self-concept in infancy and early childhood (see Stern,
1985; Tabin, 1985). In cognitive psychology, many models of perception, cognition, and memory without awareness have been influenced by psychoanalytic theories of the unconscious (Bornstein
& Pittman, 1992; Schachter, 1987). Similarly, cognitive and social
research on mental representations and schemas has borrowed lib-
erally from object relations theory and self psychology (Horowitz,
1991).

Thus, we have a curious situation. The prime source of psychoanalytic knowledge, the analytic hour, has until recently not been
available for empirical study. In contrast, psychoanalytic theories
of personality have been investigated extensively. Psychoanalytic
clinicians, however, tend to ignore empirical findings of any kind,
whether gathered in the consulting room or laboratory. As a result,
psychoanalysis remains relatively somnambulant, engaging in
nothing more vigorous than hairsplitting about minor theoretical
issues, while the rest of the scientific and intellectual community
continues to advance.

Empirical Data and Clinical Data
in Psychoanalysis

Whether psychoanalysis is a science and should be held to scientific accountability (Grunbaum, 1984) has occasioned long, conten-
tious, and fruitless debates with no resolution likely to occur
within any reader's lifetime. Those psychoanalysts who disparage
the relevance of empirical research base their objections on three
premises. First, such research has been criticized as *irrelevant* to the
clinical theory of psychoanalysis. This argument is circular because
it holds that what is truly psychoanalytic cannot be studied in the
laboratory, and if it can be studied in the laboratory, it cannot be
truly psychoanalytic.

The second objection to empirical data is that they are *unneces-*

sary because clinical evidence is so compelling and convincing that no independent verification is needed. However, the ongoing controversy about Freud's "seduction theory" is ample evidence that clinicians' prior beliefs and expectations strongly influence their patients' perceptions and memories (Loftus, 1993). Instead of systematically collecting data on reports of childhood sexual assaults, psychoanalysts have relied on dogma and authority. As Spence (1994) put it, "It is disturbing to recognize the power of Freud's authority and the way in which theory prevails over observation. . . . Evidence that does not support standard theory tends to be minimized or disparaged, and independent thinking tends to be discredited" (p. 4).

Finally, some psychoanalysts argued that empirical research represents a *misapplication of psychoanalytic concepts*. In this context, they contend that psychoanalysis is intended to be used to investigate intensively the psychological functioning of individuals and that the application of psychoanalytic theory to arbitrarily defined groups of people (e.g., people with hysteria, character-disordered persons, people with obsessive disorders, victims of child abuse) is inappropriate and contrary to psychoanalytic principles. For these scholars, psychoanalysis should be confined to the description and analysis of one person and is misused when applied to the aggregates that compose the raw material of personality and clinical research.

These objections are invalid. To dismiss the entire enterprise of experimental testing of psychoanalytic hypotheses is as simpleminded and naive as it is to dismiss the case history method. Experiments need not twist psychoanalytic theory into unrecognizable shape, and most of those summarized in this volume and the preceding seven in the Empirical Studies series do not. The need for extraclinical evidence to provide a more secure footing for psychoanalytic theory ought to be abundantly evident to anyone interested in the long-term welfare of psychoanalysis. Grunbaum's (1984) closely reasoned analysis of the philosophical and scientific assumptions underlying psychoanalytic theory makes explicit the great need for extraclinical, empirical support of the theory.

Relying exclusively on the case history to support the validity of psychoanalytic practice puts the whole enterprise in jeopardy, particularly when more objective forms of evidence could be marshaled. Case history data depend on the voluntary release of information by a participant in the therapeutic process. That case history material is subject to the vagaries of memory, repression, and motive cannot be denied, given the information we now have about Freud's selective reporting of Wolf Man's treatment, the vast discrepancy between the way Bettelheim described his work with children and his actual practice as others observed him, and the dramatic contrast between the number of documented occurrences of sexual contact between therapist and patient and the number of case histories that report such activity. Furthermore, case history data are limited to what the therapist is capable of noticing and is willing to report. The experimental literature amply documents the ease with which either client or clinician can influence the behavior of the other without awareness on either side (Masling, 1965, 1966).

Case material could never reveal the insights provided by objective, systematic investigations of the analytic hour, as is evident in each of the chapters reported in this volume. The me–you speech combination Spence has investigated and Strupp's (see chap. 1 in this volume) description of therapists' responses to the patient's hostility could not be discerned in case notes because these events are too subtle, and sometimes too threatening, for most therapists to notice and to report. To limit psychoanalytic knowledge to what is learned in case history reports would deprive the field of valuable, unique information, and to ignore experimental results once they are obtained produces a kind of foolish, self-blinding ritual. But all too often, that is exactly the case. Most analytic training institutes provide little or no training in research or appreciation of research results.

Ironically, the third objection to experimental treatment of psychoanalytic observations could have been made about Freud's own writings or those of most major psychoanalytic writers. Freud frequently generalized observations made from his treatment of one patient to the behavior of groups of people. For example, from the case of Schreber, he derived a general statement about the dynamics of the origins of paranoid thinking. Throughout the "Rat Man" and "Wolf Man" cases, Freud extrapolated from his observations about these and other patients and generalized about differences between hysterical and obsessive–compulsive disorders. In *Character and Anal Erotism*, Freud (1908/1959) described a cluster of traits that he found in some people: "The people I am about to describe are noteworthy for a regular combination of the three following characteristics. They are especially *orderly, parsimonious, and obstinate*" (p. 169; italics in original).

Freud's (1908/1959) assertion can be viewed as a kind of informal research study—he observed groups of people and noticed that they differed in character traits. Experimenters do the same thing, but they do it better: Their methods are more explicit, their data gathering is more systematic, and the experiment is made public so that it is available for replication by others. If psychoanalysis were restricted to hermeneutics or were confined to the construction of a narrative based on a single person's life, it would be robbed of one of its greatest merits—its heuristic value (see Kriegman, 1998). The recommendation that the psychoanalytic method be confined to hermeneutics seems to be an anachronistic version of a Luddite need to return to a simpler, purer way of gaining knowledge.

Clinical Evidence, Empirical Evidence, and the Self-Fulfilling Prophecy

Nothing in these remarks is intended to discredit or diminish the value of psychoanalytic treatment. We wish to distinguish here between treatment and the theory of personality that supports and explains it. All psychodynamic therapists have seen patients who improved considerably as a result of treatment, but the reason for behavioral and attitudinal changes may be independent of the therapist's personality theory. The power of placebo and expectancy effects can scarcely be exaggerated. Indeed, the therapeutic successes every school of psychoanalysis can point to suggest strongly that some nonspecific forces (e.g., the uncritical, accepting attitude of the therapist, the empathic therapeutic relationship) may be more relevant to change than is the therapist's theory.

Our comments speak to the wisdom of constructing a theory of personality based exclusively on material learned from the clinical interaction and to the belief of many clinicians that the words, dreams, recollections, and associations of the patient reveal some basic psychological truths. Such a theory will help greatly to understand a particular patient and might well reveal some general facets of human behavior. Indeed, as the volumes in this series demonstrate, many parts of psychodynamic theories are consistent with empirical evidence. However, to believe that everything a patient says or does originates from the patient without having been influenced in any way by the analyst is to ignore the important (but subtle, and frequently ignored) role of the therapist.

All therapists, of whatever therapeutic persuasion, carry a personality theory into the consulting room, a theory that instructs the therapist (and after a while, the patient as well) about which content is important and which is less consequential. Inevitably, the patient learns what the therapist considers important and what the therapist generally ignores. Before long, most patients know what will elicit a response and what will only produce silence. Thus, in a detailed analysis of the verbal interchange between a client and Carl Rogers, Murray (1956) demonstrated that Rogers' theory led him to intervene only for some categories of thematic material but not for others; in due time, the client talked only about the issues in which Rogers had demonstrated interest. This analysis by Murray (1956) was later confirmed by Truax (1966) for a second case of Rogers.

The subtle communication by therapist to patient is not confined to Rogerian therapy. Greenson (1967) reported this interaction with one of his analytic patients:

> He had been a lifelong Republican (which I had known) and he had tried in recent months to adopt a more liberal point of view because he knew I was a liberal and anti-Republican. He then told me that whenever he said anything favorable about a Republican politician, I always asked for associations. On the other hand, whenever he said anything hostile about a Republican, I remained silent, as though in agreement. Whenever he had a kind word for Roosevelt, I said nothing. Whenever he attacked Roosevelt, I would ask who did Roosevelt remind him of, as though I was out to prove that Roosevelt hating was infantile. I was taken aback because I had been completely unaware of this pattern. Yet, the moment the patient pointed it out, I had to agree that I had done precisely that, albeit unknowingly. (p. 272)

This self-report of Greenson is remarkable only because he had the integrity and reputation (and self-confidence) to publish it. One can dismiss it as "bad analytic practice" if one likes, but unintentional selective responding must surely happen with great frequency, even with the most experienced therapists.

Marmor (as cited in Grunbaum, 1984) provided a detailed explanation of how these unintended communications might work in an analytic session:

> In face-to-face transactions the expression of the therapist's face, a questioning glance, a lift of the eyebrows, a barely perceptible shake of the head or shrug of the shoulder all act as significant cues to the patient. But even *behind* the couch, our "uh-huhs" as well as our silences, the interest or the disinterest reflected in our tone of voice or our shifting postures all act like subtle radio signals influencing the patient's responses, reinforcing some responses and discouraging others. (p. 267)

There is nothing inherently improper about this kind of coaching by the therapist, who is, after all, being paid to help patients understand the events in their lives. Negative consequences of this process occur only if therapists are unable to acknowledge that the content of a patient's speech is partly the result of their implicit coaching. To believe that everything the patient says emerges untutored and unshaped by the therapist is to mistake a mirror for a window. It is inevitable that the patient's words (and memories) sometimes reflect both therapist and patient. The controversy about recovered memories of childhood sexual abuse demonstrates the ease with which therapists' beliefs sometimes result in distorted patient "recollections" (Loftus, 1993).

Freud, of course, was aware this sort of criticism could be made about the psychoanalytic method and vigorously defended against it:

> The danger of our leading a patient astray by suggestions, by persuading him to accept things which we ourselves believe but which he ought not to, has certainly been enormously exaggerated. An analyst would have had to behave very incorrectly before such a misfortune could overtake him; above all, he would have to blame himself with not allowing his patients to

have their say. I can assert without boasting that such an abuse of "suggestion" has never occurred in my practice. (1937/1964, p. 262)

Freud's concern about the vulnerability of psychoanalytic practice to this criticism is amply warranted, but given the ample documentation (Masling, 1965, 1966) of the ease with which patient and therapist can influence the behavior of the other without awareness on either part, his reassurance is unconvincing.

The end result of this unintentional coaching of the patient has been described by Marmor (as cited in Grunbaum, 1984):

> Patients seem to bring up precisely the kind of phenomenological data which form the theories and interpretations of their analysts! Thus each theory tends to be self-validating; Freudians elicit material about the Oedipus Complex and castration anxiety, Jungians about archetypes, Rankians about separation anxiety, Adlerians about masculine strivings and feelings of inferiority, Horneyites about idealized images, Sullivanians about disturbed interpersonal relationships, etc. (p. 289)

Modern-day psychoanalysis is marked by a large number of schools and theoretical orientations, each separated from the next by differences that are sometimes so minute they can only be observed by vigilantes in opposing camps, and each begun by a charismatic, authoritative leader—Freud, of course, as well as Anna Freud, Melanie Klein, Reik, Reich, Kohut, Jung, Kernberg, Horney, Lacan, Sullivan, Winnicott, Adler, Mahler, and Fairbairn. The existence of so many schools and versions of psychoanalytic thought is clear evidence that adherents of each school somehow derive material from their patients that supports a particular view of the world (see Masling & Cohen, 1987). As is the case with competing religions, the ideas and experiences so compelling to one school are dismissed as unpersuasive by the others. Those who deny the utility of empiricism, advocating instead a hermeneutic approach to knowledge, have yet to present a cogent, convincing explanation of this fact.

One way out of this endless morass (and the fruitless arguments based on nothing more substantial than authority and the selective release of undocumented portions of case histories) is to agree to open the psychoanalytic session to scrutiny by qualified experts

and to subject deeply held, "self-evident" beliefs to rigorous experimental tests. "Sooner or later, the central concepts [of psycho-
analysis] must be exposed to the test of the marketplace, subjected
to the traditional cross-validation and replication expected of any
empirical science" (Spence, 1994, p. 179).

Although the theme of these volumes strongly endorses the need
to employ empirical methods to investigate psychoanalytic theories, there should be no confusion about the relative contribution
of experiment and case history method: Relatively few truly creative ideas have originated in laboratory studies of personality. The
raw material of psychoanalytic thought, the good stuff, has come
primarily through the analyst–patient interaction and the case
method of presenting these ideas. Data derived from the experimental method can demonstrate the extent to which some psychoanalytic proposition is consistent with laboratory results. For example, Freud's observation of the anal triad has repeatedly been
confirmed experimentally (Masling & Schwartz, 1979), as has his
conjecture that some mental processes work below the level of conscious awareness (Bornstein, Leone, & Galley, 1987; Masling, 1992),
but his observation that females are less satisfied with their bodies
than are males has not (Fisher & Greenberg, 1985, 1996). Although
a simple demonstration of the validity of psychoanalytic hypotheses is important, more valuable are those studies that extend the
theory into previously unexplored areas.

The Empirical Studies of Psychoanalytic Theories Series

This series of books was begun with the aim of contributing to the
empirical base of psychoanalysis by presenting the best and most
current experimental work inspired by psychoanalytic theories,
thereby helping to fill a critical gap in the literature. A considerable
amount of such work has already been completed and reviewed
(see, e.g., Bornstein & Masling, 1998; Fisher & Greenberg, 1985,
1996; Kline, 1972; Masling, 1983, 1986, 1990; Masling & Bornstein,
1993, 1994, 1996; Masling & Schwartz, 1979). A scientific theory is
expected to generate data that will force it to be revised and ulti-

mately discarded. Most of the experiments reported in this series point to instances in which the theory must be modified to fit the data more closely. This slow accretion of knowledge from scientific studies will suggest how psychoanalytic theories can be modified to accommodate current information. Investigators using psychoanalytic theories should be seen less as bank auditors looking for signs of fraud than as sympathizers eager to keep the spirit of psychoanalytic inquiry alive and consistent with systematically collected scientific data.

It has now been nearly two decades since the first volume in this series was published (Masling, 1983). During that time, chapters in these books have discussed a wide range of topics, from studies of infant behavior and investigations of perception without awareness to analyses of the link between psychoanalysis and sociobiology and reviews of the literature on the psychodynamics of the self-concept. In every volume of the Empirical Studies series, authors have discussed the relationships between empirical data and clinical theory and data, and in every volume, at least one chapter has focused primarily on some aspect of psychotherapeutic work. The present book represents a landmark in the Empirical Studies series: It is the first volume devoted exclusively to empirical research on psychoanalytic and psychodynamic treatment.

The study of the psychoanalytic process goes right to the heart of what this series is all about—to contribute to the empirical base of psychoanalysis by presenting the best and more current research on psychoanalytic theory and therapy. Studies of the psychoanalytic treatment process and outcome are critical to the long-term health of psychoanalysis for two reasons. First, these studies have the potential to demonstrate that psychodynamic therapies have measurable positive effects, despite the assertions of critics to the contrary. Even more important, studies in this area may lead to improvements in psychotherapeutic techniques, refining—or even discarding—ineffective interventions. As psychoanalytic treatment becomes more effective, the theory itself can be revised to account better for the contemporary findings. The converse is also true: As the theory is revised and updated, our therapeutic technique will become more productive as well.

The authors of the chapters in this volume approach psychoanalytic theory and research from different perspectives, but they share with the editors a set of fundamental beliefs that link our diverse viewpoints and experimental procedures: First and foremost, we all agree that it is important to conduct empirical research for psychoanalytic theory building and hypothesis testing, and we all believe that psychoanalysis and psychoanalytic treatment can be most efficiently improved if clinicians attend to the wealth of empirical data already available from within and outside the discipline.

Volume 8 begins with Hans Strupp's illuminating overview of his influential research program relating the therapist's reactions to psychotherapeutic process and outcome. For more than four decades, Strupp and his colleagues have pioneered the development of empirical techniques to quantify and study patient–therapist interchanges during the course of treatment. His chapter traces his work in this domain, from early "groping efforts" of the 1950s to the present, methodologically refined and sophisticated approach that incorporates recent research on semantics, linguistics, and mutual verbal influence.

Enrico Jones and Pauline Price's compelling essay (see chap. 2) summarizes research examining "repetitive action structures" in psychoanalytic therapy. They discuss the links between these action structures and patient change, their research informing us in important ways about the mutual influence processes that occur during psychotherapy, even over extended periods. Using behavioral ratings, factor analysis, and time-series analysis, Jones and Price demonstrate how contemporary debates regarding intersubjectivity and the mutative effects of interpretation may be addressed by carefully designed analyses of ongoing patient–analyst interaction.

Blatt, Auerbach, and Aryan's analysis (see chap. 3) of changes in self and object representations during the course of insight-oriented therapy unites cognitive–developmental theory with research on psychotherapeutic process. This innovative research program has yielded a number of noteworthy findings regarding the "active ingredients" in psychodynamic psychotherapy and the processes that underlie (and undermine) therapeutic progress. Moreover, Blatt et al.'s chapter illustrates the heuristic value of psychotherapy research for testing and extending ideas in other related areas of psychology.

Paul Crits-Christoph and Mary Beth Connolly's insightful review (see chap. 4) of the empirical literature on supportive–expressive psychodynamic therapy goes beyond a straightforward testing of Freudian hypotheses. Instead, their analysis demonstrates how novel therapeutic methods may actually enhance the efficacy of psychoanalytic therapy. Their chapter illustrates how psychoanalytic concepts can be revised, updated, and integrated with ideas and findings from other areas of psychology without losing their essential psychoanalytic quality. The material covered in their review should put to rest the oft-mentioned (but incorrect) notion that psychoanalytic ideas are fixed and unchanging. On the contrary, Crits-Christoph and Connolly's chapter demonstrates that such concepts are alive and evolving, responsive to new data and new explanation.

Donald Spence (see chap. 5) focuses on the ways in which a close semantic analysis of patient–therapist interchanges can illuminate important features of therapeutic process. A central theme of his chapter concerns the psychodynamics of empathy and shared patient–therapist understanding within the analytic session. Spence places his intriguing arguments within the context of other scientific struggles to reform and refine existing methodologies and techniques. In the end, the reader gains a fuller appreciation of the processes by which investigators can come to understand the implicit, subtle, hidden processes that underlie psychotherapeutic efficacy. Only a carefully designed empirical study such as that conducted by Spence could have teased out such interesting findings; in ordinary hands, the case history method is incapable of uncovering such events.

Hartvig Dahl's engaging narrative (see chap. 6) describes the discovery and evolution of FRAMES—his innovative approach to exploring repetitive, maladaptive emotional structures both inside and outside the therapeutic hour. Dahl's ambitious, meticulous analyses of patient verbalizations reveal hidden relationship patterns that are not often captured using traditional interpretive techniques. The FRAMES approach not only has noteworthy implications for conceptions of psychodynamic therapy, but also for theoretical models of emotional dynamics, therapeutic efficiency, and patient growth and change.

Stanley Messer and Stephen Holland's chapter (see chap. 7) describes how single-case experimental designs can be used to study empirically the processes involved in insight-oriented psychotherapy. Such an approach brings ecological validity to the examination of psychotherapeutic process and outcome, while at the same time blending nomothetic and idiographic techniques to enrich the understanding of each individual client. Their work represents a powerful approach to theory development and clinical technique, without losing sight of the central purpose of any therapeutic intervention—to aid patients in their struggle for insight, growth, and positive change.

Suzanne Gassner and Marshall Bush's discussion (see chap. 8) of unconscious mental functioning and therapeutic change contributes importantly to both basic personality theory (i.e., on the nature of unconscious processing) and to therapeutic intervention. Bridging the gap between two controversial domains—unconscious cognition and experimental psychotherapy research—Gassner and Bush review the highly influential research program of the Mount Zion Psychotherapy Research Group. This work, under way for almost two decades, serves as a splendid model for present and future research efforts examining the myriad factors—obvious and subtle, direct and indirect—that influence psychotherapeutic process and outcome. At the same time, the results they report bear directly on basic personality theory.

All contributors to this series, as well as its editors, seek to keep psychoanalytic theory alive and consistent with modern scientific canon. Our tasks are to continue to investigate the extent to which psychoanalytic theories of personality have a substantial scientific base, to indicate where the theories have been found to be inadequate and flawed, and to extend psychoanalytic thinking into new areas of inquiry, hoping thereby to help reinvigorate psychoanalytic scholarship, teaching, and practice. This work must continue if we are to avoid Spence's (1994) gloomy prediction that if psychoanalysis does not alter its collection and use of data, "the enterprise Freud began with such promise (will end) up being fascinated with its own reflection—and seeing nothing else" (p. 203). As the chapters in this series demonstrate, more people are engaged in this effort than is commonly appreciated, and more progress is being achieved than is usually recognized. The work, however, is far from complete.

References

Aronson, E. (1992). *The social animal*. New York: Freeman.

Bornstein, R. F. (1992). The dependent personality: Developmental, social, and clinical perspectives. *Psychological Bulletin, 112*, 3–23.

Bornstein, R. F., Leone, D. R., & Galley, D. J. (1987). The generalizability of subliminal mere exposure effect: Influence of stimuli perceived without awareness on social behavior. *Journal of Personality and Social Psychology, 53*, 1070–1079.

Bornstein, R. F., & Masling, J. M. (1998). *Empirical studies of psychoanalytic theories: Vol. 7. Empirical perspectives on the psychoanalytic unconscious.* Washington, DC: American Psychological Association.

Bornstein, R. F., & Pittman, T. S. (1992). *Perception without awareness: Cognitive, clinical and social perspectives.* New York: Guilford Press.

Bowers, K. S., & Meichenbaum, D. M. (1984). *The unconscious reconsidered.* New York: Wiley.

Cooper, A. M. (1984). Psychoanalysis at one hundred: Beginnings of maturity. *Journal of the American Psychoanalytic Association, 32*, 245–268.

Emde, R. N. (1992). Individual meaning and increasing complexity: Contributions of Sigmund Freud and Rene Spitz to developmental psychology. *Developmental Psychology, 28*, 347–359.

Erdelyi, M. H. (1985). *Psychoanalysis: Freud's cognitive psychology.* New York: Freeman.

Fisher, S., & Greenberg, R. P. (Eds.). (1978). *The scientific evaluation of Freud's theories and therapy.* New York: Basic Books.

Fisher, S., & Greenberg, R. P. (1985). *The scientific credibility of Freud's theories and therapy.* New York: Basic Books.

Fisher, S., & Greenberg, R. P. (1996). *Freud scientifically reappraised: Testing the theories and therapy.* New York: Wiley.

Freud, S. (1953). The interpretation of dreams. In J. Strachey (Ed. and Trans.), *The standard edition of the complete psychological works of Sigmund Freud* (Vols. 4 and 5). London: Hogarth Press. (Original work published 1900)

Freud, S. (1953). Three essays on the theory of sexuality. In J. Strachey (Ed. and Trans.), *The standard edition of the complete psychological works of Sigmund Freud* (Vol. 7, pp. 125–245). London: Hogarth Press. (Original work published 1905)

Freud, S. (1959). Character and anal erotism. In J. Strachey (Ed. and Trans.), *The standard edition of the complete psychological works of Sigmund Freud* (Vol. 9, pp. 167–176). London: Hogarth Press. (Original work published 1908)

Freud, S. (1964). Constructions in analysis. In J. Strachey (Ed. and Trans.), *Standard edition of the complete psychological works of Sigmund Freud* (Vol.

23, pp. 255–270). London: Hogarth Press. (Original work published 1937)

Friman, P. C., Allen, K. D., Kerwin, M. L. E., & Larzelere, R. (1993). Changes in modern psychology: A citation analysis of Kuhnian displacement thesis. *American Psychologist, 48*, 658–662.

Greenson, R. R. (1967). *The technique and practice of psychoanalysis.* Madison, CT: International Universities Press.

Grunbaum, A. (1984). *The foundations of psychoanalysis.* Berkeley, CA: University of California Press.

Holland, N. N. (1984). Freud, physics and literature. *Journal of the American Academy of Psychoanalysis, 12*, 301–320.

Holt, R. R. (1992). The contemporary crises of psychoanalysis. *Psychoanalysis and Contemporary Thought, 15*, 375–402.

Horowitz, M. J. (1988). *Psychodynamics and cognition.* Chicago: University of Chicago Press.

Horowitz, M. J. (1991). *Person schemas and maladaptive interpersonal patterns.* Chicago: University of Chicago Press.

Kline, P. (1972). *Fact and fantasy in Freudian theory.* London: Methuen.

Kriegman, D. (1998). Interpretation, the unconscious, and analytic authority: Toward an evolutionary, biological integration of the empirical–scientific method with the field-defining, empathic stance. In R. F. Bornstein and J. M. Masling (Eds.), *Empirical studies of psychoanalytic theories: Vol. 7. Empirical perspectives on the psychoanalytic unconscious* (pp. 187–272). Washington, DC: American Psychological Association.

Loftus, E. F. (1993). The reality of repressed memories. *American Psychologist, 48*, 518–537.

Masling, J. M. (1965). Differential indoctrination of examiners and Rorschach responses. *Journal of Consulting Psychology, 29*, 198–201.

Masling, J. (1966). Role related behavior of the subject and psychologist and its effects upon psychological data. In D. Levine (Ed.), *Symposium on motivation* (pp. 67–104). Lincoln, NE: University of Nebraska Press.

Masling, J. (Ed.). (1983). *Empirical studies of psychoanalytical theories* (Vol. 1). Hillsdale, NJ: Analytic Press.

Masling, J. (Ed.). (1986). *Empirical studies of psychoanalytic theories* (Vol. 2). Hillsdale, NJ: Analytic Press.

Masling, J. (Ed.). (1990). *Empirical studies of psychoanalytic theories* (Vol. 3). Hillsdale, NJ: Analytic Press.

Masling, J. (1992). What does it all mean? In R. F. Bornstein & T. S. Pittman (Eds.), *Perception without awareness* (pp. 259–277). New York: Guilford Press.

Masling, J., & Cohen, I. S. (1987). Psychotherapy, clinical evidence, and the self-fulfilling prophecy. *Psychoanalytic Psychology, 4*, 65–79.

Masling, J. M., & Bornstein, R. F. (Eds.). (1993). *Empirical studies of psychoanalytic theories: Vol. 4. Psychoanalytic perspectives on psychopathology.* Washington, DC: American Psychological Association.

Masling, J. M., & Bornstein, R. F. (Eds.). (1994). *Empirical studies of psycho-analytic theories: Vol. 5. Empirical perspectives on object relations theory.* Washington, DC. American Psychological Association.

Masling, J. M., & Bornstein, R. F. (1996). *Empirical studies of psychoanalytic theories: Vol. 6. Psychoanalytic perspectives on developmental psychology.* Washington, DC: American Psychological Association.

Masling, J., & Schwartz, M. (1979). A critique of research in psychoanalytic theory. *Genetic Psychology Monographs, 100,* 257–307.

Murray, E. J. (1956). A content-analysis method for studying psychotherapy. *Psychological Monographs, 70* (13, Whole No. 420).

Norcross, J. C., Karg, R. S., & Prochaska, J. O. (1997). Clinical psychologists in the 1900s: Part I. *The Clinical Psychologist, 50,* 4–9.

Rogers, C. R. (1942). The use of electrically recorded interviews in improving psychotherapy. *American Journal of Orthopsychiatry, 12,* 429–434.

Schachter, D. L. (1987). Implicit memory: History and current status. *Journal of Experimental Psychology: Learning, Memory and Cognition, 13,* 501–518.

Shapiro, T., & Emde, R. N. (1995). *Research in psychoanalysis: Process, development, outcome.* Madison, CT: International Universities Press.

Silverman, L. H. (1976). Psychoanalytic theory: The reports of my death are greatly exaggerated. *American Psychologist, 31,* 621–637.

Singer, J. L. (1990). *Repression and dissociation.* Chicago: University of Chicago Press.

Spence, D. P. (1994). *The rhetorical voice of psychoanalysis: Displacement of evidence by theory.* Cambridge, MA: Harvard University Press.

Stern, D. N. (1985). *The interpersonal world of the infant.* New York: Basic Books.

Tabin, J. K. (1985). *On the way to self.* New York: Columbia University Press.

Truax, C. B. (1966). Reinforcement and nonreinforcement in Rogerian psychotherapy. *Journal of Abnormal Psychology, 71,* 1–9.

Uleman, J. S., & Bargh, J. A. (1989). *Unintended thought.* New York: Guilford Press.

Wolitzky, D. L. (1990). Pathways to psychoanalytic cure. *Contemporary Psychology, 35,* 1154–1155.

1

Negative Process:
Its Impact on Research, Training, and Practice

Hans H. Strupp

In this chapter I attempt to trace the evolution of the Vanderbilt research program, which has become known for its emphasis on what my colleagues and I have termed *negative process* or *negative complementarity*. Much of this work has been carried out over the past 25 years by the Vanderbilt psychotherapy research team, although its beginnings date back to my groping efforts in the early 1950s.

Background and Theoretical Orientation

From the beginning, my research has been anchored in psychodynamic theory, with a significant influence coming from neo-Freudian thinking. The latter influence derives from the formal training I received at the Washington School of Psychiatry when it was functioning as an analytic training institution under the leadership of its founder, Harry Stack Sullivan. As a clinical psychologist whose academic training predominantly followed the Boulder model, my first allegiance has always been to empirical data. Accordingly, in studying therapeutic techniques, it has been more important to me what therapists do than what they might say they do or what theoretical writings might prescribe.

For similar reasons, the "purist" distinction between "psychoanalysis" and various forms of psychoanalytic psychotherapy has continued to impress me as spurious, and claims about the alleged uniqueness of psychoanalysis seem to have been dictated by political rather than by scientific considerations. In my opinion, *psychoanalytic psychotherapy* is the proper generic term, and psychoanalysis is merely a specialized variant of psychoanalytic psychotherapy. Many writings on this topic seem to have generated more heat than light.

From the beginning of my career, two questions have been central to my thinking: What is the nature of the psychotherapeutic influence? What is the nature of therapeutic change? Fundamentally, these may reduce to a single question. The most detailed account of my theoretical position may be found in *Psychotherapy in a New Key* (Strupp & Binder, 1984). This book was intended as a so-called treatment manual, that is, a reasonably specific and detailed account of our theoretical position as it had evolved to that time, together with relatively specific recommendations for training and practice. I have never believed, nor do I believe now, that it is possible for a treatment manual to function as a cookbook. Instead, the practice of psychotherapy demands a great deal of improvisation and, apart from some basic guidelines, always calls for ingenuity and finely honed skills.

Although the Vanderbilt program of research, as will become apparent, has dealt with what I have called *time-limited dynamic psychotherapy* (TLDP), I have never been a staunch advocate of brief psychotherapy, although, as it turned out, our approach proved to be in the spirit of the time. For personal and theoretical reasons, my major commitment has been to long-term intensive psychotherapy—psychoanalysis, if you will. Without pursuing this topic in detail, I firmly believe that psychotherapy, in the best sense of the word, is a growth process, and personality growth, like education, cannot be hurried. My basic reason for studying time-limited forms of dynamic therapy has been one of research economy. I have proceeded on the assumption that the psychological processes of primary interest operate equally in time-limited therapy as they do in the more protracted forms. Another compelling reason is that the cost of studying more extended forms is utterly forbidding. Thus, because researchers' time and resources are severely limited, they have no choice but to strive for parsimony. For all of these reasons, I feel justified in claiming that my program of research, although not specifically focused on psychoanalysis, is relevant to psychoanalysis. I also believe that I have been faithful to Freud's original credo of transference, countertransference, and resistance.

As will soon become apparent, as a researcher I was quickly attracted to issues of transference and countertransference. To anticipate a point to be developed at greater length later, I became aware that even well-trained therapists, contrary to what one might expect, were not immune to what my colleagues and I came to call "negative complementarity." Nor had their personal therapy—admittedly few of our participating therapists had undergone a full-fledged training analysis—equipped them to avoid the traps of negative countertransference. It is arguable whether a "regular" training analysis ever fully accomplishes this goal; however, I firmly believe that traditional training programs—even those conducted within psychoanalytic institutes—do not nearly emphasize potential pitfalls of this kind as much as they should. Thus, it is an exceptional therapist who is entirely adequate to the task.

Negative Complementarity: Early Research Evidence

Systematic empirical research in psychotherapy began in the 1940s (Strupp & Howard, 1992), and within a few years the first evidence appeared concerning the powerful influence of negative process. I was initially interested in the empirical study of therapeutic techniques—what therapists do, in contrast to theoretical statements of what they might say they do. For tactical and practical reasons, analog studies appeared to be a reasonable approach. To this end, I asked experienced psychotherapists to respond to therapy situations that were presented initially in written form (Strupp 1955a, 1955b, 1995c) and later via a film of an initial interview.

Surprisingly it emerged that respondents to a film that portrayed an angry, hostile, and provocative patient soon developed negative reactions that appeared to influence the degree of empathy communicated in their hypothetical communications to the patient as well as their supposedly objective diagnostic and prognostic judgments, treatment plans, and so on. I speculated that a respondent's negative reaction to the patient—such attitudes seemed to emerge within minutes of watching the film—might have highly deleterious effects on the potential therapeutic relationship and its outcome. In one of the studies, Strupp and Williams (1960) found that therapists had more positive attitudes toward a patient who appeared to be more highly motivated for therapy and less disturbed. *Psychotherapists in Action* (Strupp, 1960) summarized this early work.

In a final analog study, Strupp and Wallach (1965) found that therapists seemed to confound their personal reactions to a patient with their clinical judgments. On the basis of this work and influences from my neo-Freudian Sullivanian training, I developed my conception of the therapeutic process (Strupp, 1962a, 1973, 1978). The establishment and maintenance of a positive therapeutic relationship appeared to be a necessary context for therapeutic change to take place. This good relationship—or therapeutic alliance—serves as a "power base" from which the therapist exercises a range of "influencing strategies." The combination of a positive therapeutic relationship and appropriate technical interventions will produce maximum change in the patient. The therapist's contribution to interferences with a good therapeutic relationship commonly was considered to be the result of countertransference, which, as Strupp (1962b) pointed out, was usually described as gross and relatively enduring reactions. However, the analog studies suggested that a much more frequent form of countertransference consisted of personal reactions by the therapist that were ubiquitous, continuous, and infinitely more subtle. I concluded that therapists needed to be especially careful about maintaining their composure and, as their highest priority, to adhere to an empathetic, respectful stance toward their patients. Under these circumstances and with a reasonably competent and emotionally healthy therapist, the failure to maintain a positive relationship was assumed to result from relationship or motivational deficiencies (or both) on the part of the patient.

Vanderbilt I and the Leitmotif of the Vanderbilt Studies

In the late 1960s and the early 1970s, the problem of the therapists' negative personal reactions to their patients had receded to the background. During this time, psychotherapy researchers interested in the nature of the therapist's influence focused on the more general question of the differential influence of "specific" (technique) versus "nonspecific" (relational or common) factors. "Vanderbilt I" was a large-scale process—outcome study aimed at determining the differential influence on treatment outcome of these two factors. The design compared treatments conducted by trained therapists (representing relationship plus technique factors) with treatments conducted by college professors who had a reputation for being helpful to students (presumably representing solely relationship factors). The hypothesis was that if techniques made a significant independent contribution to therapy outcome, treatments conducted by the professional therapists would have significantly better outcomes. In fact, group comparisons of treatment outcome failed to detect statistically significant differences (Strupp & Hadley, 1979).

Subsequent detailed analyses showed that the overall group comparisons hid considerable variability in outcomes for individual dyads. For the professional therapists, treatment outcomes ranged from large changes to no change, with the large changes being greater than those produced by the college professors. All therapists had good- and poor-outcome cases, and none had predominantly one or the other type of outcome. These analyses also revealed that the quality of the therapeutic alliance in the early sessions predicted treatment outcome (Gomes-Schwartz, 1978; Hartley & Strupp, 1983; Keithly, Samples, & Strupp, 1980; Moras

& Strupp, 1982). My colleagues and I continued to believe that if the therapist provided an "average expectable" interpersonal climate, personality characteristics of the patient were the primary determinant of the quality of the alliance. Although the therapeutic alliance is a transactional concept, contributions to it were still conceived of in terms of isolated, intrapsychic variables. A few years later, however, using therapeutic alliance ratings from the Vanderbilt I data, Suh, O'Malley, and Strupp (1986) analyzed the progressive development of the alliance over the first three sessions of treatment. We discovered that poor outcomes were associated with the lack of alliance development over the first three treatment sessions or with alliance deterioration over this period of time. It appeared that the fate of the alliance was determined early in therapy and resulted from the mutual influences of patient and therapist on one another, particularly negative reactions of the therapist to provocative patient behavior (Henry & Strupp, 1994).

Before this quantitative analysis of therapeutic interactions relevant to alliance formation, I conducted a set of systematic qualitative studies that revealed striking differences in the quality of interpersonal interactions in the therapies. To obtain a fine-grained picture of the therapeutic processes associated with differential outcome with the Vanderbilt I therapists, I introduced the use of "research-informed case studies" (Soldz, 1990). Specifically, each professional therapist had a good- and a poor-outcome case, respectively. Quantitative data were used to identify and characterize some of these patient–therapist dyads, on which I then conducted qualitative analyses (Strupp, 1980a, 1980b, 1980c, 1980d). Over the course of these analyses, I altered my conception of the therapist's role in the therapeutic process substantially. The first analysis revealed that the therapist preferred the patient who was more receptive to his technical approach (all therapists and patients were men), and this patient had the better outcome (Strupp, 1980a). Relying on my previous conception of factors that contribute to a good alliance, I concluded that when the therapist provides a warm and positive interpersonal climate, patient factors determine the quality of the alliance. My main criticism of this therapist was that he could have been more flexible in his technical approach to the patient.

By the time I had completed the analyses of treatments conducted by two other professional therapists, each of whom clearly preferred one patient over the other, regardless of whether these preferences were acknowledged, I had rediscovered the problem of therapists' personal reactions to all forms of patient hostility:

> As therapists we have not adequately faced up to the negative reactions engendered in us by patients who bring to our offices the products of their unhappy life experiences. . . . Thus, major deterrents to the foundation of a good working alliance are not only the patient's characterological distortions and maladaptive defenses but—at least equally important—the therapist's personal reactions. Traditionally these reactions have been considered under the heading of countertransference. It is becoming increasingly clear, however, that this conception is too narrow. The plain fact is that any therapist—indeed any human being —cannot remain immune from negative reactions to the suppressed and repressed rage regularly encountered in patients with moderate to severe disturbances. (Strupp, 1980d, p. 953)

I concluded these analyses by noting that

> in our study we failed to encounter a single instance in which a difficult patient's hostility and negativism were successfully confronted or resolved. . . . Therapists' negative responses to difficult patients are far more common and far more intractable than has been generally recognized. (Strupp, 1980d, p. 954)

With the evidence impossible to ignore, the study of therapists' reactions to and management of negative process became the explicit leitmotif of the Vanderbilt psychotherapy research team.

Even more convincing evidence of a powerful influence of negative process was offered in a reanalysis of the cases that I had originally examined qualitatively. Samples of interactions from these patient–therapist dyads were coded using the Structural Analysis of Social Behavior (SASB) interpersonal process rating system (Benjamin, 1974; Henry, Schacht, & Strupp, 1986). This subsequent analysis fully confirmed my earlier observations. There was significantly more negative process coded in the poor-outcome cases. In these cases, both patient and therapist communications toward each other were significantly more hostile. There were higher levels of negative complementarity, defined as one hostile verbalization directly evoking a hostile response, and there were more "multiple communications," defined as mixed interpersonal implications within a statement (e.g., a statement that simultaneously supports and blames). These analyses were conducted on data obtained early in the therapies, suggesting again that negative process can begin early in treatment and is not easily rectified.

A subsequent replication of this study with a different sample of patients and therapists, along with more sophisticated outcome measures, produced identical findings (Henry, Schacht, & Strupp, 1990). On the basis of these two studies, my collaborators and I concluded that the detrimental influence of negative process cannot be overestimated: "Whereas the absence of a negative interpersonal process may not be sufficient for therapeutic change, the presence of even relatively low levels of negative therapist behavior may be sufficient to prevent change" (Henry et al., 1990, p. 773). Because in both studies the therapists were all well-trained and experienced clinical psychologists and psychiatrists, we raised a concern about possible deficiencies in therapy training programs:

> Apparently, even well-trained professional therapists are surprisingly vulnerable to engaging in potentially destructive interpersonal process [and] . . . traditional training methods have not adequately prepared many therapists to expertly perceive and respond to the potential interpersonal process meanings and effects of their interactions. (Henry et al., 1990, pp. 773–774)

One likely consequence of hostile interactions between a patient and a therapist is their progressive emotional disengagement from each other, a process certain to doom the treatment. Evidence for this conclusion was produced in a study using a variant of the "research-informed case study" method (Wiseman, Shefler, Caneti, & Ronen, 1993). These researchers looked at two cases that had good and poor outcomes, respectively, and were conducted by the same therapist. Although Strupp (1980a, 1980b, 1980c) had conducted broad qualitative analyses, Wiseman et al. (1993) systematically identified theoretically significant events over the course of the therapies and then examined the therapeutic processes within these events with the aid of ratings from the Vanderbilt Psychotherapy Process Scale. They discovered that the poor-outcome case was characterized from the middle through the end of treatment by (a) a sharp decrease in the therapist's focus on relevant content; (b) a decline in patient involvement and a lack of decline in patient hostility, which had declined in the good-outcome case; and (c) a lack of increase in therapist warmth and friendliness, which had increased in the good-outcome case. Taken together, these findings indicate interpersonal disengagement by both parties in the poor-outcome treatment.

Further confirmation of the robust association between negative process and treatment outcome was produced by another research team, who completed new SASB codings not only of segments of early sessions but also of midtreatment sessions and final sessions from the original Vanderbilt I patient–therapist dyads (Tasca & McMullen, 1992). This group approached the data from the theoretical perspective that characterized a course of therapy as developing through three stages: early-stage alliance building, midstage confrontational work, and late-stage consolidation of alliance and work. Tasca and McMullen's main interest was in testing hypotheses concerning the association between the stages of therapy and interpersonal complementarity. However, their strongest finding replicated the work of the Vanderbilt investigators: "The hostility that emerged from the very beginning of unsuccessful cases was pervasive across sessions" (Tasca & McMullen, 1992, p. 519). In other words, the unsuccessful patient–therapist dyads produced significantly more negative complementarity interactions throughout treatment. Furthermore, this negative process was most observable in the early and late stages in which the therapy stage theory would predict that alliance building and alliance consolidation, respectively, would be most crucial.

Tasca and McMullen (1992) also analyzed sequences of negative complementary interactions and discovered that the patients in unsuccessful dyads made significantly more attempts to initiate hostile interchanges than the patients in successful dyads. These evidently were individuals who manifested particularly hostile maladaptive interpersonal patterns as part of their psychopathology. This type of patient poses especially difficult management problems for their therapist: The results imply that clients in this study were responsible for attempting to pull therapists into a hostile exchange in therapy and, by extension, for an unsuccessful outcome. However, one must question the inability of therapists in this sample to deal with client hostility in a "therapeutic manner" (Tasca & McMullen, 1992, p. 521). Kiesler and Watkins (1989) used a different method for assessing interpersonal complementarity in therapy dyads but also confirmed that, at least early in treatment, hostile patients exert a particularly strong influence on the quality of therapeutic interactions, contributing more than the therapist to alliance deterioration as both parties disengage from each other.

Using entirely different methods of rating process and outcome, Klee, Abeles, and Muller (1990) also found evidence that patients can pull therapists into patterns of hostile interaction. One of the aims of their study was to investigate patient and therapist contributions to the therapeutic alliance. They found that when patients made "negative contributions" to the therapeutic alliance from the beginning of treatment, their therapists also made frequent hostile interventions. The negative contributions to the alliance of patients did not affect their therapists' tendency to make positive contributions to the alliance. This suggests that although therapists may try strenuously to maintain a positive stance, they still are vulnerable to the hostile acts of their patients. Of related interest is the multivariate sequential analysis of patient and therapist contributions to the alliance tracked over the course of two therapies (Hentschel & Bijleveld, 1995). These researchers adduced evidence of the mutual influence that both parties have on one another, and they noted the particularly rapid influence of patient actions on therapist contributions to the therapeutic alliance. To summarize, one primary challenge for the therapist's skill is to avoid being recruited by the patient as a coparticipant in the patient's unconscious scenarios.

Vanderbilt II and the Continuing Struggle With Negative Process

In the 1980s the Vanderbilt group designed and began the "Vanderbilt II" project, which investigated changes in therapist performance after a 1-year manual-guided training program in TLDP (Strupp, 1993). The therapists were 16 experienced psychiatrists and psychologists who treated bona fide patients. The study used a pre- to posttreatment repeated measures design, which permitted observation of within-therapists changes from an established base-line of performance. The therapy model examined the detection and management of maladaptive interpersonal patterns, with particular emphasis on their enactment within the therapeutic relationship (Strupp & Binder, 1984).

The training was found to increase the therapists' adherence to the techniques prescribed by the manual, and when, as part of the training, they viewed tape-recorded therapy sessions they also keenly observed their own and their peers' interpersonal process. Contrary to expectations, however, the training did not significantly improve the therapists' capacity to monitor and manage the interpersonal processes within the therapeutic relationship. In fact, there was evidence of an increase in hostile and complex communications as reflected in the SASB codes, attributable primarily to increased therapist activity as part of a short-term treatment approach (Henry, Strupp, Butler, Schacht, & Binder, 1993). The findings from that study suggested that negative process is difficult to control, let alone eradicate, even when the therapy model and associated training is designed specifically to deal with it. As Henry et al. put it, a little bit of bad process can go a long way.

This conclusion was further supported by another analysis of the Vanderbilt II data, which examined the overall effectiveness of the participating therapists (Najavits & Strupp, 1994). Effectiveness (as indicated by treatment outcome) varied across the therapists and across patients for each therapist. Particularly interesting was the finding that the relative effectiveness of each therapist was not affected by the training program. A clear association was demonstrated between effectiveness and negative process, with the more effective therapists evidencing far fewer SASB codings of hostile behavior (e.g., blaming and belittling, and ignoring and rejecting). It also is interesting that the more effective therapists tended to be more self-critical, suggesting that they engaged in more self-reflection and self-monitoring. It would make sense that the capacity for self-monitoring would help to minimize becoming snared in negative process.

The research team conducted an intensive qualitative analysis of a posttraining therapy with poor outcome by one of the therapists who participated in the Vanderbilt II study. This analysis illustrates the enormous difficulties associated with managing negative process: therapists' underestimation of its influence and the limitations of training in improving relevant skills (Strupp, Schacht, Henry, & Binder, 1992). The patient was a narcissistically fragile man who hid his intense psychic distress behind a mask of bravado. Pervasive negative complementarity doomed any possibility for a therapeutic alliance to develop. On the one hand, "the pejorative connotation of the therapist's communications was often indirect, implicit, and/or embedded in messages carrying a double meaning" (Strupp et al., 1992, p. 204). On the other hand, in one session, for example, the patient engaged in a lengthy tirade about professionals who abuse their power, particularly doctors, yet in a post-session evaluation of the session the therapist observed, "and other than the antipathy toward professions in general, very little was able to be captured about dealing with the transference" (Strupp et al., 1992, p. 199). The therapist clearly had not mastered one of the most important skills associated with the treatment model in which he had been trained: the detection of implicit references to problems in the therapeutic relationship (Strupp & Binder, 1984). Yet, this therapist evidenced a good conceptual understanding of transference and countertransference.

Although my colleagues and I have given primary attention to the problem of negative process, by no means are we, as therapists, immune to its effects. Strupp (1990) published the case of a woman seen in therapy that was videotaped for use in the training of the Vanderbilt II therapists and in which the therapeutic process ran aground. The treatment ended prematurely after 13 sessions, when in anger the patient precipitously terminated. Early in the treatment of this professional woman, she and I identified a prepotent interpersonal theme of feeling exploited by and disappointed in men as well as a conviction that men could not understand her experience. Both patient and therapist struggled with the manifestations of this theme within the therapeutic relationship but eventually succumbed to it. As I observed after the patient quit,

> I was disappointed by what I experienced as a defeat. I also reacted with anger to what I experienced as false accusations

(e.g., the charge that I had made "typically Freudian" interpretations). I tried conscientiously to help the patient but recurrently felt frustrated and discouraged. I respected Helen's (a pseudonym) intellect and achievements and felt compassionate toward her predicament. There remained, however, an undercurrent of anger, continually fueled by her rage. One might argue that these feelings complemented precisely the patient's unconscious intent, in other words, they pointed to a central transference problem. I tried to avoid a power struggle but, in the end, failed. (Strupp, 1990, p. 655)

The writings of Wile (e.g., 1984) vividly illustrate the deleterious consequences of accusatory and pejorative communications by psychoanalytic psychotherapists. For the most part, Wile did not attribute these communications to therapists' negative countertransference but instead viewed them as being anchored in the dictates of psychoanalytic theory. In his view, psychoanalytic terminology and formulations invariably tend to have an accusatory and pejorative quality that may, of course, be intensified by the therapist's personal reactions to the patient. Wile cited the case histories of Kohut and Kernberg in support of his contention.

The writings of Wachtel (e.g., 1993) provide detailed documentation from a wide variety of clinical material on the subject of negative complementarity and pejorative communications. A brief example illustrates one of Wachtel's major messages: The patient, a painfully shy young woman, had been sitting for a long time in an uncomfortable silence, occasionally adding that she just didn't have anything to say. Finally, at one point the therapist said to her, "I think you're silent because you're trying to hide a lot of anger." (Notice the confrontive quality of this statement.) Contrast this with an empathic, compassionate response: "I have the sense that you're angry but feel you're not supposed to be" or "I wonder if you're staying silent because you had better not say anything if what you're feeling is anger" (Wachtel, 1993, pp. 70–71). Wachtel's book is a major treatise devoted to the fundamental problem of negative complementarity. Comparably, the case histories from the Vanderbilt studies likewise highlight therapist deficiencies in this arena.

The Advent of Treatment Manuals and the Vanderbilt II Study

During the past 15 years, psychotherapy outcome researchers in the United States have actively investigated the development and testing of "manualized" forms of psychotherapy, exploring their relative efficacy with each other and relative to pharmacotherapy. These forms of psychotherapy are defined by a training manual that attempts to specify, in an explicit and detailed manner, the steps practitioners should pursue to conceptualize and treat their patients' psychological disorders. Therapists using these treatment approaches in outcome studies are discouraged from using any kinds of interventions not explicitly sanctioned by the treatment manual. The intention is that the use of treatment manuals in guiding training and practice within research projects will promote treatment integrity, thus allowing more precise and valid conclusions to be drawn about the usefulness of the treatment under study (Goldfried, Greenberg, & Marmar, 1990).

Would psychotherapists in clinical settings be more effective if they received manual-guided training and practiced manualized treatments instead of their customary treatment approaches? Rounsaville, O'Malley, Foley, and Weissman (1988) noted that "systematic evaluations of the efficacy of manual-guided training [itself], or of the basic parameters of training programs . . . have yet to be performed for any type of psychotherapy" (p. 682). Convincing evidence that treatment manuals improve outcomes has yet to be provided and would require demonstrations that "therapists trained in a manual-guided approach are more effective than therapists practicing a similar type of therapy without the benefit of manualized training" (Rounsaville et al., 1988, p. 685). This issue has particular significance for the contemporary therapeutic community. As the demand for accountability rises and third-party payments shrink, more therapists are likely to want and receive continuing education in manualized short-term treatment approaches. How effective is such training in meeting the criterion of improving the outcomes of psychotherapy?

The Vanderbilt II project (Strupp, 1993) was designed to answer this question with regard to one form of brief manualized therapy,

TLDP (Strupp & Binder, 1984). It specifically examined whether training therapists in this modality would improve their ability to skillfully manage the vicissitudes of the therapeutic relationship and increase their therapeutic effectiveness. The design of the study may be unique, in that it did not compare therapists administering theoretically contrasting treatments but examined the performance of the same set of therapists before and after a year of training in TLDP. Thus, by having therapists serve as their own controls, we hoped that the study of the effects of training on therapeutic efficacy could be made more precise.

The exact nature of the hypothesized benefits of training in TLDP relates to the reasons for the development of this modality. TLDP grew out of the findings from the earlier Vanderbilt I study. That study, as I have tried to show, was designed to test the relative contributions of so-called specific (i.e., technical) and nonspecific (i.e., relational) factors. My colleagues and I found, among other things, that experienced psychodynamic therapists, supposedly well-trained in managing the intricacies of the therapeutic relationship, showed surprisingly hostile countertransference reactions to resistant patients who had a negative initial relationship with the therapist. Accordingly, it seemed reasonable to hypothesize that the poor outcomes in this group of patients resulted from specific technical deficiencies that might be overcome through additional training in the observation, management, and clinical use of the therapeutic relationship. A particular technical adjustment thought to be necessary was an earlier and much more systematic examination of the interpersonal process between patient and therapist than usually occurs in practice. Thus, TLDP was developed as a form of brief dynamic therapy that in particular emphasizes the importance of early and consistent exploration of the transference in the here and now.

Initial analyses of the Vanderbilt II data investigated the effects of the TLDP training on therapists' in-session behaviors. Henry, Strupp, et al. (1993) reported that after training, therapists were more active and exhibited greater adherence to TLDP-consistent interventions but that they also exhibited as much or more negative behavior toward patients than before training. Thus, the training did not reduce the hypothesized effect of negative countertransference reactions. Henry, Schacht, Strupp, Butler, and Binder

(1993) investigated trainer teaching style, therapist experience level and introject, and patient difficulty as mediators of therapist response to treatment. They found, for example, that therapists with more punitive introjects tended to show greater technical adherence but poorer interpersonal processes.

In a new study based on the same data, Bein et al. (1997) investigated whether TLDP training would increase therapeutic effectiveness. Because TLDP, at least in part, was specifically developed to help therapists become more effective with "difficult" patients, Bein et al. were particularly interested in studying this issue. Accordingly, they formulated two major questions: (a) Did TLDP training in general improve therapist effectiveness? (b) Was TLDP training differentially more beneficial in improving therapist effectiveness with more difficult patients?

The strategy of Bein et al. (1997) for assessing posttraining skills with TLDP focused on determining, for each of the 32 cases under study, whether it had been conducted with at least an acceptable level of skill. Because therapists had treated only one patient during their training, Bein et al. believed that setting a higher standard of competence was unrealistic. To measure TLDP adherence, Butler, Henry, and Strupp (1996) had developed the Vanderbilt Therapeutic Strategies Scale, but there was no measure of TLDP skill. Because Bein et al. were not attempting a fine-grained assessment of skill, they believed it would be possible to make reasonably accurate assessments without developing a TLDP skill measure or reviewing a large number of sessions per case. They also believed that, although clearly desirable, it was not strictly necessary to distinguish the "TLDP learners" from "TLDP nonlearners." The number of posttraining cases judged to have been conducted skillfully would provide a rough indication of the extent to which TLDP had been learned by the therapist sample at large. Therapist skill at TLDP was assessed on a case-by-case basis by two judges who both had experience teaching TLDP to therapists in training.

Bein et al. (1997) found that 8 of the 32 posttraining cases (25%) had been judged to have conducted TLDP with at least a minimal level of skill. Nine of the therapists did not conduct a posttraining case with at least minimal skill, 6 conducted one of the two cases they had treated with at least minimal skill, and 1 therapist conducted both cases skillfully. Their analyses of the data provided no support for either of their hypotheses about the beneficial effects of TLDP training. Most of their significance tests failed to yield a statistically significant result, although they had acceptable power.

In summary, the Bein et al. (1997) semiformal assessment of the skillfulness of the posttraining therapies provided no evidence that most of the project therapists achieved an acceptable level of mastery of TLDP. Even if the tally of the number of TLDP-skillful cases were off by 50%, it still seems implausible that the majority of the project therapists had reached a reasonable level of competence. Bein et al. felt safe in suggesting that the 9 therapists who did not conduct a minimally skillful posttraining case were not "TLDP learners" and that some, but probably not all, of the remaining 7 therapists had been learners. Bein et al. frequently found therapists spontaneously asking patients about their feelings about the therapeutic relationship or offering hasty transference interpretations that were not adequately grounded in previous session material. They also found that when therapists did offer appropriate transference interpretations, they often seemed unsure of how to follow up to deepen the patient's emotional experience and self-understanding. These common behaviors were taken as evidence of therapists still struggling to consolidate a basic level of competence at a new approach to treatment. Whether skillfully and faithfully conducted TLDP is an effective treatment, such treatment was not administered to most of the posttraining patients.

Why did the therapists not learn more from the year-long training? A study of the audiotapes of the training sessions currently in progress may yield useful information about the strengths and weaknesses of the training that had been offered. In addition, it is valuable to compare the intensity of the manual-guided training and supervision provided in the study with that provided in other studies of manualized treatments. For example, in the National Institute of Mental Health Collaborative Study of Depression (Elkin, Parloff, Hadley, & Autry, 1985), the interpersonal psychotherapy therapists had three to five videotaped training cases for which they received individual supervision for each therapy session. Therapists who did not achieve a high level of skill during training were removed from the project, and a lower level of supervision was continued during the official project therapies (Rounsaville et al., 1988). By contrast, the Vanderbilt II therapists had a single training case, received no individual supervision, were never removed from the project, and received little supervision with their posttraining cases. However, providing the kind of training the interpersonal psychotherapy therapists received to an appreciable proportion of the therapeutic community is economically unfeasible; the level of training provided by the Vanderbilt II project is much closer to what is viable for meeting real-world training needs. How much and the kind of training required to bring most therapists to a reasonable level of mastery of TLDP remains unanswered.

Finally, it seems important to distinguish two important issues regarding the value of manual-based training and manualized therapies in clinical settings. The first regards training: Are therapists trained more effectively if their training emphasizes the use of treatment manuals? For example, will graduate students more quickly master basic therapy skills and more coherently develop a theoretical orientation if treatment manuals are used in their training and their clinical supervisors emphasize the value of adherence to these manuals? Will the use of treatment manuals promote the establishment of sound habits of mind regarding case formulation and treatment planning?

The second question concerns practice: Would most therapists be more effective if they strictly adhered to a manualized therapy as opposed to practicing a more idiosyncratic, technically eclectic brand of therapy? Meehl (1954) and others have shown that clinicians conducting psychological testing often overestimate their ability to integrate and draw valid conclusions from the large body of data such testing generates and that empirically derived formulas frequently outperform the assessment of experts. Similarly, there are some seldom-recognized cognitive biases that limit clinicians' abilities to process complex clinical situations accurately. Could it be that, analogously, most psychotherapists overestimate their ability to improvise productively and would be better served adhering to an established and clearly articulated therapeutic approach?

The foregoing kinds of questions are related but distinct. One could imagine, for example, that novice therapists would typically profit from manual-guided training but that experienced therapists would typically be hampered by closely adhering to a manualized form of treatment.

Implications for Training

The research studies described in this chapter clearly have important implications for the training of therapists. To explore some of these, let me begin by asking why therapists in the Vanderbilt II study did not learn more from the year-long training in a manualized form of psychotherapy.

Beyond their agreement to participate in the project, the therapists in that study were under no obligation to adopt TLDP principles and techniques. They had completed their formal training as psychiatrists or clinical psychologists, had been engaged in private practice for several years, had received supervision as part of their doctoral or postdoctoral training, and considered themselves—one can safely assume—competent practitioners. They were presumably interested in a worthwhile learning experience and felt free to adopt or to ignore the principles and techniques emphasized in the training. For their part, Bein et al. (1997) were eager to keep the therapists interested and motivated in remaining in the study, which involved a major commitment (e.g., treating two patients for up to 25 hr before training, participating in the year-long training program for 2 hr per week, treating a patient under supervision during training, and treating two additional patients after training). Therapists received payment for the treatments but not for the training. Unlike graduate students or residents in psychiatry, who must strive to attain passing grades, no such strictures applied. By contrast, in the National Institute of Mental Health Collaborative Study of Depression, much more intensive training was provided. For example, therapists continued to receive supervision after their training, and in a few instances therapists whose performance was judged to be substandard were replaced.

After having studied the therapists' performance after TLDP training, Bein et al. (1997) concluded that the changes in technique had been relatively superficial. Specifically, they found that although the therapists tended to "adhere" to a greater extent to the

TLDP principles, more thoroughgoing changes in their performance were largely absent. Therapists often "delivered" TLDP interventions in a fairly forced and mechanical manner, suggesting that adherence to particular aspects of a protocol and skillful performance were far from identical. Most problematic were therapists' attempts to use TLDP-specific interventions dealing with the therapeutic relationship. In particular, they were often premature in addressing the therapeutic relationship before a pattern had been explored sufficiently to permit plausible connections between the patient's concerns outside of therapy and specific events in therapy. Furthermore, whereas therapists made greater use of TLDP-specific techniques (e.g., focusing on the patient–therapist relationship, addressing transactions in the here and now), they also, as might be expected, made extensive use of numerous other techniques that were already part of their therapeutic repertoire.

Among other possible improvements, it might have been preferable to use novice therapists rather than practitioners who already had several years of postgraduate experience and had developed a style of their own. The use of beginning therapists also might have resulted in a more homogeneous sample, but individual differences would still have persisted and exerted a considerable influence.

More important, therapists' newly acquired TLDP skills were filtered through their preexisting personal dispositions, which were unlikely to be significantly altered through a program of manualized study. Specifically, my colleagues and I found that therapists whose introject ratings emerged as self-controlling and self-blaming showed the highest technical adherence to TLDP. When we examined treatment outcomes as a function of the therapist's introject, we found that self-controlling and self-blaming therapists had significantly poorer outcomes than those of therapists having different introject patterns (Henry, Schacht, et al., 1993). Finally, therapists with self-indicting introjects were judged to display in their therapy sessions the least warmth and friendliness, and their patients showed the highest level of hostility. In summary, these therapists were not interchangeable units, and their adoption of techniques could not be standardized.

To state the basic point more boldly: Psychotherapy in general, and the therapeutic relationship in particular, represents a broad and multifaceted social influence, and it appears highly artificial —indeed, fallacious—to presume that it can be reduced to a few simple parameters. Furthermore, the most essential therapist characteristics cannot be culled out of some sort of "psychic centrifuge" for the purposes of empirical study. As Lambert (1989) noted, "the therapist is more than the sum of the dimensions (and interaction of dimensions) that is usually studied in traditional process and outcome research" (p. 471). Standing in isolation, the therapist's demographic characteristics, attitudes, values, professional affiliations, and techniques have little to do with the ability, as a person, to relate comfortably with others, to serve as a model for adult living, to be sensitive to subtle but essential interpersonal dynamics, and to allow oneself to be privy to the unfolding of the patient's cyclical maladaptive patterns while appropriately maintaining professional distance (this is no small order). Although techniques may be taught and rotely implemented, it is the therapist who provides the *élan vital* to these lifeless abstractions. Indeed, some master therapists may have difficulty teaching their strategies to others because their techniques are intertwined with their very being.

In a recent article dealing with the future role of the university in the computer age, an observation of Noam (1995), a professor of finance and economics at Columbia University, has impressive significance for the enterprise of psychotherapy as well: "True teaching and learning are more than information and its transmission. *Education is based on mentoring, internalization, identification, role modeling, guidance, socialization, interaction, and group activity* [italics added]" (p. 249). With equal validity one might say that psychotherapeutic treatment is considerably more than the application of techniques set forth in a treatment manual. As a large psychodynamic literature has long attested, therapeutic change is likewise a function of mentoring, internalization, identification, role modeling, guidance, socialization, and interaction.

Early in the history of psychoanalysis, Freud characterized psychotherapy as a form of "aftereducation" (*Nacherziehung*); in other words, a teaching and learning process (Alexander & French, 1946). He understood that psychotherapy is not a treatment except in a metaphoric sense and that it can never be a product of a commodity delivered by a technician to a passive individual. As has frequently been discussed over the years, the therapist functions as a teacher and mentor whose attitudes and values the patient internalizes and with whom he or she identifies; furthermore, the therapist functions as a model of adult living and provides guidance as well as a benign and nurturing social milieu in which the patient can "grow" and mature. In the therapeutic context, too, the therapist is in a position to demonstrate to the patient beliefs and patterns of behavior that have been self-defeating, painful, and troublesome. In other words, the therapist effectively mediates unlearning that is typically a prerequisite to new learning. Clearly, such a corrective emotional experience cannot be prescribed, easily packaged, and dispensed.

To return once again to the alleged distinction between "psychoanalysis" and "psychoanalytic psychotherapy": Whereas the general principles of what constitutes therapeutic unlearning and learning are well understood, their application in a specific case often calls for consummate empathic understanding, sensitivity, tact, and skill on the therapist's part. It is an intricate and intuitive process in which each therapeutic hour may become an artistic creation that is highly personalized and tailored to the needs of the individual patient at a particular time. Therapists need to determine the center of the patient's current difficulty and to frame their communications in a way that is most helpful to the patient at this juncture. This often means "not getting in the way," staying out of power struggles, and avoiding interpretations that might be complementary to the patient's provocations. In each instance, there are probably a number of ways in which this can be accomplished, with no single sure-fire formula for success. On the other hand, there are undoubtedly many ways in which the therapist can interfere with, undercut, sabotage, or otherwise derail the therapeutic process.

How does the therapist acquire the requisite skills? Like any complex and intricate process, it takes time, effort, instruction, and practice. Toward this goal a treatment manual can be a useful beginning or a reference. Perhaps this is the most that can be expected.

Instruction in psychotherapy, like the practice of therapy, has become briefer and often provides little opportunity to practice and explore the gamut of issues confronted in therapy. I feel strongly that psychotherapy training has not kept pace with the times: It has remained essentially unchanged over the past 80 years and has, for the most part, remained unsystematic. In particular, it is just beginning to make use of modern technology (e.g., CD-ROM), which undoubtedly will come to play a major role in presenting to students various technical problems and serve as a vehicle for learning and discussion.

One of the most important lessons from the Vanderbilt studies is the need for a good theory of therapeutic practice. As Lewin noted many years ago, there is nothing as practical as a good theory. In the Vanderbilt I study, my colleagues and I discovered that the college professors, although highly competent in interpersonal relationships, lacked a theory of psychotherapy. They repeatedly noted that after a few sessions with their patients, they "ran out of material to talk about." In short, they were floundering. My colleagues and I also discovered—if further evidence were required—that trained psychotherapists use more than "a bag of tricks" in relating to and communicating with their patients. They need to know where they want to go and how to get there, what to do and what not to do, how to say it using language and metaphor individually tailored to each patient, how and when to do it—in short, they need a conceptual road map. Finally, it has become abundantly clear that these skills are not acquired in a few easy lessons; they call for intensive training over an extended period of time, the apparent results of the Vanderbilt I study to the contrary notwithstanding.

References

Alexander, F., & French, T. M. (1946). *Psychoanalytic therapy: Principles and applications*. New York: Ronald Press.

Bein, E., Anderson, T., Strupp, H. H., Henry, W. P., Schacht, T. E., Binder, J. L., & Butler, S. F. (1997). *The effects of training in time-limited dynamic psychotherapy: Changes in therapeutic outcome*. Manuscript submitted for publication.

Benjamin, L. S. (1974). Structural Analysis of Social Behavior. *Psychological Review, 81,* 392–425.

Butler, S. F., Henry, W. P., & Strupp, H. H. (1996). Measuring adherence in time-limited dynamic psychotherapy. *Psychotherapy, 32,* 629–638.

Elkin, I., Parloff, M., Hadley, S., & Autry, J. (1985). NIMH Treatment of Depression Collaborative Research Program: Background and research plan. *Archives of General Psychiatry, 42,* 305–316.

Goldfried, M., Greenberg, L., & Marmar, C. (1990). Individual psychotherapy: Process and outcome. *Annual Review of Psychology, 41,* 659–688.

Gomes-Schwartz, B. (1978). Effective ingredients in psychotherapy: Prediction of outcome from process variables. *Journal of Consulting and Clinical Psychology, 46,* 1023–1035.

Hartley, D. E., & Strupp, H. H. (1983). The therapeutic alliance: Its relationship to outcome in brief psychotherapy. In J. Masling (Ed.), *Empirical studies of psychoanalytical theories* (Vol. 1, pp. 1–37). Hillsdale, NJ: Analytic Press.

Henry, W. P., Schacht, T. E., & Strupp, H. H. (1986). Structural Analysis of Social Behavior: Application to a study of interpersonal process in differential psychotherapeutic outcome. *Journal of Consulting and Clinical Psychology, 54,* 27–31.

Henry, W. P., Schacht, T. E., & Strupp, H. H. (1990). Patient and therapist introject, interpersonal process, and differential psychotherapy outcome. *Journal of Consulting and Clinical Psychology, 58,* 768–774.

Henry, W. P., Schacht, T. E., Strupp, H. H., Butler, S. F., & Binder, J. L. (1993). The effects of training in time-limited dynamic psychotherapy: Mediators of therapist's response to training. *Journal of Consulting and Clinical Psychology, 61,* 441–447.

Henry, W. P., & Strupp, H. H. (1994). The therapeutic alliance as interpersonal process. In A. O. Horvath & L. S. Greenberg (Eds.), *The working alliance: Theory, research and practice* (pp. 51–84). New York: Wiley.

Henry, W. P., Strupp, H. H., Butler, S. F., Schacht, T. E., & Binder, J. L. (1993). The effects of training in time-limited dynamic psychotherapy: Changes in therapist behavior. *Journal of Consulting and Clinical Psychology, 61,* 434–440.

Hentschel, V., & Bijleveld, C. J. H. (1995). It takes two to do therapy: On differential aspects in the formation of therapeutic alliance. *Psychotherapy Research, 5,* 22–32.

Keithly, L. J., Samples, S. J., & Strupp, H. H. (1980). Patient motivation as a predictor of process and outcome in psychotherapy. *Psychotherapy and Psychosomatics, 33,* 87–97.

Kiesler, D. J., & Watkins, L. M. (1989). Interpersonal complementarity and the therapeutic alliance: A study of relationship in psychotherapy. *Psychotherapy, 26,* 183–196.

Klee, M. R., Abeles, N., & Muller, R. T. (1990). Therapeutic alliance: Early indicators, course, and outcome. *Psychotherapy, 27,* 166–174.

Lambert, M. J. (1989). The individual therapist's contribution to psychotherapy process and outcome. *Clinical Psychology Reviews, 9,* 469–485.

Meehl, P. E. (1954). *Clinical versus statistical prediction*. Minneapolis: University of Minnesota Press.

Moras, K., & Strupp, H. H. (1982). Pre-therapy interpersonal relations, a patient's alliance, and outcome in brief therapy. *Archives of General Psychiatry, 39*, 405–409.

Najavits, L. M., & Strupp, H. H. (1994). Differences in the effectiveness of psychodynamic therapists: A process-outcome study. *Psychotherapy, 31*, 114–123.

Noam, E. M. (1995). Electronics and the dim future of the university. *Science, 210*, 247–249.

Rounsaville, B. J., O'Malley, S., Foley, S., & Weissman, M. M. (1988). The role of manual-guided training in the conduct and efficiency of interpersonal psychotherapy for depression. *Journal of Consulting and Clinical Psychology, 56*, 681–688.

Soldz, S. (1990). The therapeutic interaction: Research perspectives. In R. A. Wells & V. J. Gianetti (Eds.), *Handbook of the brief psychotherapies* (pp. 27–54). New York: Plenum.

Strupp, H. H. (1955a). An objective comparison of Rogerian and psychoanalytic techniques. *Journal of Consulting Psychology, 19*, 1–7.

Strupp, H. H. (1955b). Psychotherapeutic technique, professional affiliation, and experience level. *Journal of Consulting Psychology, 19*, 97–102.

Strupp, H. H. (1955c). The effect of the psychotherapist's personal analysis upon his techniques. *Journal of Consulting Psychology, 19*, 197–204.

Strupp, H. H. (1960). *Psychotherapies in action*. New York: Grune & Stratton.

Strupp, H. H. (1962a). The therapist's contribution to the treatment process: Beginning and vagaries of a research program. In H. H. Strupp & L. Luborsky (Eds.), *Research in psychotherapy* (Vol. 2, pp. 25–40). Washington, DC: American Psychological Association.

Strupp, H. H. (1962b). Patient-doctor relationships: Psychotherapist in the therapeutic process. In A. J. Bachrach (Ed.), *Experimental foundations of clinical psychology* (pp. 576–615). New York: Basic Books.

Strupp, H. H. (1973). On the basic ingredients of psychotherapy. *Journal of Consulting and Clinical Psychology, 41*, 1–8.

Strupp, H. H. (1978). Suffering and psychotherapy. *Contemporary Psychoanalysis, 14*, 73–97.

Strupp, H. H. (1980a). Success and failure in time-limited psychotherapy: A systematic comparison of two cases (Comparison 1). *Archives of General Psychiatry, 37*, 595–603.

Strupp, H. H. (1980b). Success and failure in time-limited psychotherapy: A systematic comparison of two cases (Comparison 2). *Archives of General Psychiatry, 37*, 708–716.

Strupp, H. H. (1980c). Success and failure in time-limited psychotherapy: With special reference to the performance of a lay counselor (Comparison 3). *Archives of General Psychiatry, 37*, 831–841.

Strupp, H. H. (1980d). Success and failure in time-limited psychotherapy:

Further evidence (Comparison 4). *Archives of General Psychiatry, 37,* 947–954.

Strupp, H. H. (1990). The case of Helen R. *Psychotherapy: Theory, Research and Practice, 27,* 644–656.

Strupp, H. H. (1993). The Vanderbilt psychotherapy studies: Synopsis. *Journal of Consulting and Clinical Psychology, 61,* 431–433.

Strupp, H. H., & Binder, J. L. (1984). *Psychotherapy in a new key: A guide to time-limited dynamic psychotherapy.* New York: Basic Books.

Strupp, H. H., & Hadley, S. W. (1979). Specific versus nonspecific factors in psychotherapy: A controlled study of outcome. *Archives of General Psychiatry, 36,* 1125–1136.

Strupp, H. H., & Howard, K. I. (1992). A brief history of psychotherapy research. In D. Freedheim (Ed.), *History of psychotherapy: A century of change* (pp. 309–334). Washington, DC: American Psychological Association.

Strupp, H. H., Schacht, T. E., Henry, W. P., & Binder, J. L. (1992). Jack M: A case of premature termination. *Psychotherapy, 29,* 191–206.

Strupp, H. H., & Wallach, M. S. (1965). A further study of psychiatrists' responses in quasi-therapy situations. *Behavioral Science, 10,* 113–134.

Strupp, H. H., & Williams, J. V. (1960). Some determinants of clinical evaluations of different psychiatrists. *Archives of General Psychiatry, 2,* 434–440.

Suh, C. S., O'Malley, S. S., & Strupp, H. H. (1986). The Vanderbilt Process Measures: The Psychotherapy Process Scale (VPPS) and the Negative Indicators Scale (VNIS). In L. S. Greenberg & W. M. Pinsof (Eds.), *The psychotherapeutic process: A research handbook* (pp. 285–324). New York: Guilford Press.

Tasca, G. A., & McMullen, L. M. (1992). Interpersonal complementarity and antitheses within a stage model of psychotherapy. *Psychotherapy, 29,* 515–523.

Wachtel, P. L. (1993). *Therapeutic communication.* New York: Guilford Press.

Wile, D. B. (1984). Kohut, Kernberg, and accusatory interpretations. *Psychotherapy, 21,* 353–364.

Wiseman, H., Shefler, G., Caneti, L., & Ronen, Y. (1993). A systematic comparison of two cases in Mann's time-limited psychotherapy: An events approach. *Psychotherapy Research, 3,* 227–244.

2

Interaction Structure and Change in Psychoanalytic Therapy

Enrico E. Jones and Pauline B. Price

There is a long-standing debate among psychoanalytic clinicians concerning the nature of therapeutic action. This scientific and clinical discourse has been organized around two principal hypothesized sources of therapeutic action: (a) interpretation and psychological knowledge and (b) interpersonal interaction. Those who emphasize the importance of interpretation view as decisive the patient's self-knowledge, understanding, and insight. Interactive models, in turn, emphasize interpersonal and relationship factors, such as empathy, a sense of safety, the containment of feelings, and therapeutic alliance. These ideas parallel the debate concerning the usefulness of a "one-person" as opposed to a "two-person" psychology for conceptualizing therapeutic process. The question is whether psychological processes can be conceptualized as being within the mind of an individual, or whether primary attention should be given to an individual's experience of the external, particularly of the therapist. A similar parallel has emerged in discussions of the relative importance of specific as opposed to nonspecific effects of interventions that have so dominated the field of psychotherapy research in recent decades. *Specific factors* are well-defined, intentional actions on the part of the therapist that are linked to a particular theory about patient change, such as interpretation or linking past experience to the present. *Nonspecific factors* are qualities inherent in any positive human relationship that felicitously affect an individual's expectations or morale.

The dialogue concerning whether therapeutic action can be located in the achievement of psychological knowledge through uncovering meaning, or through interpersonal interaction, has from the beginning constituted an important tension for psychoanalytically informed technique. Interaction was presumed to be a process similar to interpersonal influence, or indirect suggestion. Freud (1921/1955) considered suggestibility, or the tendency to be influenced without adequate rational foundation, to be an irreducible, fundamental fact in mental life. It was at base an expression of an emotional tie, of love or libido or sexual instinct. As Freud more fully understood the phenomenon of transference, psychoanalytic thinking took a position in strong opposition to the use of hypnosis and has since been cautious about the purposeful or unwitting use of the analyst's authority to influence patients. As the early form of interpretation analysis, in which the aim was to make the unconscious conscious, evolved into resistance, or defense, analysis, analysts became more attentive to the role of relational aspects. Freud stated his understanding of this component of therapeutic action in several essays:

> Personal influence is our most powerful dynamic weapon. . . .
> The neurotic sets to work because he has faith in the analyst,
> and he believes him because he acquires a special emotional
> attitude towards the figure of the analyst. . . . We make use of
> this particularly large suggestive influence. Not for suppressing
> symptoms . . . but as a motive force to induce the patient to
> overcome his resistances. (Freud, 1926/1959, pp. 224–225)

Strachey (1934) proposed a more formal role for relationship factors in his view that patient change is made possible by alterations in the ego occurring as a consequence of the analyst's suggestion that the patient become more tolerant of threatening and conflicted mental contents. "Mutative interpretations" effected change partially by means of the analyst's influence as a more tolerant auxiliary superego. The patient is given permission to consciously experience some threatening emotion or idea ("You can allow yourself to experience your hostility and hatred"). Here, then, the role of the therapist's suggestive influence is an important factor in the change process, although applied in a limited, articulated, and self-conscious way. Some modern defense analysis-oriented theorists such as Gray (1994) argue that using positive transferences to overcome resistance, although still widely done, relies too much on indirect suggestion and the use of authority. He noted that in Strachey's conceptualization, an important element of therapeutic action is the gradual replacement of the primitive superego by the internalization of the more benevolent attitude of the therapist, processes that occur outside the patient's awareness. He emphasized instead the importance of helping patients develop the capacity for self-observation and for focusing on conflict and defensive processes that can be consciously and directly observed.

Interaction-oriented theorists emphasize the possibilities offered by a new object relationship to permit the resumption of developmental processes that are hypothesized to have been arrested by trauma or deficiencies in early interpersonal relations. There are several viewpoints within "interactional" or "intersubjective" approaches, and they derive both from conventional ego psychology or modern structural theory (e.g., Weiss & Sampson, 1986) as well as object relations theory (Mitchell, 1993; Modell, 1976). Although all these theories emphasize the therapeutic action of interpersonal interaction, they differ in their explanation of the nature of the psychological processes by which a new kind of interpersonal experience effects change. Loewald (1960), for example, thought of therapeutic action as a process that was parallel to ego development, particularly early identification through introjection of the mother's image of the child. He held that if analysis was to be a process leading to structural change, interactions of a comparable nature would have to take place. The reemphasis of interactional approaches on the role of trauma and the experience of the early parent–child relationship in the etiology of mental problems has led to greater attention to the emotional climate in which treatment takes place and raises the question of whether interaction is necessarily indirect suggestion (Kohut, 1984; Winnicott, 1965). The interpersonal interaction models assume a strong developmental point of view. They construct an analogy between the interpersonal, empathic bond between the therapist and patient and that between the parent and child and hold that uninterpreted aspects of interaction are equally or even more mutative than achieving psychological knowledge through the interpretive process.

Interactional models have been criticized for placing too much emphasis on the role of external influences and for conceptualizing motivation, intent, and instrumentality as having primarily external sources. Human motivation has its source primarily in reaction to important objects. Relational thinkers conceptualize both the transference and resistance as being the creation of the interaction between the patient and therapist rather than as being located within the patient (Sugarman & Wilson, 1995). It is assumed, for example, that defensive processes are catalyzed by failures in the therapist's empathy or by some misunderstanding by the therapist. The patient is seen as instrumental only in the realm of adaptively oriented object seeking; deviation from benign object seeking is seen as resulting from the failure of an external object. During development, it is the relational or empathic failure of the mother; during treatment, it is the failure of the therapist (Murray, 1995). It has been argued that interactional approaches may encourage selective expression, particularly of anxiety-relieving, protection-seeking transferences to an authority figure perceived as benign, affectionate, and approving but at the cost of participating in an illusion of safety from criticism, punishment, and loss of love. The exploration by the patient and therapist of a need for the therapist's constant empathic mirroring or containment of troublesome feelings may be avoided, and aggressive, hateful, or sadomasochistic transferences may be suppressed.

Repetitive Interaction Structures

A model of therapeutic action has been advanced (Jones, 1997) that addresses the complementary roles of interpretation and interaction. It brings together these polarities in a new framework that emphasizes the presence and meaning of repetitive patterns of interaction in the therapy relationship. The model is longitudinal and emphasizes the ongoing analytic or therapeutic process. It has as its central postulate *repetitive interaction structures*, defined as repeated, mutually influencing interactions between the therapist and patient, as a fundamental aspect of therapeutic action. Repetitive interaction structures provide a way of formulating and empirically operationalizing those aspects of the analytic process that have come to be termed *intersubjectivity, transference–countertransference enactments*, and *role responsiveness*. In this model, insight and relationship are inseparable because psychological knowledge of the self can develop only in the context of a relationship in which the therapist endeavors to understand the mind of the patient through the medium of their interaction.

The patient and therapist interact in repetitive ways; these slow-to-change patterns of interaction likely reflect the psychological structure of both the patient and therapist, regardless of whether psychic structure is conceptualized in terms of object representations or compromise formations and impulse-defense configurations. Therapeutic action is located in the experience, recognition, and understanding by both the patient and therapist of these repetitive interactions. Causal influences are not assumed to flow only in the direction of therapist to patient. The nature of the patient's influence on the therapist and on the emerging patterns of relationships are considered, along with the manner in which the therapist's interventions mobilize patient change, providing a framework in which mutual or reciprocal influence processes between the patient and therapist can be taken into account. Repetitive interaction structures allow the consideration of both the intrapsychic and interpersonal interaction by recognizing the intramental as an important basis for what becomes manifest in the interpersonal or interactive field. It differs from other research-derived constructs, such as Luborsky's Core Conflictual Relationship Theme (Luborsky & Crits-Christoph, 1988), which locates the conflict in the patient and captures how these conflicts are experienced in the relationship with the therapist and important others. By contrast, repetitive interaction structures is an interactive concept. It refers not only to how the patient's conflicts are represented in the transference but also the characteristic manner in which the therapist reacts to these conflicts. In addition, it comprises important aspects of the change process by linking interaction, interpretation, and the patient's growing capacity for self-knowledge.

Innovations in Research Method: Quantitative Single-Case Studies

Studying psychoanalytic constructs requires innovative research strategies, particularly new quantitative methods for the study of single cases (Jones, 1993b). The renewed interest in the intensive study of the individual case has been prompted by a confluence of several influences in clinical research and practice. First, there has been a growing recognition of the limitations of controlled clinical trials to inform researchers about how patients change and that understanding the processes that promote therapeutic change will require a close analysis of the therapist–patient interaction. Process research that derives its data from larger samples of patients and therapists rests on two assumptions: (a) The interpersonal processes that occur have fixed meanings independent of context and (b) such processes discretely and uniquely contribute to outcomes (Shoham-Salomon, 1990). In this "decontextualized" conception of process, therapist actions (e.g., confrontation or interpretation) are assumed to have a fixed meaning (i.e., the same significance for process regardless of accuracy, timing, or importance), and they contribute to patient change directly regardless of what else is occurring between the therapist and patient. However, the meaning of events in psychotherapy is determined by context, making it difficult to identify simple, direct associations between particular therapist actions or patient behaviors and treatment outcome in group data or samples of treatments (Jones, Cumming, & Horowitz, 1988).

A second reason concerns the need to test clinical theoretical models. Although comparative treatment outcome studies can confirm the efficacy of the treatments under investigation, the probative value of such studies for the treatment models' underlying clinical constructs is indirect and limited (Persons, 1991). Finally, it has often been pointed out that treatment research has had little influence on either psychoanalytic theory building or clinical practice. The primary means of clinical inquiry, teaching, and learning in psychoanalysis has been, and still remains, the case study method, which is grounded in the tradition of naturalistic observation. Statements about psychotherapy that are derived from group data typically have little direct relevance for the clinical problems that are presented to the analytic therapist, so that much of the therapy research enterprise has remained peripheral to clinical practice and to the major theoretical and intellectual currents in psychoanalysis.

Although the study of individual cases has long been a fundamental source of data for psychoanalysis, there are long-recognized difficulties in using data so derived for hypothesis testing or for the verification of clinical constructs: the problem of assessing the reliability of case study data (i.e., the manner in which observations are selected and recorded); the difficulty in choosing among alternative interpretations of the same observations; the sources of uncontrolled variation; the problems in comparing one case study with another; and the difficulty in replication (Jones, 1993a). What is needed is a formalization of the case study method in ways that are consonant with the requirements of empirical science.

The Berkeley Psychotherapy Research Project is developing a longitudinal model for the study of single cases using quantitative methods. The approach takes into account the interaction of multiple variables or influences in clinical treatments. Specific processes are viewed as conjointly defining the meaning of an event; one element (e.g., transference interpretation) becomes more fully understood relative to others. Process is considered to be a sequence of events that extends over time and is studied as interrelated configurations or patterns of relationships among variables along temporal dimensions (Jones & Windholz, 1990). This strategy takes into account time, context, and the effect of previous hours on subsequent events in therapy. Within this framework, any given interaction is best understood within a sequence of actions that extend over time. Conventionally, samples of patient and therapist behavior or speech are used to predict outcome or to examine session differences or contrasts between therapies. Little attention is given to how the pattern of therapeutic interaction changes over the course of treatments. The strategy followed in this research is distinguished from traditional studies of process by focusing on patterns of patient–therapist interaction within and across therapy sessions and exploring the association of structure and sequence of interaction with patient change.

The research program applies an innovative set of methods in intensive single-case designs to identify the presence of repetitive interactions structures and to determine whether they are causally linked to patient change. Descriptive ratings of therapy sessions are made using the Psychotherapy Process Q-set (PQS; see below). Luborsky's (1953, 1995) P-technique is then applied to these ratings. The P-technique is a factor analysis of repeated measures within the same patient–therapist pair to identify potential underlying structures of interaction. Time series analysis (TSA; Gottman, 1981), a quantitative technique that can assess changes over time, is then used to examine the *temporal unfolding* of these factors along with patient change measures. TSA requires the repeated measure of a set of variables over time within the individual case and attempts to understand temporal variations or change in the scores of certain of these variables as a function of other variables (Czogalik & Russell, 1995; Jones, Ghannam, Nigg, & Dyer, 1993). In our study, two longer term psychoanalytic therapies were selected because they had contrasting outcomes: one successful and a second in which the patient reported little measurable change. There were three research questions: (a) whether there would be meaningful structures of patient–therapist interaction; (b) whether these would differ across the two treatments; and (c) how changes in structures of interaction might be associated with patient improvement.

Method

Patients and Treatments

The two treatments studied were conducted as part of a research program studying longer term psychotherapies for major depressive disorder. Patients referred to the research project were assessed using the following intake procedure: (a) a videotaped semistructured interview based on the Schedule for Affective Disorders and Schizophrenia (SADS-I; Endicott & Spitzer, 1977) and resulting in a Research Diagnostic Criteria (RDC) diagnosis (Spitzer, Endicott, & Robins, 1979); (b) a second 90-min videotaped life history interview covering areas of distress and symptomatology, current life circumstances, and history of interpersonal relationships; and (c) a battery of pretherapy self-report measures. Patients met the following inclusion criteria: a definite diagnosis of major depressive disorder on the RDC; a score of 16 or higher on the Beck Depression Inventory (BDI; Beck, Ward, Mendelson, Mock, & Erbaugh, 1961); and a score of 14 or higher on the Hamilton Rating Scale for Depression (HRSD; Hamilton, 1967). Therapies were conducted over a 2- to $2^1/_2$-year period, twice weekly; all treatment hours were video- and audio-recorded. Assessments were conducted every 16 sessions (see below for a description of measures). Follow-up assessments were conducted, when possible, 6 months and 1 and 2 years after treatment to track the stability of levels of improvement. Therapists were experienced practitioners whose routine and preferred approach to treatment was longer term psychodynamic psychotherapy.

Assessment of Treatment Outcome

The BDI (Beck et al., 1961) is a 21-item self-report measure designed to assess current syndromal depression. Respondents are instructed to complete each item in terms of how they have felt over the preceding week. The BDI has shown good concurrent validity when compared with psychiatric ratings of depression in both clinical populations and college students (Bumberry, Oliver, & McClure, 1978).

The SCL–90–R (Derogatis, Lipman, Rickels, Uhlenhuth, & Covi, 1974) is a multidimensional self-report inventory of symptoms, which has demonstrated both good reliability and sensitivity to change in psychotherapy, and is a widely used symptom change measure. The Automatic Thoughts Questionnaire (ATQ; Hollon & Kendall, 1980) is a 30-item self-report instrument designed to measure the frequency and intensity of negative thoughts about the self, which cognitive–behavioral theorists posit to be an etiological source of depression. It has demonstrated ability to discriminate between depressed and nondepressed groups.

The Social Adjustment Scale (SAS; Weissman, Prusoff, Thompson, Harding, & Meyers, 1978) is a 42-question self-report instrument that measures either instrumental or expressive role performance over the past 2 weeks in six major areas of functioning: work as a wage earner, housewife, or student; social and leisure activities; relationship with extended family; marital role as a spouse; parental role; and membership in the family unit.

The Minnesota Multiphasic Personality Inventory (MMPI; Dahlstrom & Welsh, 1960) can be used to identify a wide range of clinical syndromes; particularly relevant for this study was Scale 2 (Depression), a 60-item true–false inventory embedded within the larger 550-item measure. Scale 2 of the MMPI is at least as sensitive a measure of change in depression as any of the other instruments and is far less susceptible to response sets and dissimulation.

The Inventory of Interpersonal Problems (IIP; Horowitz, Rosenberg, Baer, Ureño, & Villaseñor, 1988) is a 127-item measure designed to identify interpersonal sources of distress. The respondent is asked to consider each problem on the list and, in a format similar to that of the SCL-90–R (see above), to rate how distressing that problem has been on a scale ranging from 0 (*not at all*) to 4 (*extremely*). Horowitz et al. (1988) found that although both the IIP and symptom measures are sensitive to change early in treatment, only the IIP continues to be sensitive to change at later stages of treatment.

Every 16 sessions, the therapist and patient completed an overall change rating, a 9-point scale ranging from −4 (*very much worse*) to 4 (*very much improved*).

The PQS

The PQS (Jones, 1985) provides a basic language for the description and classification of intervention processes in a form suitable for quantitative analysis. The method is designed to be applied to an audio- or videotaped record or verbatim transcript of actual treatment hours. The PQS comprises 100 items describing patient attitudes, behaviors, or experience; the therapist's actions and attitudes; and the nature of their interaction. A coding manual (Jones, 1985) provides the items and their definitions, along with examples to minimize potentially varying interpretations. After studying a record of a treatment hour, clinical judges sort the 100 PQS items, each printed separately on cards to permit easy arrangement and rearrangement, into nine piles ranging on a continuum from (1) least characteristic (Category 1) to most characteristic (Category 9). The number of cards sorted into each pile, ranging from 5 at the extremes to 18 in the middle, or "neutral," category, conforms to a normal distribution. This distribution procedure requires judges to make multiple evaluations among items, thus reducing both positive and negative halo effects.

The Q-method has special value because it provides a way of quantifying the qualities of the therapeutic process and capturing the uniqueness of each treatment hour while also permitting the assessment of the similarities or dissimilarities between hours and patients (see Block, 1961/1978). The instrument addresses key questions concerning unit of analysis, content and coverage, questions of sampling, the use of inference, and the role of theoretical perspective (Jones, Hall, & Parke, 1991). The PQS can account for the interaction of multiple influences in psychotherapeutic treatments. Specific processes are conceptualized as conjointly defining the meaning of an event; one element becomes more fully understood relative to others.

The judges of our study, a group of eight research-oriented clinicians and advanced graduate students in clinical psychology, received training in the application of the Q-sort method. Videotapes of every second hour of these two cases (as well as other treatments under study) were completely randomized, and independent Q-ratings were made by two judges who did not know one another's ratings. When agreement was below .50, a third rater was added. Interrater reliability was calculated using the Pearson product–moment correlation coefficient; average interrater reliability for the 167 hr rated for our study achieved .80 (Spearman–Brown corrected; range = .66–.94). Q-sort composites (i.e., Q-ratings meaned across judges) were used in all subsequent analyses.

Results

Patient A.: A Successful Treatment

After the two treatments under study had been completed, five psychoanalytic clinicians viewed the 90-min intake interviews for the two patients and were asked to create a case formulation. They did not know the treatment outcome and had no other information about the case beyond that contained in the initial interview. Using a variant of Caston's (1993) consensus method for developing case formulations, the clinical judges were asked to group their inferences about the case in five theoretically relevant domains: (a) conflictedness; (b) defense-impulse configurations; (c) historical antecedents; (d) wishes; and (e) transference. The resulting array of clinical propositions about the case generated by each judge was then divided into thought units and listed. Only those propositions that appeared in the material of at least three of the five judges were included in the case formulations, which are rendered in narrative form below. This method provides the basis for consensually derived case formulations.

Ms. A., a college student, was 21 years old at the beginning of treatment. She was seen for 126 sessions over a 21-month period. The immediate impetus for her seeking therapy was her depression in reaction to the sudden onset of a serious mental disorder in an older sister with whom she had a close relationship.

The clinical judges saw Ms. A. as conflicted about autonomy and independence, and guilty and inhibited about self-assertion, aggression, and competitiveness. She was conflict avoidant and relied on denial, especially of her anger and defiance, as her primary psychological defense. She tended to displace important affects, especially from her mother to her sister. She was fearful of authority figures and was generally compliant and eager to please. Ms. A. wished for both a greater sense of independence and more closeness with her parents. She also wanted to have better relationships with men.

The clinical judges agreed that Ms. A. had suffered significant trauma in early life. Her childhood was characterized by frequent relocations. She lived with her parents and older sister until the age of 7 years, at which point her parents divorced. Her father remarried shortly thereafter, and she then lived with her father, siblings, and a stepmother, along with the stepmother's children. The stepmother became the dominant figure in her life while her father withdrew emotionally, becoming preoccupied with work. Ms. A. described a bleak existence in which she had a heavy load of chores, and her stepmother was frequently physically abusive.

Ms. A. felt there was something wrong with her but that if she continued to work hard, she would eventually be accepted into the family. She also reported being sexually abused over a period of years by her stepmother's sons. Finally, in her midteens she left to live with her mother.

Patient A.: assessment of change. Figure 1 plots scores on several symptom measures over the course of treatment. Evaluating change in the single case does not allow researchers to compare such change directly with that of other patients, as is possible in large-sample studies. This problem was addressed by estimating the clinical significance of patient change using the method suggested by Jacobson and Truax (1991), which determines whether the patient achieves a postscore on a measure that is more likely to belong in the functional than the dysfunctional population. A cutoff score was calculated using the means and standard deviations from normative data for functional and dysfunctional populations for all measures for which this information was available, and it was then determined whether Ms. A. crossed the cutoff point in the direction of a functional sample from pre- to posttest. Patient A.'s treatment was, by all indexes of patient change, successful. Her symptom scores and problem indexes demonstrated clinically significant change, and she maintained these gains at 6-month and 1-year follow-ups (see Table 1 and Figure 1). Patient A. met criteria for clinically significant change both posttherapy and at 1-year follow-up on the BDI, the General Severity Index (GSI) of the SCL-90–R, the ATQ, the Depression scale of the MMPI, the SAS, and the IIP. There was a large negative correlation between the GSI and treatment session number ($r = -.82$), demonstrating a significant association between patient improvement and length of treatment.

P-technique: identifying interaction structures. To determine whether structures of interaction could be identified, we subjected the Q-ratings for each of the treatment hours ($n = 63$) to an exploratory factor analysis (principal-components method). The factor analysis yielded three conceptually interpretable clusters after varimax rotation that accounted for 37% of variance in Q-sort descriptions. The items that best defined the clusters are listed in Table 2. Factor 1 was labeled *Collaborative Exploration*; Factor 2, *Ambivalence/Compliance*; and Factor 3, *Provoking Rescue*. Factor scales were constructed by averaging the relevant PQS items for each of

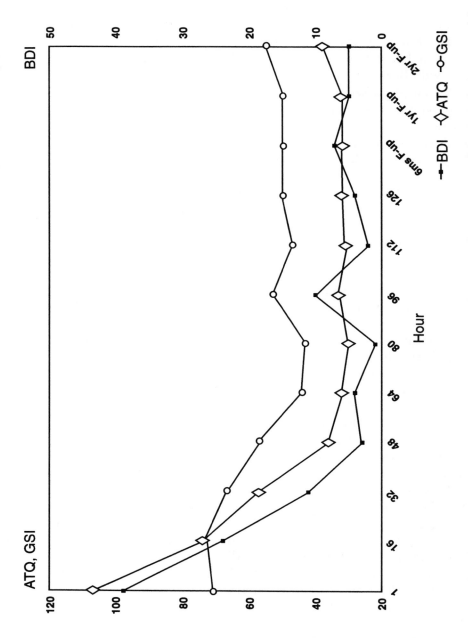

Figure 1. Plot of scores on Ms. A.'s symptom measures over the 21-month treatment and at 6-month, 1-year, and 2-year follow-ups. Beck = BDI Depression Inventory; ATQ = Automatic Thoughts Questionnaire; GSI = General Severity Index of the SCL-90–R; F-up = follow-up.

Table 1

Patient A. and Patient B. Scores on Assessment Measures

Measure	Patient A.			Patient B.		
	Pretherapy	Posttherapy	1-Year follow-up	Pretherapy	Posttherapy	1-Year follow-up
SADS RDC	Major depressive disorder	—	—	Major depressive disorder	—	—
Hamilton Rating Scale for Depression	30	—	—	23	—	—
Beck Depression Inventory	40	3[a]	4[a]	18	12[a]	17
SCL-90–R (GSI)	71	50[a]	50[a]	81	74[a]	75
Automatic Thoughts Questionnaire	107	32[a]	32[a]	68	54[a]	64
MMPI-2 Depression scale	62	42[a]	47[a]	92	77	73
Social Adjustment Scale	2.65	1.42[a]	1.69[a]	2.33	1.56[a]	1.78[a]
Inventory of Interpersonal Problems	2.64	0.34[a]	0.79[a]	1.41	1.62	1.39
Patient change rating (−4 to 4)	—	4	3	—	3	2
Therapist Change Rating (−4 to 4)	—	2	—	—	2.5	—

Note. SADS RDC = Schedule for Affective Disorders and Schizophrenia Research Diagnostic Criteria; GSI = General Severity Index; MMPI-2 = Minnesota Multiphasic Personality Inventory-2. Dashes indicate that data were not available.
[a]Patient met criteria for clinically significant change.

Table 2

Patient A.: Repetitive Interaction Structures

Q-item no. and factor	Loading
Factor 1: Collaborative Exploration	
73. The patient is committed to the work of therapy.	.77
95. Patient feels helped.	.70
97. Patient is introspective, readily explores inner thoughts and feelings.	.70
88. Patient brings up significant issues and material.	.65
55. Patient conveys positive expectations about therapy.	.63
72. Patient understands the nature of therapy and what is expected.	.63
10. Patient seeks greater intimacy with the therapist.	.57
32. Patient achieves a new understanding or insight.	.56
Factor 2: Ambivalence/Compliance	
58. Patient resists examining thoughts, reactions, or motivations related to problems.	.71
8. Patient is concerned or conflicted about his or her dependence on the therapist (vs. comfortable with dependency or wanting dependency).	.65
49. The patient experiences ambivalent or conflicted feelings about the therapist.	.64
44. Patient feels wary or suspicious (vs. trusting and secure).	.63
87. Patient is controlling.	.57
20. Patient is provocative, tests limits of the therapy relationship. (N.B. Placement toward uncharacteristic end implies patient behaves in a compliant manner.)	.51
Factor 3: Provoking Rescue	
12. Silences occur during the hour.	.78
13. Patient is (not) animated or excited.	.73
15. Patient does not initiate topics; is passive.	.63
61. Patient feels shy and embarrassed (vs. unselfconscious and self-assured).	.63
54. Patient is (not) clear and organized in self-expression.	.60
41. Patient's aspirations or ambitions are (not) topics of discussion.	.58
25. Patient has difficulty beginning the hour.	.57
74. Humor is (not) used.	.57
94. Patient feels sad or depressed (vs. joyous or cheerful).	.56

continued

Table 2 (*Continued*)

Q-item no. and factor	Loading
Factor 3: Provoking Rescue	
59. Patient feels inadequate and inferior (vs. effective or superior).	.55
56. Patient (does not) discuss experiences as if distant from his or her feelings. (N.B. Rate as neutral if affect and import are apparent but modulated.)	.55
52. Patient relies upon therapist to solve her problems.	.50
69. Patient's current or recent life situation is (not) emphasized in discussion.	.50

the three clusters after reversing the coding of the items that were negative indicators of the factors. The alpha reliabilities were .86, .78, and .89, respectively.

Patient A.: TSA. We hypothesized that decline in the intensity and frequency of certain interaction structures would be related to patient improvement. It is, of course, more difficult to infer causation from quantitative single-case designs than from randomized clinical trials. However, single-case designs have an advantage in affording multiple observations of the same variables taken at regular time intervals (i.e., time series data). In addition to knowing the magnitude of change in a variable, one also knows when that change occurred relative to changes in other variables. Causality can therefore be inferred inductively using TSA. The basic logic is as follows: If, for example, the factor labeled Collaborative Exploration influenced symptom improvement, then a score on the SCL-90−R at a given time should be predictable from past levels of Collaborative Exploration above and beyond what is predictable from knowing previous SCL-90−R scores alone. Furthermore, the influence should be unidirectional (i.e., SCL-90−R scores should not predict future Collaborative Exploration above and beyond what could be predicted from past Collaborative Exploration).

Gottman and Ringland's (1981) statistical approach formally tests this logic. Their bivariate TSA is designed to determine whether one series of scores (e.g., on an outcome measure) may be predicted from the history of another series of scores (e.g., Collaborative Exploration) controlling for autocorrelation (or correlation across time) within the first series. Predicting one series from the history of the other is called *cross-regression*, whereas predicting a series from its own history is called *autoregression*. Four regression equations (models) are built for each series. The models differ with respect to the number of autoregressive and cross-regressive terms that they contain. The number of terms in a model corresponds to the number of lags (i.e., the number of data points into the future that are used in the regression equation). Likelihood ratio tests are then used to discover which model best describes the series with the minimum number of terms. The unidirectionality of influence is then tested by transposing the predicted and predicting series and repeating the procedure (Pole & Jones, 1998).

Scores on the four process factors for each rated treatment hour ($n = 63$) and GSI scores were subjected to a TSA to determine whether one series was partially predictable from another. Because GSI scores from the SCL-90–R were obtained only after every 16th session, the values of the missing scores were estimated by calculating a moving average (Jones et. al., 1993). Estimating so many data points was deemed justifiable when cross-correlations of the true GSI scores confirmed the results of the TSA. Table 3 illustrates the procedure applied to the factor Provoking Rescue, the only factor that unambiguously predicted changes in scores on the symptom measure. For each factor the procedure first constructs four regression models (i, ii, iii, and iv). Models listed under Provoking Rescue attempt to predict scores on the Provoking Rescue factor. Models listed under GSI attempt to predict the GSI score. The number of autoregressive terms in each model is given under columns A and C. The number of cross-regressive terms is given under columns B and D. The first model is always given 10 autoregressive terms and 10 cross-regressive terms; it is designed to be oversized (i.e., it uses an arbitrarily large number of terms to predict a given time series; see Gottman, 1981, for details). The column marked *SSE* gives the sum of squared error, an index of variability left unexplained. The objective of the TSA is to minimize *SSE* while minimizing the number of terms in the equation. The goal is to explain the greatest variance with the simplest model. Model ii contains the smallest number of autoregressive terms and cross-regressive terms. This is the simplest model that controls for au-

Table 3

Summary of Time Series Analysis for Patient A.

Model	A		B	SSE	C		D	SSE
	Provoking Rescue				GSI total score			
i	10		10	40.47	10		10	17.19
ii	4		0	57.49	2		5	7.07
iii	4		0	57.49	2		0	9.68
iv	10		0	48.09	10		0	15.13
i vs. ii	$Q(16) = 18.59$, *ns*				$Q(13) = -47.00$, *ns*			
ii vs. iii	$Q(0) = 0$, *ns*				$Q(5) = 16.00$, $p < .01$			
iii vs. iv	$Q(6) = 9.46$, *ns*				$Q(8) = -23.64$, *ns*			
Conclusions:	GSI ↛ Provoking Rescue				Provoking Rescue → GSI			

Note. The bivariate time series analysis (Gottman & Ringland, 1981) is conducted by comparing four types of regression equations (models) to determine the smallest model (minimum number of terms) that minimizes residual error of prediction. Values under columns A and C represent the number of autoregressive terms in each model. Values under columns B and D represent the number of cross-regressive terms in each model. *SSE* = sums of square error (unexplained error variance when a given model is applied). Pairwise comparisons between the four models are evaluated using the *Q* statistic, whose significance can be estimated using a chi-square table. GSI = General Severity Index of the SCL-90–R. Comparisons of Model i versus Model ii and Model iii versus Model iv represent internal checks of the model, whereas the comparison of Model ii versus Model iii indicates the presence or absence of predictability of one series from the other, controlling for autocorrelation. Causality → is implied when Model ii is the best model; ↛ = causality not implied.

tocorrelation and also uses information from the other series. For example, Model ii under Provoking Rescue predicts scores on this factor using four autoregressive terms and no cross-regressive terms, but it leaves a larger residual (*SSE*) than Model i. Model iii also predicts Provoking Rescue with four autoregressive and no cross-regressive terms. Model iv predicts the factor with the maximum autoregressive terms and no cross-regressive terms. It is the oversized, purely autoregressive model.

The next step is to test which of these best fits the data given the goals of minimizing both the number of terms and the residual error. This is accomplished using a likelihood ratio comparison. The comparison is evaluated using a Q statistic, which has a chi-square distribution. This is best illustrated by examining the results displayed under the heading GSI total score. A comparison of Models i and ii revealed that the two were not significantly different in their ability to explain variability, $Q(13) = -47.0$, ns. In this case, Model ii is superior because it has fewer terms. A comparison between Models ii and iii revealed a significant difference in their ability to explain variability, $Q(5) = 16.0$, $p < .01$. Model ii is better because it left a smaller residual. Finally, the comparison between Models iii and iv also revealed no significant differences, $Q(8) = -23.64$, ns, suggesting that Model iii is better because it has fewer terms. However, as we have seen, Model ii is superior to Model iii. Model ii is therefore best for predicting the GSI score. Patient symptom change is best predicted by a Lag 2 autoregression and a Lag 5 cross-regression. Note the comparisons under Provoking Rescue revealed no significant differences between the residuals left by any of the models. Both Models ii and iii have the smallest number of terms, and GSI scores contribute nothing to the prediction of changes on the Provoking Rescue factor. We can therefore conclude that the bivariate TSA demonstrates that shifts in Provoking Rescue influence changes on Patient A.'s symptom scores.

Patient B.: An Unsuccessful Treatment

Mr. B. was a 29-year-old single man who had an advanced degree in a business-related field. He was seen for a total of 208 treatment sessions over a $2^1/_2$-year period. His presenting complaint was a long-standing depression and anxiety, which had recently become particularly acute. Mr. B. felt isolated and lonely, and pressured by his job, where he felt he had to work under disinterested authority figures. He lacked self-confidence and was deeply pessimistic about his future. He also reported a variety of somatic complaints that he believed were related to stress and anxiety.

Clinical judges viewed Mr. B. as conflicted about closeness and intimacy as well as commitment. He was seen as using primarily cognitive defenses, such as intellectualization and isolation, as well as somatization, to ward off feelings of sadness and anger. They understood the origins of Mr. B.'s difficulties to stem from the death of his mother at the age of 12, unresolved grief at her loss, and his identification with a depressed, pessimistic, and emotionally withdrawn father. This was judged to be the source of his difficulty in being aware of and expressing affect; he tended to shut off or repress his feelings. Mr. B. was seen as wishing to repair the loss of his mother, to achieve intimacy with women, and to be strong and successful. The judges predicted that his primary transferences toward the therapist would be a yearning for a mother figure and struggles around submitting to, or defeating, authority figures.

Patient B.: assessment of change. Mr. B.'s symptom scores fluctuated considerably, and at termination he was somewhat improved, although at 1-year follow-up he had returned to pretreatment levels on some indices (see Table 1). Figure 2 plots some of the symptom measures over the course of treatment. Mr. B. met criteria for clinically significant change at posttherapy on the BDI, ATQ, and SAQ, but not on the SCL-90–R, the IIP or the Depression scale of the MMPI. At the 1-year follow-up, Mr. B. met criteria for clinically significant change only on the SAS. There was no correlation between session number and score on the GSI Total Score of the SCL-90–R.

P-technique: identifying interaction structures. As with Ms. A., Q-ratings were obtained for every other treatment hour ($N = 104$) in completely randomized order and subjected to a factor analysis. The factor analysis yielded three conceptually interpretable clusters after varimax rotation that accounted for 34% of the variance. The items that best defined these factors are listed in Table 3. Factor 1, which was similar in content to the first factor for Patient A., was identically labeled as *Collaborative Exploration*; Factor 2 was labeled *Resistant and Withdrawn*, and Factor 3 was labeled *Angry Interaction* (see Table 4). The alpha reliabilities were .82, .75, and .82, respectively.

TSA. The scores on the four process dimensions for each rated treatment hour ($N = 104$) and the GSI of the SCL-90–R were subjected to a TSA to determine whether one series of scores was partially predictable from another. As with Patient A., SCL-90–R scores were obtained only after every 16th session, with the values of the missing scores estimated by calculating a moving average. Estimating so many data points was deemed justifiable when cross-correlations of the true GSI scores confirmed the results of the TSA, presented in Table 5. A comparison of the four models

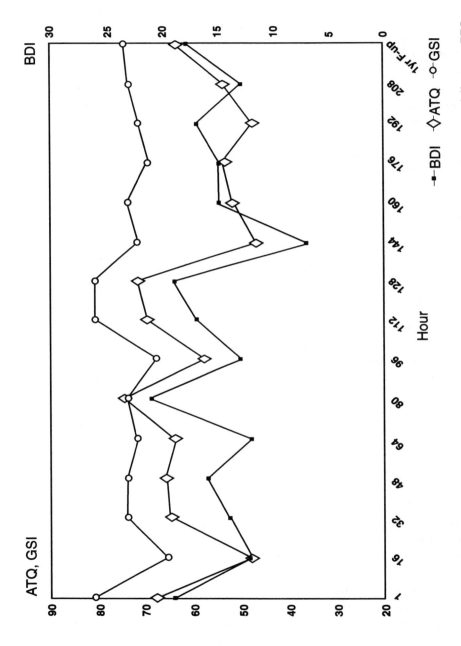

Figure 2. Plot of scores on Mr. B.'s symptom measures over the 2½-year treatment and at 1-year follow-up. BDI = Beck Depression Inventory; ATQ = Automatic Thoughts Questionnaire; GSI = General Severity Index of the SCL-90–R; F-up = follow-up.

Table 4

Patient B.: Repetitive Interaction Structures

Q-item no. and factor	Loading
Factor 1: Collaborative Exploration	
97. Patient is introspective, readily explores inner thoughts and feelings.	.81
88. Patient brings up significant issues and material.	.71
73. The patient is committed to the work of therapy.	.62
10. Patient seeks greater intimacy with the therapist.	.61
55. Patient conveys positive expectations about therapy.	.53
33. Patient talks of feelings about being close to or needing someone.	.52
32. Patient achieves a new understanding or insight.	.50
72. Patient understands the nature of therapy and what is expected.	.50
Factor 2: Resistant and Withdrawn	
58. Patient resists examining thoughts, reactions, or motivations related to problems.	.73
15. Patient does not initiate topics; is passive.	.70
12. Silences occur during the hour.	.58
25. Patient has difficulty beginning the hour.	.50
44. Patient feels wary or suspicious (vs. trusting and secure).	.49
Factor 3: Angry Interaction	
14. Patient does not feel understood by therapist.	.66
9. Therapist is distant, aloof (vs. responsive and affectively involved).	.64
31. Therapist (does not) ask for more information or elaboration.	.64
42. Patient rejects (vs. accepts) therapist's comments and observations.	.60
77. Therapist is tactless.	.57
87. Patient is controlling.	.57
65. Therapist (does not) clarify, restate, or rephrase patient's communication.	.54
39. There is a competitive quality to the relationship.	.53
24. Therapist's own emotional conflicts intrude into the relationship.	.52
30. Discussion centers on cognitive themes (i.e., about ideas or belief systems).	.51

Table 5

Summary of Time Series Analysis for Patient B.

Model	Collaborative Exploration			GSI total score		
	A	B	SSE	C	D	SSE
i	10	10	77.3	10	10	97.9
ii	1	2	84.1	2	0	15.2
iii	1	0	136.3	2	0	15.2
iv	10	0	95.8	10	0	764.4
i vs. ii	$Q(17) = 7.86$, ns			$Q(18) = -608$, $p < .001$		
ii vs. iii	$Q(2) = 45.40$, $p < .001$			$Q(0) = 0$, ns		
iii vs. iv	$Q(9) = 33.12$, ns			$Q(8) = -367$, $p < .001$		
Conclusions:	GSI → Collaborative Exploration			Collaborative Exploration ↛ GSI		

	Angry Interaction				GSI total score		
i	10	10		40.3	10	10	64.1
ii	8	9		40.8	2	0	15.2
iii	8	0		62.3	2	0	15.2
iv	10	0		60.4	10	0	764.6

Angry Interaction:

i vs. ii $Q(3) = 1.0$, ns
ii vs. iii $Q(9) = 39.9$, $p < .001$
iii vs. iv $Q(2) = 2.9$, ns
Conclusions: GSI → Angry Interaction

GSI total score:

i vs. ii $Q(18) = -134$, $p < .001$
ii vs. iii $Q(0) = 0$, ns
iii vs. iv $Q(8) = -367$, $p < .001$
Conclusions: Angry Interaction → GSI

Note. The bivariate time series analysis (Gottman & Ringland, 1981) is conducted by comparing four types of regression equations (models) to determine the smallest model (minimum number of terms) that minimizes residual error of prediction. Values under columns A and C represent the number of autoregressive terms in each model. Values under columns B and D represent the number of cross-regressive terms in each model. SSE = sums of square error (unexplained error variance when a given model is applied). Pairwise comparisons between the four models are evaluated using the Q statistic, whose significance can be estimated using a chi-square table. GSI = General Severity Index of the SCL-90-R. Comparisons of Model i versus Model ii and Model iii versus Model iv represent internal checks of the model, whereas the comparison of Model ii versus Model iii indicates the presence or absence of predictability of one series from the other, controlling for autocorrelation. Causality → is implied when Model ii is the best model; ↛ = causality not implied.

predicting Collaborative Exploration revealed that the best model was Model ii, indicating that the GSI of the SCL-90–R predicted the factor scores above and beyond what could be predicted from Collaborative Exploration's own history. On the other hand, the comparison of models predicting SCL-90–R GSI scores indicated that Model ii was not superior and that adding cross-regressive terms (Collaborative Exploration) did not improve prediction. In other words, symptom scores predicted Collaborative Exploration. Symptom scores also added to the predictability of Angry Interaction. Interestingly, changes in patient symptom level signaled changes in the structure of the interaction, rather than changes in the interaction predicting patient symptom improvement, as with Ms. A. When Mr. B. was more symptomatic and depressed, this indicated that he and his therapist would be less involved in collaborative exploration and more inclined to become caught up in angry interactions in the next sessions.

Discussion

The results of this study demonstrate the value of quantitative single-case designs in testing hypotheses about the nature of therapeutic action in analytic therapies. It also demonstrates the usefulness of statistical procedures such as the P-technique in identifying interaction structures and TSA in linking the reduction of the intensity and frequency of these interactions to patient improvement. Clinical judges' formulations of the two cases were reflected in the types of interaction structures that emerged for each. The clinical judges thought Ms. A., despite her experience of relatively severe early trauma, had the capacity to develop a strong positive transference to the therapist. Mr. B. was assessed as being more difficult to treat because he relied on obsessional and intellectually oriented defenses, his distance from his feelings, and his inclination to be caught up in struggles around submitting to, or defeating, authority figures. The process data demonstrated that although one important structure of interaction was similar across the two cases (collaborative exploration), other repetitive structures (e.g., provoking rescue for Ms. A. and angry interaction for Mr. B.) were case specific. The Collaborative Exploration factor was virtually identical (except for one Q-item) in each of the cases. The replication of this factor, and its specific item content, is noteworthy. This factor included the following Q-items: Patient is committed to the work of therapy; Patient brings up significant issues and material; and Patient feels helped. This factor likely represents that aspect of therapist–patient interaction often termed *therapeutic alliance*. Interestingly, collaborative exploration did not predict patient symptom change. Perhaps this kind of interaction is necessary to sustain a therapeutic relationship but insufficient to promote patient change.

Therapeutic action, at least for Ms. A., was located in the case-specific interaction structure, provoking rescue. This interaction structure of Ms. A. and her therapist was captured by the following Q-items (among others): Silences occur during the hour; Patient does not initiate topics; Patient is passive; Patient feels shy and embarrassed; Patient is not clear and organized in self-expression; Patient feels sad and depressed; Patient feels inadequate and inferior; and Patient relies upon therapist to solve her problems. This repetitive interaction was characterized by the patient's passivity and lengthy silences, accompanied by depressed affect, a strong sense of inadequacy, inferiority and humiliation, and a wish to rely on the therapist to solve her problems. Reduction in the intensity and frequency of this interaction correlated strongly with length of treatment ($r = -.71, p < .05$). The following is an illustration of this kind of interaction taken from a verbatim transcript that had a high score on this factor. Earlier in the session, Ms. A. discussed her feeling of frustration that she was not doing anything, although she knew she was taking all the necessary steps to pursue her goals. There are many lengthy pauses and silences during this hour.

> THERAPIST: You'd mentioned something to the effect of being frustrated in here, but you haven't said a whole lot about what that's about or what's behind it.

> PATIENT: (Pause) I just wonder why—I wonder if—y'know (pause)—if I'll ever resolve all these issues, or if I just bring them up. I guess I wonder if it's worth it or how it's worth it.

> THERAPIST: Is it related at all to what you said earlier today about maybe wanting something more in terms of support from people? Perhaps I'm in that category.
>
> PATIENT: Yeah, I don't say very much. (Pause) I don't say anything.
>
> THERAPIST: So maybe part of what you were saying earlier today was indirectly related to me, in terms of perhaps wishing and wanting someone might be giving you more advice and being supportive or kind of giving you that guidance that you feel that you'd want. Even though you're taking all these steps, doing all these things.
>
> PATIENT: (Silence) Hm. It's like—all the steps aren't recognized. They're seen as things.
>
> THERAPIST: As opposed to?
>
> PATIENT: (Pause) Steps! Steps that get somewhere.

During these repetitive interactions, there was a strong implicit, and often explicit, demand on the therapist to fill the painful silences and to deliver transformative explanations. The therapist, on his part, often felt ineffective and was prompted to become more active in drawing the patient out and rescuing them both from her tortured silences. The therapist was nevertheless able to interpret this pattern as, among other meanings, a way of avoiding the pain associated with talking about herself, reflecting on past traumas, and the fear of making herself vulnerable by revealing herself. This repetitive interaction structure also represented an unconscious effort to provoke the therapist into pursuing her, which may have repeated in the transference the traumatic sexual abuse the patient had experienced in childhood and early adolescence. TSA demonstrated that the slow decline in frequency and intensity of this interactive pattern predicted Ms. A.'s improvement in both her depression and her daily functioning.

Mr. B. demonstrated modest symptom change after more than 2 years of twice-weekly psychotherapy. The therapist–patient interaction structure labeled *angry interaction* was captured by the following Q-items: Patient does not feel understood; Therapist is distant, aloof; Patient rejects therapist's comments and observations; Therapist is tactless; Patient is controlling; There is a competitive quality to the relationship; Therapist's own emotional conflicts intrude into the relationship (or countertransference); and Discussion centers on cognitive themes. The following excerpt illustrates this kind of repetitive interaction taken from the verbatim transcripts of a session that had one of the highest scores on this factor. Earlier Mr. B. had asked his therapist to reduce his already low fee even more.

> THERAPIST: What seems to start that? That process of disavowing intent? They ... *they* have put me here in this situation. They've put me in the awkward situation that I have to say to you that the arrangement that I said would be temporary may need to endure. You know, yesterday you were fine, but it's like, sorry I'm late, I missed the bus. If the bus hadn't come so early I would have been here.

> PATIENT: But, yeah, on another occasion, when I just said sorry I'm late, you said, "Well, you didn't even bother to say why you were late this time." It was like, well, what do I do? You know, it was, like, that's a nicety, that's what people say. That's just what you do. I mean, what's the alternative?

> THERAPIST: What we're talking about, the issue you raise is about your aggression. And what we're talking about, I think, is the difficulty you have in taking responsibility for your aggression.

> PATIENT: Mhm-hm. . . . Can you say more about that?

> THERAPIST: And that comes out either in what you called yesterday an "obtuseness"

> PATIENT: Mhm-hm. Mhm-hm.

> THERAPIST: as you provoke other people, hurt other people's feelings, that it comes out in a disavowal of responsibility. Things conspire to put you in a situation where you can't do what you've agreed to do or what other people want you to do. I was thinking of the way yesterday's hour

began with your being late and then forgetting your checkbook. We talked about it later. You said, "Yeah. It's just like, if it's not one damn thing, it's another." Your father's phrase. Afterwards, it occurred to me that you don't think: if *I* don't do one damn thing, *I* do another.

PATIENT: Hm. Hm.

THERAPIST: Well, it's externalized.

PATIENT: Right.

THERAPIST: It's not something you're doing. Something else has put you in this situation of having created with me a false agreement.

PATIENT: Hm-hm.

THERAPIST: It isn't that you failed to get the details right.

PATIENT: I see. So, in other words, it's that you would say it differently. That would constitute taking responsibility?

THERAPIST: That's the business about finding a technology (to find the right words to say to others). I don't think it'll work to try to learn the words that I would use.

PATIENT: Well, other than punching my boss in the nose, what would constitute being responsible for my aggression?

THERAPIST: Well, say more.

PATIENT: Well, I mean, say "Excuse me, but I'm a very aggressive person. I'm going to have to punch you in the nose." I don't think that's going to be socially acceptable. You could say it's a technology not to punch my boss in the nose. However, it's not something I'm going to do. Ergo, it makes me wonder what would constitute being responsible for my own aggression?

These repetitive interactions were tense, competitive, and intellectualized exchanges in which the patient attempted to control the therapist and in which the patient did not feel understood and rejected the therapist's attempts to help. The therapist, in turn, was less tactful and had to struggle with angry, contemptuous countertransference reactions. In our example, the therapist attempts to interpret the patient's evident hostility and simultaneous disavowal of such feelings. However, in the face of the patient's rigid defenses, the therapist reacts with frustration, annoyance, and some punitiveness.

The causal direction of the relationship of interaction structures to symptom change was different from those with Ms. A. and her therapist. With Mr. B., symptom scores predicted the levels and frequency of interaction patterns. In other words, lower levels of depression and symptom scores predicted higher levels of collaborative exploration, and higher symptom scores predicted more frequent and intense angry interaction. Mr. B. was more capable of working in collaboration with the therapist, and less likely to provoke tense, angry exchanges, when he felt less depressed and anxious. There was no decline in the intensity and frequency of this interaction structure during the therapy (the correlation between therapy session number and this factor was $-.06$, ns). This angry interaction structure was perhaps insufficiently interpreted and understood, and we conclude that this unanalyzed, and relatively unchanging interaction pattern was associated with the patient's reporting only little improvement at termination. There is, in short, preliminary evidence that the reduction in frequency and intensity of repetitive interaction patterns of this type, through their interpretation and mutual understanding by therapist and patient, is mutative.

We have been able to demonstrate empirically the presence of repetitive interaction structures. They also can, of course, be routinely observed in clinical practice. The repetitive interaction structure construct has much in common with already familiar theoretical and technical language, such as analyzing the transference in the here and now and working through. However, it provides an empirically derived underpinning for aspects of these concepts. Moreover, the repetitive interaction construct helps specify the two-person interaction patterns that emerge in psychotherapy. It refers not only to how the patient's conflicts are represented in the transference but also to the therapist's reactions to these conflicts. The construct provides a means for bridging theories of therapeutic action by insight and by relationship in emphasizing the intrapsychic as the basis of what is manifest in the interactive field.

We posit a relationship between repetitive interaction structures and the patient's overall mental structure. Following Kernberg's (1980) conceptualization, mental structure and unconscious mental life can be viewed as being determined by real and fantasied (drive-derived) interpersonal interactions that are internalized as a complex world of self and object representations. Impulse and defense find expression through an internalized object relation that has an emotional cast and meaning. Intrapsychic conflict is not simply conflict between impulse and defense, but between two opposing sets of internalized object relations, or self and object representations under the impact of an affect disposition. Pathology is associated, among other things, with both a lack of organization and integration of such mental structures. Repetitive interaction structures animate, in the interactive field, aspects of both the patient's and the therapist's mental structure (see Jones, 1997).

We theorize that the experience, identification, and understanding of repetitive interaction structures is mutative by way of recovering threatening ideas and feelings and the consequent reorganization and integration of usually primitive, repudiated unconscious mental structures with more complex, differentiated, and conscious mental structures. Recognition of repetitive interaction structures also can promote the development of previously inhibited mental processes by engaging and mobilizing in them the therapist–patient interaction (Fonagy, Moran, Edgcumbe, Kennedy, & Target, 1993; Fonagy, Moran, & Target, 1993). The recognition of repetitive interaction structures permits changes in mental representations by providing an opportunity to bring to a conscious state and systematically explore the mental representations expressed in the interaction. In this way mental representations acquire greater internal cohesion or consolidation, links are fostered between representational structures, and new representations of both internal states and perceptions of the external are created. Integration of previously isolated or conflicted representations permits the achievement of a greater sense of subjectivity, a better integrated self-concept, and a more consistent representational world.

Our study findings have implications for process–outcome research strategies in underscoring the complexity of causal relations in psychotherapy. Our data suggest that although there may be similarities in interaction structures across patients (e.g., collaborative exploration), there also are crucial differences. It is unlikely that a particular therapist action, or even certain kinds of processes, invariably signify something fixed for all patients. The subjective meaning of observable processes will vary across patient–therapist pairs. If differing causal relations can be identified in only two cases, this could easily account for the difficulty in identifying significant process–outcome correlations in conventional studies relying on group designs that average effects across samples of patients and therapists. A focus on the variability within the therapist–patient relationship must remain the very core of psychoanalytic process research.

References

Beck, A. T., Ward, C. H., Mendelson, M., Mock, J. E., & Erbaugh, J. K. (1961). An inventory for measuring depression. *Archives of General Psychiatry, 4*, 561–571.

Block, J. (1978). *The Q-sort method in personality assessment and psychiatric research.* Springfield, IL: Charles C Thomas. (Original work published 1961)

Bumberry, W., Oliver, J. M., & McClure, J. N. (1978). Validation of the Beck Depression Inventory in a university population using psychiatric estimate as a criterion. *Journal of Consulting and Clinical Psychology, 46*, 150–155.

Caston, J. (1993). Mannequins in the labyrinth and the couch-lab intersect. *Journal of the American Psychoanalytic Association, 41*, 51–65.

Czogalik, D., & Russell, R. (1995). Interactional structures of therapist and client participation in adult psychotherapy: Technique and chronography. *Journal of Consulting and Clinical Psychology, 63*, 28–36.

Dahlstrom, W. G., & Welsh, G. S. (Eds.). (1960). *An MMPI handbook.* Minneapolis: University of Minnesota Press.

Derogatis, L. R., Lipman, R. S., Rickels, K., Uhlenhuth, E. H., & Covi, L. (1974). The Hopkins Symptom Checklist (HSCL): A self-report symptom inventory. *Behavioral Science, 19*, 1–15.

Endicott, J., & Spitzer, R. L. (1977). A diagnostic interview: The Schedule for Affective Disorders and Schizophrenia. *Archives of General Psychiatry, 35,* 837–844.

Fonagy, P., Moran, G. S., Edgcumbe, R., Kennedy, H., & Target, M. (1993). The roles of mental representations and mental processes in therapeutic action. *Psychoanalytic Study of the Child, 48,* 9–48.

Fonagy, P., Moran, G. S., & Target, M. (1993). Aggression and the psychological self. *International Journal of Psychoanalysis, 74,* 471–485.

Freud, S. (1955). Group psychology and the analysis of the ego. In J. Strachey (Ed. and Trans.), *The standard edition of the complete psychological works of Sigmund Freud* (Vol. 18, pp. 69–143). London: Hogarth Press. (Original work published in 1921)

Freud, S. (1959). The question of lay analysis. In J. Strachey (Ed. and Trans.), *The standard edition of the complete psychological works of Sigmund Freud* (Vol. 20, pp. 177–258). London: Hogarth Press. (Original work published in 1926)

Gottman, J. M. (1981). *Time series analysis.* New York: Cambridge University Press.

Gottman, J. M., & Ringland, J. (1981). The analysis of dominance and bidirectionality in social development. *Child Development, 52,* 393–412.

Gray, P. (1994). *The ego and the analysis of defense.* Northvale, NJ: Jason Aronson.

Hamilton, M. (1967). Development of a rating scale for primary depressive illness. *British Journal of Social and Clinical Psychology, 6,* 278–296.

Hollon, S. D., & Kendall, P. C. (1980). Cognitive self-statements in depression: Development of an automatic thoughts questionnaire. *Cognitive Therapy and Research, 4,* 383–395.

Horowitz, L. M., Rosenberg, S. E., Baer, B. A., Ureño, G., & Villaseñor, V. S. (1988). The Inventory of Interpersonal Problems: Psychometric properties and clinical application. *Journal of Consulting and Clinical Psychology, 56,* 885–892.

Jacobson, N. S., & Truax, P. (1991). Clinical significance: A statistical approach to defining meaningful change in psychotherapy research. *Journal of Consulting and Clinical Psychology, 41,* 51–65.

Jones, E. E. (1985). *Manual for the Psychotherapy Process Q-set.* Unpublished manuscript, University of California, Berkeley.

Jones, E. E. (1993a). How will psychoanalysis study itself? *Journal of the American Psychoanalytic Association, 41,* 91–108.

Jones, E. E. (1993b). Introduction to the special section on single-case research in psychotherapy. *Journal of Consulting and Clinical Psychology, 38,* 722–731.

Jones, E. E. (1997). Modes of therapeutic action. *International Journal of Psychoanalysis, 78,* 1135–1150.

Jones, E. E., Cumming, J. D., & Horowitz, M. J. (1988). Another look at the nonspecific hypothesis of therapeutic effectiveness. *Journal of Consulting and Clinical Psychology, 56,* 48–55.

Jones, E. E., Ghannam, J., Nigg, J. T., & Dyer, J. F. P. (1993). A paradigm for single-case research: The time series study of a long-term psychotherapy for depression. *Journal of Consulting and Clinical Psychology, 61,* 381–394.

Jones, E. E., Hall, S. A., & Parke, L. A. (1991). The process of change: The Berkeley Psychotherapy Research Group. In L. Beutler & M. Crago (Eds.), *Psychotherapy research: An international review of programmatic studies* (pp. 98–107). Washington, DC: American Psychological Association.

Jones, E. E., & Windholz, M. (1990). The psychoanalytic case study: Toward a method for systematic inquiry. *Journal of the American Psychoanalytic Association, 38,* 985–1015.

Kernberg, O. (1980). *Internal world and external reality.* Northvale, NJ: Jason Aronson.

Kohut, H. (1984). *How does analysis cure?* Chicago: University of Chicago Press.

Loewald, H. W. (1960). On the therapeutic action of psychoanalysis. *International Journal of Psychoanalysis, 41,* 16–33.

Luborsky, L. (1953). Intra-individual repetitive measurements (P-technique) on understanding symptom structure and psychotherapeutic change. In O. H. Mowrer (Ed.), *Psychotherapy: Theory and research* (pp. 389–413). New York: Ronald Press.

Luborsky, L. (1995). The first trial of the P technique in psychotherapy research: A still lively legacy. *Journal of Consulting and Clinical Psychology, 63,* 6–14.

Luborsky, L., & Crits-Christoph, P. (1988). The assessment of transference by the CCRT method. In H. Dahl, H. Kaechele, & H. Thomae (Eds.), *Psychoanalytic process research strategies* (pp. 99–108). New York: Springer-Verlag.

Mitchell, S. A. (1993). *Hope and dread in psychoanalysis.* New York: Basic Books.

Modell, A. (1976). "The holding environment" and the therapeutic action of psychoanalysis. *Journal of the American Psychoanalytic Association, 24,* 285–308.

Murray, J. F. (1995). On objects, transference, and two-person psychology: A critique of the new seduction theory. *Psychoanalytic Psychology, 12,* 31–41.

Persons, J. B. (1991). Psychotherapy outcome studies do not accurately represent current models of psychotherapy: A proposed remedy. *American Psychologist, 46,* 99–106.

Pole, N., & Jones, E. E. (1998). The talking cure revisited: Content analysis of a two year psychodynamic psychotherapy. *Psychotherapy Research, 8,* 171–189.

Shoham-Salomon, V. (1990). Interrelating research processes of process research. *Journal of Consulting and Clinical Psychology, 58,* 295–303.

Spitzer, R. L., Endicott, J., & Robins, E. (1979). *Research Diagnostic Criteria (RDC) for a selected group of functional disorders* (3rd ed.). New York: New York State Psychiatric Institute.

Strachey, J. (1934). The nature of therapeutic action in psychoanalysis. *International Journal of Psycho-Analysis, 15,* 127–159.

Sugarman, A., & Wilson, A. (1995). Introduction to the special section: Contemporary structural analysts critique relational theories. *Psychoanalytic Psychology, 12,* 1–8.

Weiss, J., & Sampson, H. (1986). *The psychoanalytic process: Theory, clinical observation and empirical research.* New York: Guilford Press.

Weissman, M. M., Prusoff, B. M., Thompson, W. D., Harding, P. S., & Meyers, J. K. (1978). Social adjustment by self-report in a community sample and in psychiatric outpatients. *Journal of Nervous and Mental Disease, 166,* 317–326.

Winnicott, D. W. (1965). *The maturational processes and the facilitating environment.* Madison, CT: International Universities Press.

Representational Structures and the Therapeutic Process

Sidney J. Blatt, John S. Auerbach, and Mosen Aryan

In modern psychoanalytic thought, mental representation is considered to be a central construct for understanding psychological

This chapter presents findings from investigations that were originally conducted by the Object Representation Research Group at Yale University, chaired by Sidney J. Blatt, and was originally presented at a workshop sponsored by the National Institute of Mental Health on Cognitive Science and Psychodynamics, Washington, DC, June 5–6, 1993. The data were gathered through the efforts of Rebecca Behrends and Cathy Havican. We thank them and the members of our research group—Basil Anton, Rebecca Behrends, Susan Bers, Diana Diamond, Rand Gruen, Rebecca Johnston, Nadine Kaslow, Richard Kravitz, Roberta Stiel, and Helen Sayward—for their valuable comments and suggestions. We also are indebted to Howard Kurtzman of the National Institute of Mental Health for his comments on this chapter and to David Stayner for his assistance in scoring the Object Relations Inventory protocols.

development and functioning. In this chapter, we attempt to demonstrate that mental representation also is central to an understanding of psychological change in the psychotherapeutic process. In particular, we demonstrate that clinical improvement in intensive, psychoanalytically oriented inpatient treatment is linked to change and growth in patients' representations of self and others. We also show how a systematic examination of patients' mental representations contributes to an understanding of the mechanisms of therapeutic change in psychoanalysis and psychoanalytic psychotherapy.

Mental Representations in Psychoanalytic Developmental Theory

According to psychoanalytic developmental theory, children transform early interactions with primary caregivers into cognitive–affective schemas of self and other (e.g., Ainsworth, 1969, 1982; Beebe & Lachmann, 1988; Blatt, 1991, 1995; Bowlby, 1969, 1973, 1988; Lichtenberg, 1983; Mahler, Pine, & Bergman, 1975; Main, Kaplan, & Cassidy, 1985; Piaget, 1945/1962; Stern, 1985). These cognitive–affective schemas, or representations of self and others, not only bear the imprint of significant early interpersonal interactions but also express the developmental level and other important aspects of psychic life (e.g., impulses, affects, drives, and fantasies; Beres & Joseph, 1970; Blatt, 1974; Sandler & Rosenblatt, 1962). These schemas are continually constructed and revised over the life cycle, and they have conscious and unconscious cognitive, affective, and experiential components. They can involve veridical representations of consensual reality, idiosyncratic and unique constructions, or primitive and pathological distortions that suggest psychopathology (Blatt, 1991, 1995).

Cognitive–affective schemas are the templates or prototypes that structure how one thinks and feels about others and about oneself (Ainsworth, 1982; Blatt, 1974; Bowlby, 1988; Bretherton, 1985; Lichtenberg, 1983; Main et al., 1985; Stern, 1985). They derive from and determine the experience of the self in interpersonal relationships (Beres & Joseph, 1970; Blatt & Lerner, 1983; Jacobson, 1964). Observations in developmental psychology and psychoanalysis are consistent with recent findings in cognitive science, information processing, and social cognition about the centrality of these schemas of self and others as heuristic prototypes for understanding social interaction and interpersonal behavior (e.g., Anderson, 1983; Auerbach, 1993; Blatt, 1991, 1995; Brewer & Nakamura, 1984; Fiske & Taylor, 1984; Gardner, 1985; Horowitz, 1988; Mandler, 1988; Markus, 1977; Nelson & Grundel, 1987; Westen, 1991).

Schemas of self and others are constructed in interpersonal transactions that begin with the infant–caregiver relationship. These schemas unfold in response to the child's experience of the demands of the life cycle. When developmental demands are age appropriate and not too severe, the existing cognitive structures evolve to accommodate the experienced perturbations. The relational attunement between caregiver and infant in patterns of engagement and disengagement in the early months of life (e.g., Beebe & Lachmann, 1988; Stern, 1985) and in patterns of attachment and separation in the first half of the second year (e.g., Ainsworth, 1982; Bowlby, 1988) contributes to the development of representations of significant caring figures and the self (Bretherton, 1987; Diamond & Blatt, 1994; Levy, Blatt, & Shaver, 1998; Stern, 1985; Zeanah & Anders, 1987). When these enduring cognitive–affective structures derive from relatively satisfactory caring experiences, they facilitate the development of an increasingly mature concept of interpersonal relatedness and a differentiated and cohesive identity (Blatt & Blass, 1990, 1992; Loewald, 1960, 1978; Mahler et al., 1975; Sandler & Rosenblatt, 1962; Winnicott, 1965). Despite many variations, both inter- and intraindividual, in the rate at which these cognitive–affective schemas develop or become more sophisticated (Fischer, 1980), these representations of self and other unfold in a gradual but orderly sequence, from enactive, affective, and physicalistic to symbolic and abstract (Blatt, 1974; Bruner, 1964; Damon & Hart, 1988; Horowitz, 1972). Developmental stages, although highly dependent on the psychosocial contexts and environments in which they emerge, thus retain a crucial degree of temporal coherence (Damon & Hart, 1988). As a result of the gradual transformation of representational capacities in response to immediate life circumstances, increasingly mature schemas come to organize, shape, and guide subsequent interpersonal behavior. When life demands are severe, developmentally inap-

propriate, or both, however, they can overwhelm the child's capacities for accommodation and thereby compromise the development of these interpersonal schemas. Specific disturbances in the
structure of these cognitive–affective schemas are related to different forms of psychopathology (Blatt, 1991, 1995).

Research on mother–infant interaction in the first 3–4 months
of life (e.g., Stern, 1985) demonstrates that the subtle vicissitudes
of the relational attunement between caregiver and infant interact
with inborn capacities to facilitate the development of mental representations of self and others. Furthermore, observations of the
processes of attachment and separation during the first half of the
second year of life provide perhaps the clearest examples of the
relationship between quality of interpersonal interactions and the
construction of cognitive–affective schemas. Attachment patterns
in children 12–18 months of age are relatively stable over time
(Ainsworth, 1982; Bretherton, 1985) and influence a wide range of
behavior, even as late as preadolescence (e.g., age 11; Elicker &
Sroufe, 1992). They also have cross-generational continuity; for example, mothers' caregiving behavior is congruent with their reports of the care they received as children from their own mothers.
Reports by pregnant women about their early childhood experiences with their mothers are congruent with the subsequent care
they provide their infants (Fonagy, Steele, & Steele, 1991; Main
et al., 1985; Slade & Aber, 1992; Virtue, 1992). In addition, these
attachment patterns are related to important cognitive differences
in adults, such as the degree of cohesion and consistency of narrative reports adults construct in describing their early life experiences (Main et al., 1985).

The behavioral and cognitive consistency of attachment patterns
suggests that, in the first 18 months of life, the child establishes
internal working models of attachment relationships—"a set of conscious and unconscious rules for the organization of information
relevant to attachment and for obtaining or limiting access to that
information, that is, to information regarding attachment-related
experiences, feelings and ideations" (Main et al., 1985, p. 67).
Rather than constructing static representations of the self, others,
or specific attachment-related transactions, infants form prototypic
schemas involving invariant dimensions of early, affectively
charged relationships (Bretherton, 1987; Kernberg, 1994; Loewald,

1960; Stern, 1985; Zeanah & Anders, 1987). Within a context of mutual interactive regulation between babies and their caregivers (Beebe & Lachmann, 1988; Stern, 1985), experiences of gratification and frustration, of union and disruption in relatedness, constitute the basic materials from which infants construct these prototypes (Behrends & Blatt, 1985; Blatt & Blass, 1990, 1996). These mental representations or internal working models are formed early in life and vary in their level of flexibility, adaptiveness, and maturity. They are central to the development of a sense of self and others, and they pervasively influence the nature and quality of interpersonal relationships throughout the life cycle.

The development of representations of self and others reflects two independent but interrelated developmental lines: (a) the formation of a cohesive, realistic, essentially positive, increasingly differentiated, and integrated self-definition or identity and (b) the establishment of a capacity for increasingly mature, satisfying, empathically attuned, complementary interpersonal relationships. A dialectic tension between these two developmental lines, self-definition and relatedness, establishes a fundamental dynamic in personality development, a dynamic that leads to constructive psychological functioning. An increasingly differentiated, integrated, and mature sense of self is contingent on the establishment of satisfying interpersonal experiences, and, conversely, the establishment of increasingly satisfying interpersonal experiences is contingent on the development of a more mature self-definition and identity. In normal personality development, these two developmental processes evolve in an interactive, reciprocally balanced, mutually facilitating way (Blatt & Blass, 1990, 1996; Blatt & Shichman, 1983). New representational structures emerge from this interactive process between the formation of an increasingly cohesive and essentially positive sense of self and the development of an increasingly reciprocal, empathically attuned relatedness to others.

Over the past 20 years, investigators have developed methods to systematically assess the development of both normal and disturbed self and object representation (for reviews, see Blatt & Lerner, 1983; Stricker & Healy, 1990; Westen, 1991). Mayman (1967), one of the early investigators in this area, examined the thematic content of representations in projective test data and evaluated the extent to which human figures are described as differentiated, diverse, alive, and involved in benevolent and reciprocal interactions. Mayman and colleagues, evaluating these thematic dimensions in Rorschach responses (Mayman, 1967; Urist, 1977), dreams (Hatcher & Krohn, 1980; Krohn & Mayman, 1974), and early memories (Mayman & Faris, 1969; Ryan & Bell, 1984), found that the content of representations corresponded to independent estimates of clinical progress in the treatment of psychotic patients. Cook, Blatt, and Ford (1995) found that the content and structure of object representations on the Rorschach at the beginning of long-term intensive, inpatient treatment of seriously disturbed young adults predicted the extent of their therapeutic gain.

Over the course of development from preadolescence (ages 10–11) to early adulthood (age 30), the representations of the human figures in Rorschach responses of normal individuals become more "accurately perceived, well-articulated, full human figures involved in appropriate, integrated, positive and meaningful (benevolent) interactions" (Blatt, Brenneis, Schimek, & Glick, 1976, p. 367). The developmental level of representations of human figures on the Rorschach also discriminates narcissistic from borderline pathology (Farris, 1988); schizophrenic from borderline patients (Spear, 1980; Spear & Sugarman, 1984); psychotic from nonpsychotic patients (Ritzler, Wyatt, Harder, & Kaskey, 1980); and opiate-addicted from nonaddicted individuals (Blatt, Berman, et al., 1984; Blatt, McDonald, Sugarman, & Wilber, 1984). In addition, it discriminates among neurotic, outpatient borderline, inpatient borderline, and schizophrenic patients (Lerner & St. Peter, 1985). Changes in object representation also correlate significantly with independent estimates of clinical improvement in long-term intensive treatment. Among seriously disturbed inpatients, therapeutic gain was significantly related to a decreased investment in inaccurate representations of human figures in inpatients (Blatt & Ford, 1994) and to an increased investment in accurate representations in outpatients (Blatt, 1992; Kavanagh, 1985).

Blatt and colleagues (Blatt, Chevron, Quinlan, Schaffer, & Wein, 1988; Blatt, Wein, Chevron, & Quinlan, 1979) also developed procedures for evaluating the content and structure of open-ended descriptions of self and significant others (e.g., parents, significant other, and therapist). Integrating concepts of psychoanalytic and cognitive developmental theorists, Blatt (1974) formulated five levels of cognitive development in the concept of the object—sensorimotor, perceptual, external iconic, internal iconic, and conceptual—that form a developmental progression in the construction of the object. In addition, open-ended descriptions of self and other were assessed for three qualitative or thematic factors: benevolence, punitiveness, and striving (Blatt et al., 1988, 1979; Quinlan, Blatt, Chevron, & Wein, 1992).

The cognitive level was significantly lower, and there were significantly fewer nurturant themes, in the descriptions of parents by depressed than nondepressed young adults (Blatt et al., 1979). The same pattern of results was found among psychiatric, as compared with nonpsychiatric, individuals (Bornstein & O'Neill, 1992). Nonpsychiatric individuals could be distinguished from borderline patients by the degree of differentiation and cognitive complexity of their descriptions of others (Marziali & Oleniuk, 1990). Changes in both the cognitive level and the qualitative (or thematic) dimensions of representations of self and parents also correlated significantly with independent estimates of therapeutic progress of seriously disturbed adolescent and young adult inpatients in long-term, psychodynamically oriented treatment (Blatt, Stayner, Auerbach, & Behrends, 1996; Blatt, Wiseman, Prince-Gibson, & Gatt, 1991). Changes in the cognitive level of object representation also were found to parallel changes in independently reported aspects of the transference relationship in long-term, psychoanalytically oriented inpatient treatment of a schizophrenic patient and a borderline patient (Gruen & Blatt, 1990).

Mental Representations and the Treatment Process

The research findings cited above suggest that the construction of cognitive–affective schemas has important implications for the study of the therapeutic process. If various forms of psychopathology involve distortions of object and self-representation, and if satisfactory childhood attachments in normal development result in the formation of increasingly mature interpersonal schemas, then, by analogy, constructive interactions between patient and therapist should facilitate revisions of object and self-representations and lead to a more integrated and mature sense of self and others (Blatt, Wild, & Ritzler, 1975). The therapeutic relationship should create a process through which impaired interpersonal schemas are relinquished, reworked, and transformed into more adaptive cognitive–affective representations of self and others. Toward the end of treatment, representations should be more differentiated and integrated, with indications of a greater capacity for mutual interpersonal relatedness.

From a different, and complementary, perspective in psychoanalytic thought, many researchers (e.g., Gill & Hoffman, 1982; Horowitz, 1979; Luborsky, 1984; Schacht, Binder, & Strupp, 1984; Weiss & Sampson, 1986) have studied precisely these hypotheses. Starting from the assumption that psychoanalysis and psychoanalytic therapy are processes through which patients explore and come to revise maladaptive representations of self and significant figures, each of those investigators devised a method for coding patients' therapy verbalizations to identify characteristic schemas of interpersonal transactions. The simplest of these coding methods, Luborsky's (1984) Core Conflictual Relationship Theme (CCRT), analyzes patients' interpersonal schemas in terms of three components: (a) wishes of the self, (b) expected responses from others, and (c) consequent responses of the self. Luborsky and Crits-Christoph (1990) have found evidence that patients' representations of self and others change in the course of psychoanalytic psychotherapy. Specifically, they observed that patients' wishes changed little during treatment but that their expected responses from others and from themselves with regard to those wishes became less negative and more positive. The strength of process methods like the CCRT in the study of mental representations lies in their focus on changes in the *content* of these interpersonal schemas (e.g., the affective tone of representations of self and others), but they neglect the *structural* aspects (i.e., the cohesion, differentiation, and integration) of representations that are emphasized in our developmental approach. Thus, process methods like the CCRT and the projective methods that we use are complementary.

Adopting a developmental approach, we investigated the role of representational structures in the therapeutic process by studying the relationship of changes in schemas of self and significant others during the treatment process to an independent assessment of clinical change. We evaluated open-ended descriptions of self and significant others given by seriously disturbed adolescent and young-adult inpatients at the beginning and toward the end of intensive, long-term inpatient treatment that included psychodynamically oriented psychotherapy at least three times weekly. We related change in these spontaneous descriptions of self and significant figures (i.e., mother, father, and therapist) obtained at admission and discharge to changes in the level of psychological functioning as independently assessed from clinical reports prepared routinely at these same times by a multidisciplinary treatment team that included the patient's individual therapist.

Whereas our previous studies (e.g., Blatt et al., 1991, 1996; Diamond, Kaslow, Coonerty, & Blatt, 1990) were concerned primarily with whether change in object representation predicted change in clinical and psychosocial functioning, here we evaluate the level of object representation at the start of treatment, the degree of change in this variable over the course of long-term hospitalization, and the level of object representation at discharge after at least 1 year of treatment. We attempted to delineate differences in the degree of change in object representation between patients who were independently judged to have improved and those who did not. We expected that the representations of self and others of patients who showed therapeutic improvement would differ, both at admission and after extensive treatment, from those of patients who showed less clinical improvement. Thus, we wanted to determine whether the correlation of changes in self- and object descriptions with independent estimates of therapeutic change we reported earlier (Blatt et al., 1996) was the consequence primarily of growth in object relations in patients who improved most clinically or of a decline in patients who were relatively unresponsive to treatment.

Method

Participants

Participants were 40 seriously disturbed inpatients (17 young men and 23 young women) whose mean age was 17.75 years (SD = 4.12) on admission to the Yale Psychiatric Institute and whose mean Full Scale IQ was 100.40. All patients were hospitalized at least 12 months during the 1980s. More than 90% of the patients were White, and all but one was single at the time the data were gathered. At admission, they had a complex array of diagnoses from the third edition of the *Diagnostic and Statistical Manual of Mental Disorders* (*DSM-III*; American Psychiatric Association, 1980). These included conduct disorder; major depression, with and without psychotic features; bipolar disorder; atypical psychosis (psychotic disorder not otherwise specified); schizophrenia; schizoaffective disorder; severe personality disorders; and a variety of substance abuse disorders. The predominant *DSM-III* diagnosis was severe personality disorder, usually with concomitant conduct disorder, depression, or both ($n = 30$). In addition, 6 patients were diagnosed as schizophrenic, 1 as schizoaffective, and 3 as psychotically depressed. All patients had previously been in outpatient therapy and could accurately be characterized as severely impaired. Almost all (>90%) had at least one previous brief psychiatric hospitalization. According to admission reports, the mean number of prior hospitalizations was 2.77, and the mean length of these prior hospitalizations was 8.6 months.

All patients in this study received similar multifaceted, psychodynamically oriented inpatient treatment comprising individual and group psychotherapy three times weekly; milieu therapy, including a privileges system based on behavioral contingencies; involvement in community responsibilities and triweekly community meetings; weekly individual family and multifamily therapy; occupational and recreational therapy; and psychopharmacological evaluation and treatment. Patients who had not finished high school also attended an accredited special school run by hospital staff and specially trained teachers. Treatment teams included a combination of psychiatrists, psychologists, social workers, teachers, and occupational and recreational therapists. Each patient was assigned both an individual therapist, who was responsible for conducting psychoanalytically oriented psychotherapy with the patient, and a ward group administrator, who conducted the patient's group psychotherapy and coordinated all other aspects of the patient's treatment. For each patient, the individual therapist and ward group administrator were usually different people, although on rare occasions an individual clinician occupied both roles with a given patient. All individual therapists and ward group administrators were either MDs or PhDs, and some individual therapists had many years of clinical experience.

Data

Estimates of the patients' level of clinical functioning were derived from comprehensive case records assembled during the entire period of hospitalization, from the first month of inpatient treatment until discharge. Comprehensive treatment evaluations prepared by the clinical staff at admission and 6-month intervals included reports by individual, group, family, occupational, and recreational therapists; nursing staff reports; school behavior and progress reports; and reports by ward group administrators (experienced clinicians who oversaw clusters of 7–9 patients). Also contained in these case records were comprehensive admission and discharge evaluations and the results of a complete psychological assessment battery given during the first month of hospitalization.

Global Assessment Scale

The Global Assessment Scale (GAS; Endicott, Spitzer, Fleiss, & Cohen, 1976) was used to assess patients' overall clinical functioning. The GAS, a unidimensional scale, assesses overall clinical functioning and the severity of psychiatric disturbance with well-specified scale points for each of 10 intervals, ranging from a high score of 91–100 for "superior functioning in a wide range of activities, life problems never seem to get out of hand, [person] is sought by others because of his warmth and integrity, no symptoms" (p. 768); to a score of 51–60 at midrange for "moderate symptoms or generally functioning with some difficulty (e.g., few friends and flat affect, depressed mood and pathological self doubt, euphoric mood and pressured speech, moderately severe antisocial behavior" (p. 768); to a low score of 1–10 for "needs constant supervision for several days to prevent hurting self or others (e.g., requires an intensive care-unit with special observation by staff), makes no attempt to maintain minimal personal hygiene, or serious suicidal act with clear intent and expectations of death" (p. 768). The GAS is especially sensitive to changes in clinical functioning and severity of psychiatric disturbance (Endicott et al., 1976) as expressed in clinical case records or in clinical observation and interviews. Interrater reliability in four studies ranged from .69 to .85 (Endicott et al., 1976).

In our study, an independent judge, an experienced clinical psychologist, rated the independently prepared clinical case records with the GAS at admission and discharge. This judge had previously achieved a high level of reliability (intraclass correlation = .87; Shrout & Fleiss, 1979) in making GAS ratings on a sample of chronically disturbed outpatients. The case records used to derive GAS ratings included behaviorally oriented summaries prepared by nursing staff, the psychiatrist or psychologist administratively in charge of the case, and the social work, occupational, and teaching staff as well as by the group therapist, the individual therapist, and any special consultants.

The mean GAS score for our sample was 33.75 at admission and 43.25 at discharge. GAS scores of 31–40 "indicate major impairment in several areas, such as work, family relations, judgment, thinking, or mood . . . or some impairment in reality testing or communication (e.g., speech at times obscure, illogical or irrelevant) or a single suicide attempt" (Endicott et al., 1976, p. 768). GAS scores of 41–50 indicate "serious symptomatology or impairment in functioning that most clinicians would think obviously requires treatment or attention (e.g., suicidal preoccupation or gesture, severe obsessional rituals, frequent anxiety attacks, serious antisocial behavior, compulsive drinking, mild but definite manic syndrome)."

Descriptions of Significant Figures

All patients in this study were treated during a 3-year period in which inpatients who agreed to participate were given the Object Relations Inventory (ORI), an open-ended interview, at admission, discharge, and intervening 6-month intervals. On the ORI, participants are asked to describe each of the following significant figures: mother, father, significant other (friend, relative, etc.), pet, self, and individual therapist. After each description, the interviewer asks the patient to elaborate on each adjective used in describing the figure. For example, if a patient describes his or her mother as "overbearing and cold," the interviewer asks at the end of the description, "What do you mean when you say she is overbearing?" and "What do you mean when you say she is cold?" The interviewer then asks the patient to describe the next figure in the series (e.g., father) and to elaborate on each adjective in that description.

The ORI was initially administered by a postdoctoral psychology fellow or a predoctoral psychology intern to each participant as part of a battery of standard psychological tests given to all patients shortly after admission to the hospital. Thereafter, it was administered by a trained research assistant who had been instructed to record all responses verbatim. Because our primary interest was in the relationship between the treatment process and the development of object representations, we restrict our analyses in this chapter to the following four figures: mother, father, therapist, and self. Furthermore, for purposes of statistical analysis, only the descriptions obtained in the admission psychological testing and at discharge (or at the last point in treatment) were evaluated. The point during treatment from which case records were selected for GAS ratings was coordinated with that at which significant-figure descriptions were obtained. Judges scoring these descriptions did not know the identity of the patients, the patients' GAS scores, or the point in treatment at which the description was collected; they made various ratings in random order.

Assessment of Descriptions of Self and Others

To rate ORI responses, Diamond, Blatt, Stayner, and Kaslow (1991) developed a scale, the Differentiation–Relatedness Scale, that assesses the developmental level of two fundamental dimensions of self and object representation: (a) the differentiation of self from others and (b) the establishment of increasingly mature levels of interpersonal relatedness. Relying on clinical observations and theoretical formulations about early processes of boundary articulation (Blatt & Wild, 1976; Jacobson, 1964; Kernberg, 1976), the processes of separation–individuation (Mahler et al., 1975), the formation of the self (Stern, 1985), and the development of increasingly mature levels of interpersonal relatedness (Blatt, 1991, 1995), this scale distinguishes several levels of differentiation (Coonerty, 1986) in the articulation and stabilization of concepts of self and others and of their interrelationship. In general, higher ratings of descriptions of self and others are based on increased differentiation and articulation, increased coordination and integration of varied aspects of experience, and an increased appreciation of mutual and empathically attuned relatedness or a growing awareness that reciprocal relational matrices contribute to the construction of the sense of self and of others. Using a detailed manual that includes several examples at each level (Diamond et al., 1991), judges rate the level of differentiation-relatedness of descriptions of self and of significant others.

The Differentiation–Relatedness Scale distinguishes among the following levels: a lack of basic differentiation between self and others (1 and 2); the use of mirroring (3), self–other idealization or denigration (4), and an oscillation between polarized negative and positive attributes (5) as maneuvers to consolidate and stabilize representations; an emergent differentiated, constant, and integrated representation of self and others with increasing tolerance for ambiguity (6 and 7); self and others as empathically interrelated (8); self and others in reciprocal and mutually facilitating interactions (9); and reflectively constructed, integrated representations of self and others in reciprocal and mutual relationships (10).[1] This scale is based on the assumption that development moves toward the emergence of (a) a consolidated, integrated, and individuated sense of self-definition and (b) empathically attuned, mutual relatedness with significant others (Blatt & Blass, 1990; Jordan, 1986; Miller, 1984; S. A. Mitchell, 1988; Stern, 1985; Surrey, 1985). Differentiation and relatedness are interactive dimensions (Blatt & Blass, 1990, 1996; Sander, 1983) that emerge in a developmental unfolding process (see also Kegan, 1982; S. A. Mitchell, 1988; Ogden, 1986). The dialectical interaction between these two dimensions facilitates the development of increasingly mature levels of both self-organization and reciprocally attuned, empathic relatedness. The scale assumes that, with psychological maturation, representations of self and others become increasingly differentiated and integrated and begin to reflect an increased appreciation of mutuality.

---

[1]For complete instructions on the Differentiation–Relatedness Scale, refer to the scoring manual (Diamond, Blatt, Stayner, & Kaslow, 1991), which can be obtained from us.

At the lowest levels, the scale reflects the compromise of boundaries in terms of basic body awareness, emotions, or thoughts. Subsequent scale points reflect a unitary, unmodulated view of self and of the other as extensions of each other or as mirrored images (i.e., images in which self and others are identical). At an intermediate level, representations are organized around a unitary idealization or denigration of self or others (i.e., around an exaggerated sense of the goodness or badness of the figure described). At the next level, these exaggerated aspects of self and others alternate in a juxtaposition of polarized (i.e., all good or all bad) extremes. Later scale points reflect an increased capacity to integrate disparate aspects of self and others and an increased tolerance for ambivalence and ambiguity.

The scale also reflects a trend toward increasing mutuality and empathy in complex interpersonal relationships. At lower levels, the sense of relatedness in representations may involve being controlled by the other (e.g., trying to resist the intrusion of an other who is experienced as bad and destructive). At increasingly higher levels, relatedness may be expressed primarily in parallel interactions, in expressions of cooperation and mutuality, in understanding the other's perspective, or in expressions of empathically attuned reciprocity. At the highest levels, descriptions will reflect a sense of one's participation in complex, relational matrices that determine perceptions, attributions, and the construction of meaning. According to these formulations, the following 10 levels can be delineated in representations of self and others.

Level 1: Basic physical cohesion or integrity of the representation of self or others is compromised. Descriptions at this level are characterized by severely compromised physical boundaries, in which basic bodily cohesion or physical integrity is lacking or breached. The body of either self or other or both may be experienced and described as permeated by or merged with the physical presence or properties of another person or something in the environment. Thoughts and feelings may seem unbounded and lack a firm sense of being anchored in a physically defined, intact, cohesive bodily self (e.g., "My thoughts are goin' out of my head, around the world"). These descriptions reflect a sense of interpersonal barrenness and may depict infusions or broadcasting of people's thoughts and feelings, as opposed to interpersonal communication across intact personal boundaries (e.g., "My upstairs neighbor watches my dreams on her TV at night when I'm asleep").

Level 2: Affective and intellectual boundaries of the representation of self or others are confused or compromised. Self and others appear physically intact, but thoughts and feelings are amorphous, undifferentiated, or confused rather than defined and distinguishable. For instance, a description may consist of a single, global quality, often an action or image (e.g., "Busy," without any elaboration). The other person or thing also may be described by naming internal affective states that lack any reference to interpersonal experience or a sense of interpersonal differentiation (e.g., "Worried. Unhappy"). It may comprise only a flood of details that fails to portray a distinguishable person to whom one is related interpersonally. It also may reflect a confusion, vagueness, or loss of mooring that includes feeling overwhelmed in trying to give the description (e.g., "It's too much for me. I don't know. Don't know"). These descriptions reflect a sense of being lost in unformed, undefined affective–cognitive experiences, rather than the higher level sense of agency involved in refusing to answer.

Level 3: Representation is described as an extension or mirror reflection of self or others. Descriptions at this level focus almost exclusively on characteristics of self and others, usually aspects of physical appearance or body shape or size, that are virtually or exactly identical (e.g., "Very pretty lady . . . she kinda looks like me. . . . We both love clothes. We fit into the same size"). These characteristics are described as unequivocally alike and often lack contextual specificity or conditionality. The other is regarded as a mirror or an extension of the self, through which a tenuous sense of consolidation and stability is maintained.

Level 4: Representation of self or others is described in unitary, unmodulated, idealized, or denigrated terms. Descriptions at this level are characterized by extreme, one-sided idealizations or denigrations of self or others. An example of a Level 4 response is a patient's description of her therapist as follows, "An ass I don't like him. (Why not?) I don't like his face. I just don't like him. Makes me feel uncomfortable. Talks with an accent." This pervasive quality lacks any reference to conditionality or any sense of qualification or modulation. Idealization and denigration may at times be included in the same description but will appear as separate static extremes (or part properties) of self or others and will lack the oscillation between extremes that is seen at the next level (Level 5). Idealization or denigration of others helps to anchor a tenuous sense of consolidation and stability. There is little or no oscillation between these polarized representations (as seen in descriptions at Level 5), but rather a marked isolation of disparate aspects of experience of the self.

Level 5: Representation dominated by experiences of self or others in polarized extremes or by an emphasis on concrete properties to stabilize a tenuous sense of self and others. Descriptions at this level are often marked by an oscillation between disparate aspects of one's experience of self and others, aspects that have been split into dramatically opposed, mutually exclusive polarities involving a pervasive, absolute quality (e.g., "He's got mood swings. Sometimes he's nice, sometimes he's real nasty. He can be pretty nice at times. That's about it"). Extremes might include, for instance, an overwhelming closeness versus an unbridgeable gulf or distance; invasive control versus abandonment; or intense rage versus idealizing love. Disparate aspects of self or others are experienced but not integrated into a multidimensional, modulated description. Self and others are described in absolute, mutually exclusive terms, with little or no sense of context or time or place.

Relatedness in Level 5 descriptions also may oscillate between defensive distancing and overidentification with others (e.g., abandonment vs. engulfing closeness). This oscillation also may appear in a preoccupation with issues of control and autonomy, with this concern reflecting an intense struggle to preserve a fragile, vulnerable, emerging sense of self from another's invasive control, rather than the less threatened, more positive emphasis on self-directedness and autonomy often seen at higher levels. Descriptions at this level can include an inordinate emphasis on concrete physical properties, bodies, or body parts, often depicted in stilted, two-dimensional, sometimes exaggerated terms. This marked focus on physical properties or concrete characteristics is viewed as another expression of an attempt to stabilize tenuous representations of self and others. This type of concrete description might reflect a more basic cognitive or developmental style, not just a defensive blocking.

Level 6: Emergent ambivalent constancy and cohesion as well as a relational alignment. Descriptions at this transitional level reflect an emerging consolidation of disparate aspects of self and others that is expressed in more integrated, stable representations (e.g., "One thing I have now which I didn't have in the past is self-confidence. I'm becoming a more social person. I care about myself. I worry about the way my room looks . . . if a picture is crooked, I have a spaz attack. I don't know if that's good or bad. . . . I mean I get so caught up in wanting everything to be perfect in my room. . . . I'm learning ways to control my temper and expressing my feelings, and I'm still writing in a journal. Most times I enjoy school. . . . I used to be petrified and hate it when I was in [her hometown]. Maybe because it's because I know everyone here. I think I want to be like my mother").

Descriptions are marked by a hesitant, equivocal, or ambivalent movement toward this integration and stabilization. Disparate aspects of self and others, and of interpersonal experience, are brought together in descriptions that include some conditional modulating phrases and a differentiation of various dimensions. These descriptions may consist simply of a list of appropriate, role-conventional characteristics (more abstract than the concrete properties or characteristics depicted in Level 5), but these characteristics do not reflect a sense of the uniqueness of the individual. Self-descriptions are often characterized by trial identifications or distinctions that also convey a sense of tentative movement toward a more individuated and cohesive sense of self. Relatedness includes an emergent and equivocal sense of tolerance for and ability to bring together divergent aspects of interpersonal experience.

Level 7: Stable, consolidated, relationally aligned self and others. Descriptions at this level reflect a consolidated, stable representation of self and others in which thoughts, feelings, needs, and fantasies are differentiated and modulated (e.g., "Funny. Caring. Good-natured. Generous with me. Tries to be understanding. Can't keep a secret very well. About 5'9", 185 lb. A little chubby. Balding. A well-meaning person. Happily married at present"). Included in this more stable representation is an increasing tolerance for and integration of disparate aspects of experiences of self and others. Characteristics and qualities are described more conditionally, with some references to temporal and environmental contexts. These descriptions are often marked by expressions of sympathetic understanding, like attempts to recognize and to consider specific situational factors that can influence another's or one's own behavior or viewpoint. Cause–effect relationships are depicted in relatively uncomplicated, largely unidirectional terms. Self-descriptions often emphasize a positive self-assertion, in which the individual's opinions, interests, and qualities are defined and articulated. Descriptions of others also tend to emphasize unique distinguishing qualities and characteristics.

Level 8: Cohesive, individuated, empathically related self and others. Descriptions at this level reflect a cohesive, nuanced, and related sense of self and others, in which varied characteristics and qualities are recognized and increasingly integrated. Aspects of the self and others that distinguish and define a unique sense of identity are emphasized. These descriptions often express an interest in understanding and differentiating feelings and motivations through interpersonal contact and communication and often involve references to potential or experienced differences between intentions and actual behavior. They also include references to the empathic use of one's own thoughts and feelings to appreciate and understand others. Behavior is often depicted in ways that suggest a complex, context-related understanding of cause and effect—in other words, a recognition that a given action may have shades of meaning, depending on its context. Descriptions at this level also include a positive emphasis on a complex independence and dependence in relationships, on career and work choices, and on future directions and possibilities, an emphasis that reflects the experience of an increasingly stable and cohesive sense of identity. For example, a patient described her therapist as follows, "I'm trying to think of a word . . . tactful in approaching subjects . . . that wasn't the word I was thinking of . . . not blunt, can say things in a better fashion. She can put things in a better way that doesn't sound too intimidating or so cruel. She's sweet, generous, and has high morals. She's a nice person. Has high standards."

Level 9: Mutually related, integrative, unfolding self and others. In addition to an integrated, cohesive sense of self and others, descriptions at this level contain depictions of mutual affective and interpersonal interactions between the self and others, in which the

behavior of one affects the other and in which each person makes
a unique contribution to the relationship. Describing her father, for
example, a patient said "My father. He's 5'10", grayish brown hair,
blue-green eyes, he's a heavyweight . . . big belly! My father's very
overprotective of me . . . he's very insecure himself about letting
me make my own moves and my own decisions. He is very caring
but, by the way he shows it, he gets angry rather than say, 'I get
angry because I care.' But he's trying to be very helpful with me
right now, with my leaving. I've learned a lot about my parents in
the last 6 months." Descriptions at this level include expressions
of empathic identification with the other's internal frame of reference and affective experience that also maintain one's own distinct,
intact sense of self. These experiences of mutual, intersubjective
relatedness are often regarded as enriching and transforming the
self. Descriptions at this level reflect an appreciation that one's
sense of self and others is continually unfolding and being articulated in complex interpersonal matrices.

*Level 10: Creative, integrative, empathically and mutually attuned self
and others.*   In addition to containing an articulated sense of integration and mutual relatedness, descriptions at this level include
a recognition that one participates in and contributes to the construction of systems of meaning that are interwoven with one's
experience of self and others. These constructions are supported
by an understanding of reality as an unfolding interplay between
objective and subjective experience, rather than as a series of facts
existing separately from one's subjective participation. Self and
others are depicted as creative constructions or narratives that
emerge from intrapersonal and interpersonal experiences and are
understood to shape and organize one's perspective on and perceptions of self–other experience. Descriptions at this level reflect
an appreciation of a creative participation in the process of constructing meaning and in the relational matrices that contribute to
an evolving sense of self and others. An example of a patient's
Level 10 response, in describing her mother, is as follows: "She's
. . . kind of neurotic . . . she tries hard with her kids and her husband. She's basically a very nice person, and I'd say she's wise
from experience, from all she's been through. She doesn't like to
hurt people, but I think she can be hurt easily. She's organized and
she's very practical, but she's got problems. . . . She knows what's

going on now, she's smart about people and things. I understand my mother a lot better now than I did when I first came to the hospital, and I know that the way I see her now is a result of my treatment. In 6 months I may see her differently."

These 10 levels of differentiation–relatedness were established on the basis of the clinical and developmental literature in psychoanalysis. As such, they reflect what are generally regarded as clinically significant distinctions in the transition from grossly pathological to intact and even healthy object relations. The scale points are thus best regarded as discrete categories, not points on a continuum. In other words, the underlying logic of this measure is ordinal, not interval or nominal. The various levels of this scale, therefore, may not be equidistant from each other, and the specific number of scale points is to some extent arbitrary. That is, new levels of differentiation–relatedness can be added given new clinical observations and theoretical formulations. Nevertheless, a clear implication of this procedure is that higher differentiation–relatedness ratings reflect a greater degree of psychological health. In theory, Differentiation–Relatedness Levels 8, 9, and 10 indicate mental health, and Differentiation–Relatedness Level 7 is a prerequisite for normal functioning. Empirical study of the relationship between differentiation–relatedness and psychosocial functioning in the normal population is necessary, however, before these statements can be made with certainty. Also note that symptom formation, although less common, less pervasive, and less severe at high levels of differentiation–relatedness, is possible at any level on this dimension, given the right set of precipitating circumstances.

Reliability of the Differentiation–Relatedness Scale was initially examined in a pilot investigation of representations of 4 severely impaired inpatients undergoing long-term inpatient treatment (Diamond et al., 1991). Two judges rated 20 descriptions and achieved an interrater reliability of .86. Reliability was further examined (Stayner, 1994) by comparing five judges' ratings of 90 descriptions, given by several members of the sample of severely impaired adolescent and young adult inpatients studied here, of mother, father, therapist, self, and a significant-other person. The five judges varied considerably in their level of clinical experience and their familiarity with the developmental conceptualizations underlying the scale. They included two experienced clinical psychologists, two experienced psychiatric aides, one of whom had related research experience, and a clinically experienced graduate student in clinical psychology. An adjusted intraclass correlation of .83 was obtained from a two-way Judges × Items analysis of variance (Shrout & Fleiss, 1979). The two judges scoring this scale in the current investigation had participated in this prior reliability study.

Test–retest reliability of ratings based on the Differentiation–Relatedness Scale was evaluated by comparing ratings of descriptions of mother and self given by 10 severely impaired adult patients in a day hospital over a 5-day period. Because of a restricted range of scores from 3 to 6, it was not possible to use parametric statistics to assess reliability. The test–retest stability of this scale appears to be substantial, however, because ratings of the differentiation–relatedness of 18 of the 20 descriptions were within 1 point of each other (Stayner, 1994). In addition, initial findings with the Differentiation–Relatedness Scale provide some preliminary support for its construct validity. In a study of 4 severely impaired inpatients, changes in level of the differentiation–relatedness of self- and object descriptions corresponded to independent qualitative ratings of clinical improvement derived from analyses of clinical case records. Ratings of the differentiation–relatedness of the descriptions also correlated positively with ratings of differentiation–relatedness derived from patients' Rorschach responses (Diamond et al., 1990).

Data Analyses

First, using the Statistical Package for the Social Sciences partial correlation statistical procedure, which establishes residualized scores of all variables by covarying out the initial value of the variables (i.e., their values at the beginning of treatment), we correlated changes in differentiation–relatedness of descriptions of self and significant others with independent estimates of therapeutic change. The use of partial correlations permits assessment of clinical change without the statistical problems ordinarily associated with difference scores, especially the compounding of error variance. Thus, the relationship of changes in the ratings of the descriptions of self and others to changes in the level of clinical functioning (GAS scores) was tested with higher order partial correlations that controlled for the initial level of both GAS scores and the ratings of the descriptions at admission. By statistically partialing out admission scores for both the quality of representation and the level of clinical functioning, we removed from later ratings of variables that part of the variance that could be predicted from the scores at admission. Partial correlations were calculated for GAS scores and differentiation–relatedness ratings derived separately from the descriptions of mother, father, therapist, and self.

Second, to assess the clinical significance of changes in differentiation–relatedness over the course of treatment, we conducted four two-way repeated measures analyses of covariance (ANCOVAs), one for each figure (mother, father, therapist, and self). The between-subjects variable was clinical improvement, with more improvement and less improvement defined by a median split of discharge GAS scores, residualized for GAS scores at admission. The residualized discharge GAS rating was chosen because it once again provided an estimate of degree of clinical change while avoiding the statistical problems associated with the use of difference scores between admission and discharge. The statistical correction provided by partialing out admission from discharge GAS scores was important in both the partial correlations and the repeated measures ANCOVAs because these two variables were significantly correlated, $r(37) = .43$, $p = .0067$. Among more improving patients, the mean nonresidualized GAS score was 34.95 ($SD = 7.51$) at admission and 48.14 ($SD = 4.88$) at discharge. Less improving patients had a mean nonresidualized admission GAS score of 32.33 ($SD = 6.19$) and a mean discharge nonresidualized GAS score of 37.56 ($SD = 5.16$). In other words, more improved patients were those whose discharge clinical functioning, statistically corrected for admission clinical functioning, was higher than the median statistically corrected discharge score.

The within-subjects variable in the ANCOVAs was defined by time in treatment (admission, or discharge). In addition, because previous results indicated that Differentiation–Relatedness Scale scores were significantly correlated with length of significant-other descriptions (Blatt et al., 1996),[2] description length, estimated on a 7-point scale from the number of lines in the description, was included as a covariate in each analysis. In other words, to account for the potentially confounding effects of verbal productivity in constructing object representations, we partialed out description length from the analyses of changes in levels of differentiation–relatedness. Alpha levels were set at .05 for all statistical analyses.

Results

The relationship of changes in the differentiation–relatedness in mental representation of self and significant others to changes in the level of general clinical function was assessed through partial correlations between residualized GAS scores (Time 2/Time 1) and residualized differentiation–relatedness of the descriptions of significant figures. Highly significant relationships were found between degree of clinical improvement and increased differentiation–relatedness in the descriptions of all four figures, especially for mother, $r(36) = .52$, $p < .0001$, therapist, $r(36) = .50$, $p < .001$, and self, $r(36) = .52$, $p < .0001$, and only secondarily for father, $r(36) = .31$, $p < .05$.[3] Therapeutic gain was thus clearly associated with significant increases in the level of differentiation–relatedness of the representation of self and of significant others.

Table 1 contains the mean Differentiation–Relatedness Scale score and mean description-length ratings at admission and discharge for all four figures described. The mean Differentiation–Relatedness Scale ratings indicated that patients showed a consistent pattern of change on this dimension. For all four significant figures, patients generally began treatment with unintegrated rep-

---

[2]In particular, at discharge, description length in the sample to be analyzed here was found to correlate significantly with differentiation–relatedness for the following three figures: father, $r(33) = .51$, $p = .002$; therapist, $r(34) = .33$, $p = .05$; and self, $r(36) = .50$, $p = .002$. In addition, at admission, these two variables were significantly correlated for the description of self, $r(37) = -.32$, $p = .047$. Mean description-length ratings are shown in Table 1.

[3]These findings are discussed in greater detail by Blatt, Stayner, Auerbach, and Behrends (1996).

Table 1

Means and Standard Deviations of Differentiation–Relatedness Scale Scores and Length Ratings in Descriptions of Significant Figures

Variable	Differentiation–relatedness				Length			
	Admission		Discharge		Admission		Discharge	
	M	SD	M	SD	M	SD	M	SD
Mother								
Less improvement (*n* = 13)	4.92	1.44	5.92	0.95	1.62	0.87	1.08	0.28
More improvement (*n* = 20)	4.70	1.26	6.45	1.47	1.20	0.89	1.35	1.14
Total (*N* = 33)	4.79	1.32	6.24	1.30	1.36	0.90	1.24	0.90
Father								
Less improvement (*n* = 15)	5.20	1.21	6.27	1.44	1.40	0.83	1.40	0.74
More improvement (*n* = 17)	4.82	1.18	6.47	1.42	1.82	1.81	1.76	1.68
Total (*N* = 32)	5.00	1.19	6.38	1.41	1.62	1.43	1.59	1.32
Therapist								
Less improvement (*n* = 13)	5.00	1.16	6.00	1.73	1.08	0.28	1.38	0.77
More improvement (*n* = 18)	5.67	0.97	7.00	1.41	1.28	0.75	1.50	0.98
Total (*N* = 31)	5.39	1.09	6.58	1.61	1.19	0.60	1.45	0.89
Self								
Less improvement (*n* = 15)	4.87	1.30	6.13	1.64	2.13	1.30	2.73	1.87
More improvement (*n* = 20)	5.10	1.12	6.70	1.38	2.30	1.49	2.95	1.85
Total (*N* = 35)	5.00	1.19	6.46	1.50	2.23	1.40	2.86	1.83

resentations that involved oscillations between polarized qualities (i.e., all-good or all-bad) or an emphasis on concrete part properties (Differentiation–Relatedness Level 5). After a substantial time in treatment, object representations of these patients were characterized by an emergent object constancy (Differentiation–Relatedness Level 6), that is, by an emergent ability to tolerate and to begin to integrate contradictory aspects of significant figures in their lives.[4] In addition, for all four significant figures, differentiation-relatedness at discharge was always higher among patients who showed marked clinical improvement than among those who had improved less, although this difference did not always reach statistical significance.

As Table 1 indicates, for all four figures (mother, father, therapist, and self), there was a significant main effect for the within-subjects variable of moment in treatment. In other words, over the course of treatment, differentiation–relatedness increased significantly for all figures assessed. For each figure described, there was a significant main effect for the within-subjects variable, moment in treatment, as follows: mother, $F(1, 30) = 21.56$, $p < .001$, $MSE = 1.23$; father, $F(1, 29) = 21.02$, $p < .001$, $MSE = 1.38$; therapist, $F(1, 28) = 8.93$, $p < .01$, $MSE = 1.56$; and self, $F(1, 32) = 18.89$, $p < .001$, $MSE = 1.31$. In other words, over the course of treatment, differentiation–relatedness increased significantly for all figures assessed—as noted, roughly from polarization and splitting to emergent object constancy.

A significant main effect also was found for the between-subjects variable, degree of clinical improvement, for the therapist description, $F(1, 28) = 4.77$, $p < .05$, $MSE = 1.85$. That is, participants with the greatest clinical improvement showed greater differentiation–relatedness in their descriptions of their therapists than did less improving patients. At admission, patients who eventually had greater improvement described their therapists in a manner that was already approaching the emergence of object constancy, but those who were to show less improvement began at the level of polarization and splitting. At discharge, patients with

---

[4]Alternatively, this emergent object constancy might be defined as a beginning capacity to maintain stable, cohesive representations of self and others despite immediate emotional disturbances in relationships with significant figures.

greater therapeutic change displayed a consolidation of object constancy (Differentiation–Relatedness Level 7), whereas patients with less improvement had just achieved the emergence of object constancy (Level 6) in their therapist descriptions. For none of the remaining three figures (mother, father, and self), however, was there a significant main effect for degree of clinical improvement with respect to differentiation–relatedness, whether at admission or at discharge. Thus, although discharge Differentiation–Relatedness Scale scores were, as previously stated, always higher among more improved patients than among those who improved less, only in the case of the therapist was this difference statistically significant. Although Differentiation–Relatedness scores and description length were significantly correlated, it should be noted that, with the exception of a between-subjects effect for the covariate length of the father description, $F(1, 29) = 8.76$, $p < .001$, $MSE = 1.69$, all other statistical tests associated with these ANCOVAs failed to reach significance.

In summary, the data presented here indicate that increases in differentiation–relatedness occur in long-term, psychoanalytically oriented, hospital-based treatment. These increases have both statistical and clinical significance. The patients entered the hospital with object representations dominated by polarization and splitting (i.e., by the keeping apart of good and bad aspects of an object representation to preserve an emotional tie to the good aspects of the object) and left treatment with their object representations involving the emergence of—or, in the case of their therapist descriptions—the consolidation of object constancy. Furthermore, these results suggest that the Differentiation–Relatedness Scale score for therapist descriptions at both admission and discharge distinguished patients who showed clinical improvement from those who did not. Patients with greater change had significantly higher Differentiation–Relatedness Scale ratings of their descriptions of their therapists. In addition, Differentiation–Relatedness Scale scores were higher for therapist than for any of the other three significant figures described, mother, father, or self.[5]

---

[5]It is important to emphasize that ratings of differentiation–relatedness of the descriptions were made by a judge who did not know the level of patients' therapeutic progress, which descriptions were from the same patient, or when in the treatment process, early or late, the descriptions were obtained.

Discussion

The results of this investigation indicate that therapeutic progress in the treatment of seriously disturbed young adults was accompanied by significant revisions of the mental representations of self and significant others (i.e., mother, father, and therapist) during the course of long-term, intensive inpatient treatment. Descriptions of self and others, especially for patients independently judged to have made considerable therapeutic progress, became more differentiated and related with treatment. Specifically, they moved from a level of polarization and splitting (i.e., overstated, one-sided, idealized, or denigrated descriptions) to levels of object constancy (i.e., involving an integration of contradictory and disparate elements). These changes in the developmental level of representations were independent of the length of the description, and they occurred in the descriptions of all four figures: mother, father, therapist, and self. Thus, from a psychoanalytic perspective, it might be argued that, through the process of long-term, psychoanalytically oriented inpatient treatment, the patients have progressed from representations dominated by polarization and splitting to representations involving evocative constancy (Adler & Buie, 1979; Blatt & Auerbach, 1988; Blatt & Shichman, 1983). Psychoanalytic theory associates these changes in mental representations with a progression from a borderline to a primitive neurotic level of personality organization (Kernberg, 1975, 1976, 1984), a shift from the paranoid–schizoid to the depressive position (Klein, 1935, 1946; cf. Blatt & Shichman, 1983), or an integration of multiple aspects (e.g., subjective with objective, private with public, or "true" with "false") aspects of the self (Auerbach, 1993; Bach, 1985; Broucek, 1991; Modell, 1993; Stern, 1985; Winnicott, 1965). Whatever descriptive terminology one prefers, however, the clinical transformation that we observed in these patients involved a shift in the level of personality organization from fragmented to more integrated representations that approached the consolidation associated with object constancy. The emergence of object constancy in this sample of seriously disturbed patients is a remarkable clinical achievement.

Case Analysis

To illustrate this developmental progress, we present a clinical example provided by the case of Patient C., a 15-year-old single White female adolescent with admission *DSM–III* diagnoses of conduct disorder, undersocialized, nonaggressive; identity disorder; mixed substance abuse, episodic (alcohol, sedative-hypnotics, marijuana, amphetamines, and phencyclidine); and mixed personality features (dependent, antisocial, narcissistic, and histrionic).[6] As this list of diagnoses suggests, her treatment team regarded her as functioning at a borderline level of personality organization. Her GAS score at admission was 34, and at discharge was 47. Her self- and object descriptions at admission and discharge are shown in Exhibit 1, and her Differentiation–Relatedness Scale scores for these descriptions are listed in Table 2.

C.'s Differentiation–Relatedness Scale scores at admission suggested that her psychological organization at that time was dominated by polarization and splitting. At discharge, approximately 30 months later, her mean Differentiation–Relatedness score was consistent with the consolidation of object, or evocative, constancy.

In particular, C.'s descriptions of her parents at admission emphasized physical descriptors and polarized, negatively charged psychological features. In describing her mother, C. made an initial attempt to integrate a depiction of her mother as being supportive with a view of her as hostile and intrusive, but eventually the negative characterizations of her mother came to dominate the representation. Indeed, C.'s initial question, "Looks *or* personality?" (emphasis added), suggested that polarized, binary thinking was central to how she thought about significant others. A focus on concrete physical details helped C. to briefly contain her highly ambivalent feelings about her mother, but ultimately her concerns with her mother's intrusiveness overwhelmed her defenses.

In her admission description of her father, C. gave no indication of ambivalent feelings. Only anger and rage were present, as C. alternated between, on the one hand, concrete physical descriptors that once again served temporarily to mute and delay expression

---

[6]This case was previously discussed by Diamond, Kaslow, Coonerty, and Blatt (1990).

Exhibit 1

Patient C.: Self- and Object Representations at Admission and Discharge

---

Admission

MOTHER: Looks or personality? 5'7", 135 lb, brown hair, blue eyes. She's usually pretty cool but can be a bitch. Her voice is whiny, very piercing.

FATHER: A dick. 6'2", heavy, short black hair. Real nasty, a real tyrant. Beady black eyes.
Inquiry: (Why do you suppose he's like that?) Cause he's an asshole. Sucks dicks for a living.

SELF: Can be tough. Give no more than I expect to get. Get hurt a lot really easily, but I cover it up with a really tough front.
Inquiry: (Why do you suppose you do that?) I don't know. Just like to help people.

THERAPIST: Really nice, quiet, calm, pretty cool. Listens to what you say.

Discharge (2¹/₂ years)

MOTHER: Honest, basic, scared, natural, kind. Nurturing when she can be.
Inquiry: (Basic?) Simple. (Scared?) Phobic. (Kind?) Nurturing.
[C. had a flat affect but was thoughtful in choosing words.]

FATHER: Depressed, personalizes things, angry. Reasonable at times.
Inquiry: (Personalizes?) When someone is cold to him, he takes it personally.

SELF: Goofy at times. Cold and appearing aloof. Smart. Personalizes things with people too much. Impulsive. Sometimes nice. [Refused inquiry.]

THERAPIST: Calm, patient, extremely smart, caring. Easy to talk with. [Refused inquiry.]

Examiner's questions are in parentheses. Examiner's editorial comments are in brackets.

Table 2

Differentiation—Relatedness Scale Scores for Patient C. at Admission and Discharge

Significant figure	Admission	Discharge
Mother	5	8
Father	4	7
Self	6	7
Therapist	6	7
Total	21	29
M	5.3	7.3

of her deeper concerns and, on the other, a hostility that was expressed through expletives involving primitive drive contents. C's regression from phallic to anal and, finally, oral themes suggested that she was unable to modulate her anger over what she regarded as her father's intrusive domination.

In marked contrast, however, to her depictions of her parents as intrusive and domineering were C.'s more nuanced and balanced descriptions of herself and her therapist. At admission, C.'s representations of these figures were consistent with the emergence of object constancy. In acknowledging the manner in which she deployed a tough façade to cover up her sensitivity and vulnerability, this young woman demonstrated an emerging capacity to overcome polarization and splitting or, alternatively, to integrate subjective and objective perspectives on the self—to recognize her own complexities. Her description of her therapist meanwhile suggested that C. had finally found someone whom she could regard, unlike her parents, as supportive, empathic, calming, and nonintrusive. To be sure, C. had not yet begun to wrestle with the negative aspects of the therapeutic relationship, but neither was she unrealistically idealizing her therapist. Thus, these higher level representations of self and therapist at admission suggested C.'s potential for substantial therapeutic gain.

At discharge, C.'s significant-figure descriptions demonstrated her consolidation of evocative constancy and her movement toward the formation of a stable identity and mutual interpersonal relationships. Gone at this point were depictions of her parents as domineering and intrusive; in place of those angry descriptions were complex appreciations of her parents' psychological struggles. In particular, C.'s mother was no longer "a bitch" but instead a frightened woman who, despite her anxiety, still tried to be nurturing. Her father was no longer "a real tyrant" but instead a depressed, angry, and hypersensitive man who, despite his psychological limitations, was capable of being reasonable with his daughter.

In her self-description, C. elaborated on the many contradictions she felt about herself (e.g., hypersensitivity vs. aloofness, goofiness vs. coldness) and demonstrated a greater integration of these various facets. In therapy, in the difficult, often shame-filled task of reconciling her subjective feelings with her objective self-perceptions, she was no longer puzzled by her contradictions but instead regarded them as accepted parts of herself. Furthermore, she also seemed to recognize that, in her hypersensitivity, she was more like her father than she had previously thought. Finally, C. went from regarding her therapist as a listener who provided empathic support to viewing her as a truly caring figure. C.'s acknowledgment of her therapist's intelligence and patience, although perhaps indicating C.'s continuing propensity for self-criticism, meanwhile suggested that C. was expressing gratitude for her therapist's help in her emotional struggles over the past $2^{1}/_{2}$ years.

Thus, by discharge, C.'s representations had reached the more mature levels of the Differentiation–Relatedness Scale, in which there was an appreciation of the potentials for relatedness between herself and others. She had achieved the realization that significant loving relationships can survive anger and conflict at a level of evocative (object) constancy. On the other hand, the reduced verbal productivity in her discharge descriptions suggested that the emotional pressures of termination—most likely the depressive feelings and apprehensions associated with the loss of her therapist and the hospital—produced a degree of regression in C.'s ability to maintain complex, nuanced representations of self and significant others in a mutual relationship. Clinical observations of increased depression in this young woman at the time of discharge, associated with earlier depressive issues of loss and of guilt over aggression, paralleled the reduced verbal productivity with which she articulated increasingly sophisticated descriptions of significant figures. Despite her depression, therefore, C. remained at the level of evocative constancy and did not return to a reliance on polarization and splitting.[7]

Factors in Therapeutic Change

The patients in our sample, like C., did not attain at termination fully mature object relations and object representations (i.e., they still did not fully appreciate the uniqueness of, and the nature of one's relatedness to, others), but their development of the capacity to tolerate ambivalent feelings about significant objects is an important and necessary step on the way to this more mature level of interpersonal relatedness. It is therefore important to determine what factors might predict this transformation in object relations and the emergence of the representational capacity for object constancy.

Our results point to the crucial role of the therapist in facilitating this clinical change. Patients with greater change, it should be recalled, had higher initial Differentiation–Relatedness Scale scores for their therapist descriptions than did patients with less change. Also, differentiation–relatedness was initially higher for therapist descriptions than for those of each of the other three figures, mother, father, or self. In contrast to the significant relationship between the degree of clinical improvement and the change in the description of the therapist, no significant relationship was found between degree of clinical improvement and level of differentiation–relatedness in initial descriptions of self, mother, and father. Thus, one might argue that more and less improving patients were equally disturbed in their object relations, at least as

---

[7]An interesting and related question is the extent to which transient mood states can affect a patient's level of differentiation–relatedness. Although this is clearly a matter for empirical study, a plausible hypothesis, as the case example suggests, is that this dimension is not impervious to fluctuations in mood but that a patient's current emotional state has increasingly less influence on the level of differentiation–relatedness as the individual's representation rises on this scale.

regards familiar figures in their lives, but the Differentiation–Relatedness Scale score revealed a crucial clinical difference concerning an important new figure—the therapist. In turn, this clinical difference suggested that patients with greater change were those most capable of constructing more complex and nuanced representations of this significant new figure. Not surprisingly, therefore, patients who eventually had greater improvement generally had higher Differentiation–Relatedness Scale scores at admission for their therapist descriptions. Long-term, psychoanalytically oriented treatment is a complex process, however, and it also may be that the patients who improved the most were those lucky enough to have therapists who facilitated the formation of complex, nuanced therapist representations.

It is noteworthy that a significant relationship between clinical improvement and changes in differentiation–relatedness in descriptions of mother, father, and self was previously found in a correlational analysis of these data (see Blatt et al., 1996). When change in clinical functioning was treated as a continuous variable (e.g., discharge GAS ratings that were residualized for GAS scores at admission), it was significantly related to change in differentiation–relatedness for all four figures—mother, father, therapist, and self—described by the patients in this sample. We did not find this relationship, however, when treating clinical improvement as a dichotomous, rather than continuous, variable. In other words, this relationship was obscured by the less sensitive dichotomous classification of more versus less improvement. That a significant effect for the therapist representation emerged in these factorial analyses, which used as an independent variable the less sensitive, dichotomous distinction (i.e., more vs. less therapeutic change) and which also controlled for description length, suggests that the results with the representation of the therapist may be a more reliable finding than those with the representation of mother and self, which were significant only in the correlational analyses.

Limitations of This Study

At least three factors limit the generalizability of our findings. First, although it is clear that differentiation–relatedness improves over the course of long-term treatment, we did not control for the effect of the actual length of time in the hospital. It is possible that patients who showed greater gains in differentiation–relatedness were those who were hospitalized longer. Note, however, that the patients in our sample had extensive psychiatric treatment before coming to our facility and had not shown clinical improvement. Insofar as they did manifest such improvement after long-term psychoanalytic hospitalization, it is plausible to argue that growth in differentiation–relatedness is due primarily to the nature of the treatment provided, not its length.[8] Furthermore, although it also is possible that the need to appear psychologically intact at discharge from the hospital may produce an artificial inflation in differentiation–relatedness, the effect of this potential confound is likely more than balanced by the apprehensions, fears, and losses associated with termination.[9]

Second, we did not control for the effects of simple maturation. That is, it is possible that the adolescent and young adult patients in this study showed improvement in differentiation–relatedness

---

[8]The comparison we are drawing here is between long-term psychoanalytic hospitalization and conventional inpatient psychiatric treatment of the 1980s. We leave open the possibility that long-term hospitalization focusing on cognitive–behavioral therapy might produce equivalent results with regard to differentiation–relatedness. Certainly, Linehan's (1993) dialectical behavior therapy has produced significant clinical improvements in outpatient borderline samples (Linehan, Armstrong, Suarez, Allmon, & Heard, 1991; Linehan, Heard, & Armstrong, 1993; Linehan, Tutek, Heard, & Armstrong, 1994) and has reduced parasuicidality in an inpatient borderline sample whose level of disturbance was comparable to what we have studied here (Barley et al., 1993); however, a change in a representational variable such as differentiation–relatedness may be less apparent in a cognitive–behavioral treatment. We are more certain that results like those obtained here could not be obtained with the conventional short-term hospitalizations of the 1980s and the still-shorter hospitalizations of today.

[9]Patient C. thus registered her highest Differentiation–Relatedness Scale scores ($M = 8$) not at discharge but 6 months earlier. At that earlier point in treatment, she had actually advanced beyond evocative constancy to representations that expressed a cohesive integrated sense of self in empathic and mutually shared relationships but then regressed somewhat from that advanced psychological level, most likely in response to the emotional pressures of termination. Indeed, at that point 6 months before discharge, she had even shown signs of having moved beyond the consolidation of object constancy to a sense of identity formation and an appreciation of mutual, empathic relatedness.

simply because they were older at discharge than at admission. Although patient age at admission might seem a useful covariate in this regard, we did not partial out this variable because doing so would oversimplify the processes through which object representations develop. Psychological maturation in our sample was a function of at least three factors: normal developmental processes, pathological developmental processes, and treatment processes. For example, among normal adolescents evaluated in a longitudinal study, structural features of object representations showed greater differentiation, articulation, and integration over a 20-year period from ages 10–11 to age 30 (Blatt et al., 1976), but it cannot be assumed that the same pattern occurs over a 1- or 2-year period among disturbed adolescents. Although growth in object representations does in fact occur in adolescents with psychological difficulties (see Westen, 1989, 1990), one cannot assume that this growth follows the same pattern or even occurs at the same rate as it does among normal teenagers. In addition, because most seriously disturbed adolescents are in treatment and because it would be difficult to collect data on a sample of equally disturbed but untreated adolescents, it is likely that treatment processes and pathological development are confounded in ways that cannot be addressed by a simple covariance of age. Again, insofar as the patients in this study had shown clinical deterioration before long-term hospitalization, and insofar as they also were getting older while they were deteriorating clinically, it is plausible to argue that the improvements in differentiation–relatedness observed in our study were due at least partly to long-term, psychoanalytically oriented treatment, not simply to adolescent development.

Third, even though it is plausible to argue that growth in differentiation–relatedness among these patients was at least partly a treatment effect, the specific agents of therapeutic change (e.g., individual therapy, family therapy, rehabilitation therapy, milieu treatment, pharmacotherapy, etc.) cannot be determined. Because most of the patients were treatment failures before their current hospitalization and interdisciplinary treatment, a plausible conclusion is that the entire intensive treatment process, not any specific therapeutic modality, was responsible for the improvements found here. Yet, the significant change in the representation of the therapist that was associated with the independent assessment of therapeutic progress suggested that the relationship with the therapist played a central role in the treatment process. It is also possible, and perhaps even likely, that significant improvements in differentiation–relatedness also would be found in descriptions of nonfamilial figures other than therapists. (Indeed, we have collected significant-other descriptions and, less systematically, descriptions of a pet from the participants in our sample, but we have not yet scored and analyzed them.) The therapist differs from the range of possible nonfamilial significant figures, however, in one crucial respect: The patients in our sample knew a great deal about their best friends and their pets and little about the lives of their individual therapists. This difference makes our findings with the therapist description even more compelling and strengthens our inference that the relationship with the therapist was central to our patients' growth in differentiation–relatedness.

Implications for Future Research

Because representations of self and others are, above all, interpersonal schemas, it is likely that the construction of these representations also is highly dependent on the capacity to create narratives in psychotherapy. A narrative, according to Bruner (1990), "is composed of a unique sequence of events, mental states, happenings involving human beings as characters or actors" (p. 43). Although interpersonal schemas are initially constructed from nonverbal (i.e., enactive, affective, and physicalistic) materials, it is ultimately through increasingly complex and sophisticated narratives (i.e., through sequential stories with plots) that children come to integrate these nonverbal materials with the verbal and the symbolic and therefore to understand themselves, others, and the meanings of interpersonal transactions. Indeed, process methods for studying psychotherapy (e.g., Luborsky's, 1984, CCRT) are attempts at schematic representation of narrative structure. Furthermore, because the psychoanalytical dialogue is constructed through narrative (Ricoeur, 1977; Schafer, 1983; Spence, 1982), it is reasonable to speculate that patients' abilities to tell stories are intimately connected to the power of psychotherapy to help them revise maladaptive self- and object representations. The significant relationship between verbal productivity, in the form of description length, and differentiation–relatedness (Blatt et al., 1996) is certainly consistent with this hypothesis. On the other hand, consistent with our developmental approach are (a) J. Mitchell's (1995) findings that the three components of the CCRT (i.e., wishes of the self, responses of others, and responses of the self) are coherently linked together among neurotic patients but not among more severely disturbed patients; (b) Main's (1995) work on the link between attachment status and coherence of attachment narratives in adults; and (c) findings by Fonagy et al. (1996) that incoherent attachment narratives in adults are related to adult psychopathology. In other words, the telling of narratives may be essential to the revision and developmental progression of self- and object representations in psychotherapy, but it is equally likely that the ability to tell coherent stories about oneself and significant others is itself a developmental achievement. Although we did not directly study the role of narrative in the construction and developmental progression of interpersonal schemas, we believe that the best route to a deeper understanding of the psychotherapeutic process is through an integration of a narrative perspective with the structural–developmental approach that we have taken here.

References

Adler, G., & Buie, D. H., Jr. (1979). Aloneness and borderline psychopathology: The possible relevance of child development issues. *International Journal of Psycho-Analysis, 60,* 83–96.

Ainsworth, M. D. S. (1969). Object relations, dependency, and attachment: A theoretical review of the mother-infant relationship. *Child Development, 40,* 969–1025.

Ainsworth, M. D. S. (1982). Attachment: Retrospect and prospect. In C. M. Parkes & J. Stevenson-Hinde (Eds.), *The place of attachment in human behavior* (pp. 3–30). New York: Basic Books.

American Psychiatric Association. (1980). *Diagnostic and statistical manual of mental disorders* (3rd ed.). Washington, DC: Author.

Anderson, J. R. (1983). *The architecture of cognition.* Cambridge, MA: Harvard University Press.

Auerbach, J. S. (1993). The origins of narcissism and narcissistic personality disorder: A theoretical and empirical reformulation. In J. M.

Masling & R. F. Bornstein (Eds.), *Empirical studies of psychoanalytic theories: Vol. 4. Psychoanalytic perspectives on psychopathology* (pp. 43–110). Washington, DC: American Psychological Association.

Bach, S. (1985). *Narcissistic states and the therapeutic process.* Northvale, NJ: Jason Aronson.

Barley, W. D., Buie, S. E., Peterson, E. W., Hollingsworth, A. S., Griva, M., Hickerson, S. C., Lawson, J. E., & Bailey, B. J. (1993). Development of an inpatient cognitive-behavioral treatment program for borderline personality disorder. *Journal of Personality Disorders, 7,* 232–240.

Beebe, B., & Lachmann, F. M. (1988). The contribution of mother-infant mutual influence to the origins of self- and object representations. *Psychoanalytic Psychology, 5,* 305–337.

Behrends, R. S., & Blatt, S. J. (1985). Internalization and psychological development throughout the life cycle. *Psychoanalytic Study of the Child, 40,* 11–39.

Beres, D., & Joseph, E. (1970). The concept of mental representation in psychoanalysis. *International Journal of Psycho-Analysis, 51,* 1–9.

Blatt, S. J. (1974). Levels of object representation in anaclitic and introjective depression. *Psychoanalytic Study of the Child, 29,* 107–157.

Blatt, S. J. (1991). A cognitive morphology of psychopathology. *Journal of Nervous and Mental Disease, 179,* 449–458.

Blatt, S. J. (1992). The differential effect of psychotherapy and psychoanalysis on anaclitic and introjective patients: The Menninger Psychotherapy Research Project revisited. *Journal of the American Psychoanalytic Association, 40,* 691–724.

Blatt, S. J. (1995). Representational structures in psychopathology. In D. Cicchetti & S. Toth (Eds.), *Representation, emotion and cognition in developmental psychopathology* (pp. 1–33). Rochester, NY: University of Rochester Press.

Blatt, S. J., & Auerbach, J. S. (1988). Differential cognitive disturbances in three types of "borderline" patients. *Journal of Personality Disorders, 2,* 198–211.

Blatt, S. J., Berman, W., Bloom-Feshbach, S., Sugarman, A., Wilber, C., & Kleber, H. D. (1984). Psychological assessment of psychopathology in opiate addicts. *Journal of Nervous and Mental Disease, 172,* 156–165.

Blatt, S. J., & Blass, R. B. (1990). Attachment and separateness: A dialectic model of the products and processes of psychological development. *Psychoanalytic Study of the Child, 45,* 107–127.

Blatt, S. J., & Blass, R. B. (1992). Relatedness and self-definition: Two primary dimensions in personality development, psychopathology, and psychotherapy. In J. Barron, M. Eagle, & D. Wolitsky (Eds.), *Interface of psychoanalysis and psychology* (pp. 399–428). Washington, DC: American Psychological Association.

Blatt, S. J., & Blass, R. (1996). Relatedness and self definition: A dialectic model of personality development. In G. G. Noam & K. W. Fischer

(Eds.), *Development and vulnerabilities in close relationships* (pp. 309–338). Hillsdale, NJ: Erlbaum.

Blatt, S. J., Brenneis, C. B., Schimek, J. G., & Glick, M. (1976). The normal development and psychopathological impairment of the concept of the object on the Rorschach. *Journal of Abnormal Psychology, 85,* 364–373.

Blatt, S. J., Chevron, E. S., Quinlan, D. M., Schaffer, C. E., & Wein, S. (1988). *The assessment of qualitative and structural dimensions of object representations* (Rev. ed.). Unpublished manuscript, Yale University, New Haven, CT.

Blatt, S. J., & Ford, R. Q. (1994). *Therapeutic change: An object relations perspective.* New York: Plenum.

Blatt, S. J., & Lerner, H. D. (1983). Investigations in the psychoanalytic theory of object relations and object representation. In J. Masling (Ed.), *Empirical studies of psychoanalytic theories* (Vol. 1, pp. 189–249). Hillsdale, NJ: Analytic Press.

Blatt, S. J., McDonald, C., Sugarman, A., & Wilber, C. (1984). Psychodynamic theory of opiate addiction: New directions for research. *Clinical Psychological Review, 4,* 159–189.

Blatt, S. J., & Shichman, S. (1983). Two primary configurations of psychopathology. *Psychoanalysis and Contemporary Thought, 6,* 187–254.

Blatt, S. J., Stayner, D., Auerbach, J. S., & Behrends, R. S. (1996). Change in object and self representations in long-term, intensive, inpatient treatment of seriously disturbed adolescents and young adults. *Psychiatry, 59,* 82–107.

Blatt, S. J., Wein, S. J., Chevron, E. S., & Quinlan, D. M. (1979). Parental representations and depression in normal young adults. *Journal of Abnormal Psychology, 88,* 388–397.

Blatt, S. J., & Wild, C. M. (1976). *Schizophrenia: A developmental analysis.* New York: Academic Press.

Blatt, S. J., Wild, C. M., & Ritzler, B. A. (1975). Disturbances in object representation in schizophrenia. *Psychoanalysis and Contemporary Science, 4,* 235–288.

Blatt, S. J., Wiseman, H., Prince-Gibson, E., & Gatt, H. (1991). Object representation and change in clinical functioning. *Psychotherapy, 28,* 273–283.

Bornstein, R., & O'Neill, R. (1992). Perceptions of parents and psychopathology. *Journal of Nervous and Mental Disorders, 180,* 475–483.

Bowlby, J. (1969). *Attachment and loss: Vol. 1. Attachment.* New York: Basic Books.

Bowlby, J. (1973). *Attachment and loss: Vol. 2. Separation, anxiety, and anger.* New York: Basic Books.

Bowlby, J. (1988). *A secure base.* London: Routledge.

Bretherton, I. (1985). Attachment theory: Retrospect and prospect. *Monographs of the Society for Research in Child Development, 50,* 3–35.

Bretherton, I. (1987). New perspectives on attachment relations: Security, communication, and internal working models. In J. Osofsky (Ed.), *Handbook of infant development* (pp. 1061–1100). New York: Wiley.

Brewer, W. F., & Nakamura, G. V. (1984). The nature and function of schemas. In R. S. Wyer & T. K. Srull (Eds.), *Handbook of social cognition.* Hillsdale, NJ: Erlbaum.

Broucek, F. J. (1991). *Shame and the self.* New York: Guilford Press.

Bruner, J. S. (1964). The course of cognitive growth. *American Psychologist, 19,* 1–15.

Bruner, J. (1990). *Acts of meaning.* Cambridge, MA: Harvard University Press.

Cook, B., Blatt, S. J., & Ford, R. Q. (1995). The prediction of therapeutic response to the long-term extensive treatment of seriously disturbed young adults. *Psychotherapy Research, 5,* 176–188.

Coonerty, S. (1986). An exploration of separation-individuation themes in borderline personality disorder. *Journal of Personality Assessment, 50,* 501–511.

Damon, W., & Hart, D. (1988). *Self-understanding in childhood and adolescence.* Cambridge, England: Cambridge University Press.

Diamond, D., & Blatt, S. J. (1994). Internal working models and the representational world in attachment and psychoanalytic theories. In M. B. Sperling & W. H. Berman (Eds.), *Attachment in adults: Clinical and developmental perspectives* (pp. 72–97). New York: Guilford Press.

Diamond, D., Blatt, S. J., Stayner, D., & Kaslow, N. (1991). *Self-other differentiation of object representations.* Unpublished manuscript, Yale University, New Haven, CT.

Diamond, D., Kaslow, N., Coonerty, S., & Blatt, S. J. (1990). Change in separation-individuation and intersubjectivity in long-term treatment. *Psychoanalytic Psychology, 7,* 363–397.

Elicker, J., & Sroufe, L. A. (1992). Predicting peer competence and peer relationships in childhood from early parent-child relationships. In R. Parke & A. Ladd (Eds.), *Family-peer relationships: Modes of linkage* (pp. 77–106). Hillsdale, NJ: Erlbaum.

Endicott, J., Spitzer, R. L., Fleiss, J. L., & Cohen, J. (1976). The Global Assessment Scale. *Archives of General Psychiatry, 33,* 766–771.

Farris, M. A. (1988). Differential diagnosis of borderline and narcissistic personality disorders. In H. D. Lerner & P. M. Lerner (Eds.), *Primitive mental states and the Rorschach* (pp. 299–337). Madison, CT: International Universities Press.

Fischer, K. (1980). A theory of cognitive development: The control and construction of hierarchies of skills. *Psychological Review, 87,* 477–531.

Fiske, S. T., & Taylor, S. E. (1984). *Social cognition.* New York: Random House.

Fonagy, P., Leigh, T., Steele, M., Steele, H., Kennedy, R., Mattoon, G., Target, M., & Gerber, A. (1996). The relation of attachment status, psychiatric classification, and response to psychotherapy. *Journal of Abnormal Psychology, 64,* 22–31.

Fonagy, P., Steele, H., & Steele, M. (1991). Maternal representations of attachment during pregnancy predict the organization of infant-mother attachment at one year of age. *Child Development, 62,* 891–905.

Gardner, H. (1985). *The mind's new science: A history of the cognitive revolution.* New York: Basic Books.

Gill, M., & Hoffman, I. (1982). A method for studying the analysis of aspects of the patient's experience of the relationship in psychoanalysis and psychotherapy. *Journal of the American Psychoanalytic Association, 30,* 137–167.

Gruen, R., & Blatt, S. J. (1990). Change in self and object representation during long-term dynamically oriented treatment. *Psychoanalytic Psychology, 7,* 399–422.

Hatcher, R., & Krohn, A. (1980). Level of object representation and capacity for intensive psychotherapy in neurotics and borderlines. In J. S. Kwawer, H. D. Lerner, P. M. Lerner, & A. Sugarman (Eds.), *Borderline phenomena and the Rorschach Test* (pp. 299–320). Madison, CT: International Universities Press.

Horowitz, M. J. (1972). Modes of representation of thought. *Journal of the American Psychoanalytic Association, 20,* 793–819.

Horowitz, M. J. (1979). *States of mind: Analysis of change in psychotherapy.* New York: Plenum.

Horowitz, M. J. (1988). *Introduction to psychodynamics: A new synthesis.* New York: Basic Books.

Jacobson, E. (1964). *The self and the object world.* Madison, CT: International Universities Press.

Jordan, J. V. (1986). *The meaning of mutuality* (work in progress papers, No. 23). Wellesley, MA: Wellesley College, Stone Center.

Kavanagh, C. G. (1985). Changes in object representations in psychoanalysis and psychoanalytic psychotherapy. *Bulletin of the Menninger Clinic, 49,* 546–564.

Kegan, R. (1982). *The evolving self: Problems and process in human development.* Cambridge, MA: Harvard University Press.

Kernberg, O. F. (1975). *Borderline conditions and pathological narcissism.* Northvale, NJ: Jason Aronson.

Kernberg, O. F. (1976). *Object relations theory and clinical psychoanalysis.* New York: Jason Aronson.

Kernberg, O. F. (1984). *Severe personality disorders.* New Haven, CT: Yale University Press.

Kernberg, O. F. (1994). Psychoanalytic object relations theories. In B. E. Moore & B. D. Fine (Eds.), *Psychoanalysis: The major concepts* (pp. 450–462). New Haven, CT: Yale University Press.

Klein, M. (1935). A contribution to the psychogenesis of manic-depressive states. *International Journal of Psycho-Analysis, 16,* 145–173.

Klein, M. (1946). Notes on some schizoid mechanisms. *International Journal of Psycho-Analysis, 27,* 99–110.

Krohn, A., & Mayman, M. (1974). Levels of object representation in dreams and projective tests. *Bulletin of the Menninger Clinic, 38,* 445–466.

Lerner, H. D., & St. Peter, S. (1985). Patterns of object relations in neurotic, borderline, and schizophrenic patients. *Psychiatry, 47,* 77–92.

Levy, K. N., Blatt, S. J., & Shaver, P. R. (1998). Attachment style and mental representation in young adults. *Journal of Personality and Social Psychology, 74,* 407–419.

Lichtenberg, J. D. (1983). *Psychoanalysis and infant research.* Hillsdale, NJ: Analytic Press.

Linehan, M. M. (1993). *Cognitive-behavioral treatment of borderline personality disorder.* New York: Guilford Press.

Linehan, M. M., Armstrong, H. E., Suarez, A., Allmon, D., & Heard, H. L. (1991). Cognitive-behavioral treatment of chronically suicidal borderline patients. *Archives of General Psychiatry, 48,* 1060–1064.

Linehan, M. M., Heard, H. L., & Armstrong, H. E. (1993). Naturalistic follow-up of a behavioral treatment of chronically suicidal borderline patient. *Archives of General Psychiatry, 50,* 971–974.

Linehan, M. M., Tutek, D. A., Heard, H. L., & Armstrong, H. E. (1994). Interpersonal outcome of cognitive behavioral treatment for chronically suicidal borderline patients. *American Journal of Psychiatry, 151,* 1771–1776.

Loewald, H. W. (1960). On the therapeutic action of psychoanalysis. *International Journal of Psycho-Analysis, 41,* 16–33.

Loewald, H. W. (1978). Instinct theory, object relations, and psychic structure formation. *Journal of the American Psychoanalytic Association, 26,* 493–505.

Luborsky, L. (1984). *Principles of psychoanalytic psychotherapy: A manual for supportive-expressive treatment.* New York: Basic Books.

Luborsky, L., & Crits-Christoph, P. (1990). *Understanding transference: The CCRT method.* New York: Basic Books.

Mahler, M. S., Pine, F., & Bergman, A. (1975). *The psychological birth of the human infant.* New York: Basic Books.

Main, M. (1995). Recent studies of attachment: Overview, with selected implications for clinical work. In S. Goldberg, R. Muir, & J. Kerr (Eds.), *Attachment theory: Social, developmental, and clinical perspectives* (pp. 407–474). New York: Guilford Press.

Main, M., Kaplan, N., & Cassidy, J. (1985). Growing points of attachment theory and research. *Monographs of the Society for Research in Child Development, 50,* 66–104.

Mandler, J. M. (1988). How to build a baby: On the development of an accessible representational system. *Cognitive Development, 3,* 113–136.

Markus, H. (1977). Self-schemata and processing information about the self. *Journal of Personality and Social Psychology, 35,* 63–78.

Marziali, E., & Oleniuk, J. (1990). Object representations in descriptions of significant others: A methodological study. *Journal of Personality Assessment, 54,* 105–115.

Mayman, M. (1967). Object-representations and object-relationships in Rorschach responses. *Journal of Projective Techniques and Personality Assessment, 31,* 17–24.

Mayman, M., & Faris, M. (1969). Early memories as expressions of relationship paradigms. *American Journal of Orthopsychiatry, 31,* 507–520.

Miller, J. B. (1984). *The development of women's sense of self* (work in progress papers, No. 84-01). Wellesley, MA: Wellesley College, Stone Center.

Mitchell, J. (1995). Coherence of the relationship theme: An extension of Luborsky's Core Conflictual Relationship Theme method. *Psychoanalytic Psychology, 12,* 495–512.

Mitchell, S. A. (1988). *Relational concepts in psychoanalysis.* Cambridge, MA: Harvard University Press.

Modell, A. H. (1993). *The private self.* Cambridge, MA: Harvard University Press.

Nelson, K., & Grundel, J. (1987). Generalized event representations: Basic building blocks of cognitive development. In M. Lamb & A. L. Brown (Eds.), *Advances in developmental psychology* (Vol. 1, pp. 131–158). Hillsdale, NJ: Erlbaum.

Ogden, T. H. (1986). *The matrix of the mind: Object relations and the psychoanalytic dialogue.* Northvale, NJ: Jason Aronson.

Piaget, J. (1962). *Play, dreams and imitation in childhood.* New York: Norton. (Original work published 1945)

Quinlan, D. M., Blatt, S. J., Chevron, E. S., & Wein, S. (1992). The analysis of descriptions of parents: Identification of a more differentiated factor structure. *Journal of Personality Assessment, 59,* 340–351.

Ricoeur, P. (1977). The question of proof in Freud's psychoanalytic writings. *Journal of the American Psychoanalytic Association, 25,* 835–871.

Ritzler, B. A., Wyatt, D., Harder, D., & Kaskey, M. (1980). Psychotic patterns of the concept of the object on the Rorschach. *Journal of Abnormal Psychology, 89,* 46–55.

Ryan, E. R., & Bell, M. D. (1984). Changes in object relations from psychosis to recovery. *Journal of Abnormal Psychology, 93,* 209–215.

Sander, L. W. (1983). Polarity, paradox, and the organizing process in development. In J. Call, E. Galenson, & R. Taylor (Eds.), *Frontiers of infant psychiatry* (pp. 315–327). New York: Basic Books.

Sandler, J., & Rosenblatt, B. (1962). The concept of the representational world. *Psychoanalytic Study of the Child, 17,* 128–145.

Schacht, T. E., Binder, J. L., & Strupp, H. H. (1984). The dynamic focus. In H. H. Strupp & J. L. Binder, *Psychotherapy in a new key: A guide to time-limited dynamic psychotherapy* (pp. 65–109). New York: Basic Books.

Schafer, R. (1983). *The analytic attitude.* New York: Basic Books.

Shrout, P. E., & Fleiss, J. L. (1979). Intraclass correlations: Uses in assessing rater reliability. *Psychological Bulletin, 86,* 420–428.

Slade, A., & Aber, L. J. (1992). Attachment, drives and development: Conflicts and convergences in theory. In J. Barron, M. Eagle, & D. Wolitsky

(Eds.), *Interface of psychoanalysis and psychology* (pp. 154–185). Washington, DC: American Psychological Association.

Spear, W. E. (1980). The psychological assessment of structural and thematic object representations in borderline and schizophrenic patients. In J. S. Kwawer, H. D. Lerner, P. M. Lerner, & A. Sugarman (Eds.), *Borderline phenomena and the Rorschach Test* (pp. 321–340). Madison, CT: International Universities Press.

Spear, W., & Sugarman, A. (1984). Dimensions of internalized object relations in borderline schizophrenic patients. *Psychoanalytic Psychology, 1*, 113–129.

Spence, D. P. (1982). *Narrative truth and historical truth: Meaning and interpretation in psychoanalysis*. New York: Norton.

Stayner, D. (1994). *The relationship between clinical functioning and changes in self and object representations in the treatment of severely impaired inpatients*. Unpublished doctoral dissertation, Teachers College, Columbia University, New York, NY.

Stern, D. N. (1985). *The interpersonal world of the infant*. New York: Basic Books.

Stricker, G., & Healy, B. (1990). Projective assessment of object relations: A review of the empirical literature. *Psychological Assessment, 2*, 219–230.

Surrey, J. L. (1985). *Self-in-relation: A theory of women's development*. Unpublished manuscript, Wellesley College, Wellesley, MA.

Urist, J. (1977). The Rorschach Test and the assessment of object relations. *Journal of Personality Assessment, 41*, 3–9.

Virtue, C. (1992). The effects of maternal object representations and psychological differentiation on early mother-infant feeding interactions (Doctoral dissertation, Cornell University, 1990). *Dissertation Abstracts International, 52*, 3917.

Weiss, J., & Sampson, H. (1986). *The psychoanalytic process: Theory, clinical observations, and empirical research*. New York: Guilford Press.

Westen, D. (1989). Are "primitive" object relations really preoedipal? *American Journal of Orthopsychiatry, 59*, 331–345.

Westen, D. (1990). Towards a revised theory of borderline object relations: Contributions from empirical research. *International Journal of Psycho-Analysis, 71*, 661–693.

Westen, D. (1991). Social cognition and object relations. *Psychological Bulletin, 109*, 429–455.

Winnicott, D. W. (1965). *The maturational process and the facilitating environment*. Madison, CT: International Universities Press.

Zeanah, C. H., & Anders, T. F. (1987). Subjectivity in parent-infant relationships: A discussion of internal working models. *Infant Mental Health Journal, 8*, 237–250.

Empirical Basis of Supportive–Expressive Psychodynamic Psychotherapy

Paul Crits-Christoph and Mary Beth Connolly

The purpose of this chapter is to present a summary of empirical evidence about the process and outcome of supportive–expressive (SE) psychodynamic therapy. We first present an overview of the place of SE therapy within the context of various psychodynamic models, particularly other models of brief dynamic therapy. This is followed by a description of refinements to SE therapy for special populations and the status of outcome data using SE therapy with these special populations. Studies of key constructs in the process of SE therapy are then presented to highlight what is known about the mechanisms of action of SE therapy.

The preparation of this chapter was funded in part by National Institute on Drug Abuse Grant U18-DA07090 and by National Institute of Mental Health Grants P50-MH-45178, K02-MH00756, and R01-MH40472.

SE Therapy in the Context of Psychodynamic Models

Psychodynamic psychotherapy continues to be a widely practiced form of psychotherapy. Although Jensen, Bergin, and Greaves' (1990) survey of 423 psychotherapists (psychiatrists, psychologists, and social workers) showed that most (68%) identified themselves as eclectic in orientation, the majority (72%) of these eclectic therapists reported that psychodynamic therapy was the orientation they used most often. An additional 17% of the therapists identified themselves as being purely psychodynamic. Within the broad dynamic therapy rubric, some form of brief dynamic therapy is commonly practiced. A survey by Levenson, Speed, and Budman (1995) showed that of 850 psychologists surveyed, 40% spent a large portion of their clinical time conducting brief therapy and that 22% of all brief therapy hours were accounted for by psychodynamic therapists. Crits-Christoph, Frank, Chambless, Brody, and Karp (1995) found that 61.5% of graduate programs in clinical psychology provided supervised clinical experiences in some version of brief dynamic therapy to their students.

There are, of course, a number of variants of both time-limited and time-unlimited psychodynamic psychotherapy. The psychodynamic rubric includes the different modes of psychotherapy based on classical Freudian, ego psychology, object relations, interpersonal, and self psychological schools of psychoanalysis. Brief dynamic therapy models aligned with the different psychoanalytic models or combinations or derivatives of these psychoanalytic models have been developed. These different brief dynamic therapy models are presented and compared by Crits-Christoph and Barber (1991), Barber and Crits-Christoph (1995), and Messer and Warren (1995).

The dynamic therapy treatment approach described in this chapter was originally put forth in a treatment manual by Luborsky (1984). The SE treatment manual covers both time-limited and time-unlimited versions of the treatment. Because most empirical research on SE therapy has been in the context of the time-limited model, we primarily discuss that variant of SE therapy.

Luborsky (1984) and Luborsky and Mark (1991) traced the origins of the SE model to Freud's chapters on technique (Freud, 1911/1958a, 1912/1958b, 1912/1958c, 1913/1958d, 1914/1958e, 1915/1958f). Subsequent writers (e.g., Bibring, 1954; Fenichel, 1945; Stone, 1951) in the psychoanalytic tradition also had a significant influence on the principles of treatment described in the SE therapy manual. The term *supportive–expressive psychoanalytic psychotherapy* was used as a label for the psychotherapy treatment implemented at the Menninger Foundation (Luborsky, Fabian, Hall, Ticho, & Ticho, 1958; Wallerstein, 1986; Wallerstein, Robbins, Sargent, & Luborsky, 1956), where Luborsky worked before coming to the University of Pennsylvania. Precursors to the formal published manual existed at the University of Pennsylvania and were used by Luborsky from about 1970 to 1984 as an aid in teaching psychotherapy to psychiatric residents.

The major aspects of the SE treatment model that can be traced back to Freud and subsequent psychoanalytic writers include the concepts of transference, insight, interpretation, and the alliance. Luborsky (1990) described 22 separate elements of Freud's (1912/1958b) observations about transference for which there is convergence between the SE operationalization of this concept and Freud's ideas. Thus, this concept in the SE model appears to have a high level of similarity to Freud's original notion of transference. However, despite these similarities, the particular operationalization of transference in the SE model, namely the patient's wishes and responses and the perceived response of other, was originated by Luborsky, Woody, Hole, and Velleco (1977).

The role of insight within psychoanalysis has evolved not only within Freud's writings but also in subsequent psychoanalytic writings. With the introduction of Freud's structural model, the goal of psychoanalysis changed from making the unconscious conscious to emphasizing the integration of intrapsychic structure. Treatment not only attempted to help the patient remember forgotten events but also helped the patient place these memories into a causal context, where they might be better integrated. Within SE therapy, the causal context, in terms of an interpersonal sequential transaction (e.g., if I wish X, the other person will do Y, and then I will feel Z), is of primary importance. Less emphasis is given to the recovery of deeply repressed memories, although such recovery of memories occurs with some patients. In most cases, the relationship patterns discussed within SE therapy are more or less readily available to consciousness. The integration (i.e., "working through") of these themes in terms of their role in current and past relationships is the main focus of treatment.

The concept of the therapeutic alliance also can be traced to Freud (1912/1958b), in terms of the "friendly and affectionate aspects of the transference which are admissible to consciousness and which are the vehicle of success" (p. 105). However, it was Greenson's (1965) later writing on the "working alliance" and Zetzel's (1958) introduction of the term *therapeutic alliance* to refer to the positive affectionate attachment to the therapist that provided the impetus for Luborsky's (1976) "helping alliance" and the emphasis on this factor within SE treatment. The main difference between Freud's original specification of these "friendly and affectionate" feelings of the patient toward the therapist and Luborsky's (1984) articulation of the helping alliance is that for Freud, this aspect of the treatment process set the stage for the role of interpretation, whereas Luborsky suggested that the alliance is a curative element in its own right. Moreover, the attempts by the therapist to bolster the alliance (i.e., the supportive component of treatment) are clearly divergent from a traditional "blank screen" therapist role.

Insight was obtained in Freudian psychoanalysis through interpretations made by the therapist. Indeed, Bibring (1954) described interpretation as the "supreme agent in the hierarchy of therapeutic principles" (p. 763). Freud (1901–1905/1953) in particular emphasized the interpretation of transference. The goal of such interpretations is to help the patient understand the way in which early relationships distort the patient's relationships in the present, particularly the relationship with the therapist. Lowenstein (1951), however, emphasized the importance of repeating interpretations across different domains of the same theme (working through) and highlighted the importance of making brief interventions using everyday language. Fenichel (1945) discussed another important issue related to interpretation: the accuracy of an interpretation.

Whereas the concept of interpretation in SE therapy is directly based on Freud's writings, certain technical differences also are evident. For example, SE therapy does not overemphasize the interpretation of themes in the relationship with the therapist. SE therapy follows Lowenstein's (1951) recommendations more closely, with emphasis placed on interpretation of themes in a variety of domains (e.g., current relationships, past relationships, therapeutic relationships), and attention to the brevity and clarity of interpretations. The concept of accuracy of interpretation discussed by Fenichel (1945) also is of central importance to SE therapy. Therapists conducting SE therapy are taught to increase their accuracy by focusing interpretations on a specific content (i.e., the patient's wish and response pattern). Thus, SE therapy has borrowed concepts regarding interpretation from a variety of post-Freudian writers.

Some other differences between the SE model and Freudian psychoanalysis also are apparent. These include the time-limited nature of one version of SE therapy. The time-limited version of SE therapy is the only one, in fact, that has been implemented in the various treatment outcome studies conducted using SE therapy. Perhaps the most important difference between Freudian psychoanalysis and SE therapy is the explicit connection of recent versions of the SE model (e.g., Crits-Christoph, Crits-Christoph, Wolf-Palacio, Fichter, & Rudick, 1995) to the interpersonal school within the psychodynamic rubric. This is characterized by a shift away from drives and instinctual wishes, with greater emphasis placed on motivations arising from interpersonal transactions. Thus, although some, but not other, aspects of Freud's treatment model are contained in the SE approach, the theory of psychopathology is more closely aligned with recent theories. Having traced the origins of SE therapy, we now discuss the main SE treatment techniques and theory of change.

The treatment manual on SE therapy specifies two main treatment components: a supportive component and an expressive, interpretative component. SE therapy, as described by Luborsky (1984), is hypothesized to work through three main curative factors: the helping alliance, self-understanding (insight) of maladaptive interpersonal patterns, and the incorporation of the treatment gains. The first goal of SE therapy is to build a supportive, collaborative therapeutic relationship. This positive alliance is built by conveying to the patient a warm, empathic relationship in which the patient and therapist are working together toward a common goal. Through the narratives told by the patient during therapy and through the therapist's own experience of the patient, the therapist unfolds the patient's maladaptive interpersonal themes using the Core Conflictual Relationship Theme method (CCRT; Luborsky & Crits-Christoph, 1990). The CCRT describes three main components of interpersonal patterns, including the patient's wishes or needs in interpersonal situations, the perceived responses of others toward the patient, and the responses of the patient. The main expressive (i.e., exploratory) technique of SE therapy is the interpretation of patient's maladaptive wish and response patterns. The SE model postulates that, through self-understanding of the maladaptive CCRT patterns, patients are able to gain new, more adaptive ways of interacting with others leading to eventual symptom alleviation.

Comparing the main facets of SE therapy with other short-term dynamic models will help clarify the unique and common features of the approach. Although models of short-term dynamic psychotherapy share a focus on both a positive therapeutic alliance and self-understanding of maladaptive interpersonal patterns, there also are important differences in these models. Strupp and Binder (1984) and Malan (1976) viewed the formation of a positive therapeutic alliance as a necessary but not sufficient condition for change in psychotherapy. In these models, the alliance serves the purpose of facilitating the exploration of the impairing relationship conflicts. By contrast, Luborsky (1984) viewed the therapeutic alliance as being curative in its own right. In fact, Luborsky (1984) suggested that the alliance may be the most potent curative factor within SE therapy.

Models of brief dynamic therapy also vary in the extent to which transference interpretations are emphasized. Malan (1976) suggested that interpretations of the therapeutic relationship are the most therapeutically effective. Strupp and Binder (1984) and Sifneos (1992) presented models of dynamic psychotherapy that focus heavily on the interpretation of the transference relationship as well. Although Luborsky (1984) also recognized the potential for interpretations of the relationship with the therapist, transference interpretations are actually relatively rare in SE therapy sessions. In fact, a recent analysis of therapist response modes in brief SE psychotherapy for depression revealed that the average SE therapy session contained an average of less than one transference interpretation (Connolly, Crits-Christoph, Shappell, Barber, & Luborsky,

1997). Instead, interpretations more often focus on understanding the pervasiveness of current maladaptive interpersonal patterns in the patient's world (i.e., relationships outside of therapy).

As psychodynamic therapy has become more focal and briefer, as in the model described here, and as cognitive therapy (CT) has been modified over the years to have more emphasis on schemas, or core beliefs, the degree of similarity of these two major modalities of treatment has increased. Despite some similarities, it is important to point out where differences remain. Some of these differences are mostly a matter of relative emphasis, and some are clear theoretical divergences.

Although CT models (e.g., Beck & Emery, 1985) have a major focus on the concept of schemas, which seems similar to the notion of core conflictual relationship themes, the SE model specifically defines the important schemas as interpersonal in nature rather than as simply beliefs about the self or the world in general. Note that the CT model does not exclude interpersonal schemas but that it does not emphasize them to the extent that the SE model does. More recently, some CT models (Safran & Segal, 1990) have begun to have a more explicit interpersonal focus.

The SE model also specifies the interpersonal pattern in terms of three sequential components: the wish, response from other, and response of self. In particular, it is the wish component that is a major difference between the SE model and the CT model. The notion that the wish drives the whole sequence is distinctively a psychodynamic one.

The SE model also has a greater emphasis on self-understanding and working through as the major elements in the change process, whereas CT emphasizes the identification of automatic thoughts, homework, exposure, and evaluating evidence for a belief. However, both treatments contain elements of all these processes, and the differences are more a matter of emphasis or terminology. In the SE model, however, at least some of the material (i.e., aspects of the CCRT pattern) is thought to be less accessible to the patient, at least initially in therapy, but the CT model assumes that material can be fairly easily accessed with some probing.

One clear difference between SE therapy and CT relates to the theory of defenses. Whereas the CT model would posit that the concept of defenses is simply another set of beliefs, the psychodynamic model adds that defenses are motivated. Because of the importance of defenses and the theory that some important material is not readily available to consciousness, the SE model, relative to the CT model, places more emphasis on the need to develop material over the course of treatment. This leads to a treatment process that is less structured than a CT process, even in a brief, focal SE therapy.

Refinements of SE Therapy for Special Populations: Clinical Models and Outcome Data

Having sketched out the main elements of SE therapy and compared these elements with other major forms of brief dynamic therapy, we now present available outcome data on the treatment. The process of obtaining empirical support for the efficacy of SE therapy begins with creating a new treatment manual that tailors the generic SE therapy approach to a specific patient population. We want to emphasize, however, that these refinements are relatively modest and that the main principles of SE therapy remain constant across different patient populations. The refinements generally concern the types of special issues that are typical of the patient population as well as a discussion of the relative emphasis on the supportive versus expressive components of treatment.

SE Therapy for Treating Generalized Anxiety Disorder

Recent research efforts (Crits-Christoph, Connolly, Azarian, Crits-Christoph, & Shappell, 1996) have included adapting SE therapy for treating generalized anxiety disorder (GAD). We therefore provide a more extensive discussion of developments in this area, beginning with the rationale for developing a dynamic therapy for GAD.

GAD is a relatively prevalent disorder that is associated with a high degree of chronicity and a moderate degree of impairment in functioning (Massion, Warshaw, & Keller, 1993; Wittchen, Zhao,

Kessler, & Eaton, 1994). Medication and cognitive–behavioral treatments have been shown to be effective in the treatment of GAD, although concerns about recurrence rates with benzodiazepines in particular (Rickels et al., 1985; Rickels, Schweizer, & Lucki, 1987) have been documented, and cognitive–behavioral treatments continue to show only modest benefits, with clinically significant change occurring in only about 50% of patients (Chambless & Gillis, 1993).

The rationale for developing an interpersonally oriented dynamic treatment for the diagnosis of GAD is based in part on emerging empirical evidence on the nature of GAD. For example, Borkovec, Robinson, Pruzinsky, and DePree (1983) have demonstrated that *worry*, the central feature of GAD, is associated with high levels of interpersonal concerns. In addition, the possible interpersonal etiological factors in GAD have been investigated by Lichtenstein and Cassidy (1991), who had patients with GAD recall memories of the nature of attachment to primary caregivers in childhood. The patients with GAD were significantly more insecurely attached and felt more rejected as children by the primary caregiver than did those without GAD. The primary pattern was one of enmeshment and role reversal (i.e., the need to protect but fear of losing the primary caregiver), with associated preoccupying anger and oscillating feelings toward the caregiver.

GAD also has been associated with a history of past traumatic events. Borkovec (1994) found that individuals meeting GAD criteria had a greater frequency of past traumatic events than those without GAD. Molina, Roemer, Borkovec, and Posa (1992) found that patients with GAD reported trauma involving death, illness, or injury at a rate 1.5 times greater than nonanxious individuals and traumas related to assault, emotional events, and miscellaneous traumas at rates four to six times greater. Moreover, Borkovec (1994) reported that although patients with GAD had higher rates of traumas related to death, illness, or injury than nonanxious individuals, they rarely worried about these events. Nonanxious individuals, however, worried about these events at a much higher rate (25%). Borkovec (1994) speculated that patients with GAD avoided thinking about those past events that they considered to be traumatic. Consistent with this speculation, Roemer, Borkovec, Posa, and Lyonfields (1991) reported that worrying appeared to distract patients with GAD from more disturbing emotional contents. From a psychodynamic perspective, worrying could be described as serving a defensive function.

This research literature on GAD and worry raises the hypothesis that GAD is linked to both an insecure or conflicted attachment in childhood and to a history of past traumas. Whether these are two independent paths to GAD or whether these factors interact (i.e., specific traumas happening to a person with insecure or conflicted attachment patterns producing the symptoms of GAD) is not clear. The data on the nature of GAD, although retrospective, are consistent with an interpersonally oriented psychodynamic perspective on GAD that emphasizes attachment patterns and disruptions in the cognitive and emotional processing of past traumatic events.

The SE treatment model for GAD (Crits-Christoph, Crits-Christoph, et al., 1995) hypothesizes that a set of dangerous or traumatic experiences, occurring at any phase of life, leads to basic schemas about oneself and other people, particularly about the ability of oneself to successfully obtain what one needs in relationships. Patients with GAD might develop schemas involving concerns about the obtainment of love, security, stability, or protection from others. At times, these concerns are associated with powerful feelings of fear so troubling that the patient is actively motivated not to think about the concerns. Defensive processes are activated that lead patients with GAD to become overly worried about other current events in their life as a way of avoiding thinking about the more difficult emotional issues. The underlying, warded-off concerns, however, continue to motivate the patient and are manifested in repetitive, maladaptive relationship patterns and worry. These relationship patterns are cyclical, that is, they end up recreating the same sort of perceived circumstances that generated the fear to begin with (e.g., expectation of losing a loved one). Such interpersonal and defensive factors are not assumed to be the only factors in the etiology or maintenance of GAD. Predisposing biological and genetic (temperament) factors also may be contributing to the symptoms of GAD.

SE psychotherapy for GAD has been refined from the generic SE model to meet the specific needs of patients with GAD treated in a 16-week format (Crits-Christoph, Crits-Christoph, et al., 1995). Four phases of treatment have been specified, including an early alliance-building phase, a middle phase that focuses on refining the patients' CCRT, a termination phase that focuses on understanding the treatment termination in light of the CCRT, and a booster phase that helps the patient internalize the treatment gains. Like the generic SE model, supportive techniques are viewed as necessary. However, the therapist's goal is not to support the patient to alleviate the anxiety symptoms completely because a mild amount of anxiety is thought to be a motivating factor. Finally, many patients with GAD report a history of traumatic events. The goal of the SE therapist is to be empathic while helping the patient understand the influence of past traumas on the CCRT.

To date, we have completed a treatment development project aimed at conducting an initial test of the usefulness of brief SE therapy for GAD. The results of this study are presented in Crits-Christoph et al. (1996) and are briefly summarized here. Twenty-six patients who met criteria for GAD (fourth edition of the *Diagnostic and Statistical Manual of Mental Disorders*; American Psychiatric Association, 1994) were offered 16 sessions of SE psychotherapy. Of the 26 patients offered treatment, 3 completed less than 12 sessions of therapy. The treatment consisted of 16 weekly sessions of SE psychotherapy plus 3 monthly booster sessions delivered by trained therapists.

The outcome results for all 26 patients who received treatment are presented in Table 1. Paired *t* tests revealed statistically significant changes across treatment for all outcome measures. In addition, hierarchical linear modeling (Bryk & Raudenbush, 1992) revealed a significant linear rate of change on the Beck Anxiety Inventory (BAI) across the 16 weeks, $t(24) = -7.0, p < .001$. Finally, the results showed no significant therapist effects for any of the symptom change measures ($ps > .40$).

Patients also were asked to rate their expectations about improvement across treatment at intake. Patients scored an average 2.6 on a scale ranging from -3 to 3, indicating that they expected a moderately large amount of improvement. At treatment termination, patients rated three 7-point scales representing their opinions about treatment. The results indicated that patients found the treatment moderately sensible ($M = 5.6, SD = 1.4$), were confident that the treatment was helpful ($M = 5.1, SD = 1.7$), and would be

Table 1

Pretreatment to Posttreatment Effects for Studies of Supportive–Expressive Psychotherapy

Measure	Generalized anxiety disorder		Depression		Opiate dependence (1990)		Opiate dependence (1995)		Avoidant personality disorder		Obsessive–compulsive personality disorder	
	ES	p	ES	p	ES	p	ES	p	ES	p	ES	p
HARS	1.41	.001							0.96	.001*	1.16	.005*
HRSD	1.15	.001	2.28	.001					1.13	.001*	1.15	.001*
BAI	1.99	.001							1.02	.001*	1.14	.001*
BDI	1.09	.001	1.91	.001	0.89	.01	0.56	.001	1.32	.001*	2.21	.001*
Worry	0.95	.001										
IIP	0.25	.026							0.88	.001*	0.41	.02*
WPDI									0.68	.10	1.71	.005

	ES	p	ES	p
GAF	−2.07	.001		
SCL-90 total	0.74	.01	0.46	.001
Maudsley	0.73	.01	0.67	.001
Employment factor	1.07	.01	0.06	ns
Drug factor	0.56	.01	0.51	.01
Legal factor	0.51	.01	−0.10	ns
Psychological	0.31	ns	0.55	.01

Note. Effect size is defined as the posttreatment mean minus pretreatment mean divided by the pretreatment standard deviation. ES = effect size; HARS = Hamilton Anxiety Rating Scale; HRSD = Hamilton Rating Scale for Depression; BAI = Beck Anxiety Inventory; BDI = Beck Depression Inventory; Worry = Penn State Worry Questionnaire; IIP = Inventory of Interpersonal Problems; WPDI = Wisconsin Personality Disorders Inventory; GAF = Global Assessment of Functioning; Maudsley = Maudsley Neuroticism score. The Employment, Drug, Legal, and Psychological factors are from the Addiction Severity Index. *p values for the slope across intake, Month 4, Month 8, and termination. All other p values for test of change from intake to termination.

confident in recommending the treatment to a friend (M = 5.4, SD = 1.9).

One session for each of the 26 patients, as well as one session from each of 23 patients receiving CT for anxiety problems, was rated for adherence and competence to the SE therapy for GAD manual. The results revealed large effects differentiating SE therapy from CT on the total competence score, $t(47)$ = 5.3, p < .0001, and the competence on expressive techniques scale, $t(47)$ = 5.9, p < .0001, and smaller effects for the competence on supportive techniques scale, $t(47)$ = 2.4, p < .02.

The results of this uncontrolled investigation suggest that SE psychotherapy is a promising treatment for GAD. Patients demonstrated broad improvements, including significant changes in symptoms of anxiety, depression, worry, and interpersonal functioning. Patients reported positive expectations of their therapy pretreatment and, after therapy, viewed their treatment as being sensible and were confident that the treatment was helpful. We are currently engaged in a controlled pilot study to examine whether SE therapy produces greater benefits than a nonspecific psychotherapy control condition.

SE Therapy for Treating Opiate Dependence

The SE model for the treatment of opiate dependence (Luborsky, Woody, Hole, & Velleco, 1995) builds on the general SE model reported by Luborsky (1984) by focusing on helping patients to understand their drug dependence in the context of maladaptive relationship patterns. Early sessions are focused on socializing patients to the psychotherapy and providing a supportive relationship. The supportive component of the treatment is viewed as being central given the tendency of opiate-dependent patients to resort to drug use in place of interpersonal relationships. Interpretive techniques are used to help patients understand the maladaptive wishes and responses associated with their drug use, with interpretations being a central element in bolstering the therapeutic relationship. SE psychotherapy for opiate dependence also maintains a focus on the patient's compliance in not taking drugs. The therapist uses such information to explore the wish and response patterns that support the patient's drug use.

Two outcome studies have examined SE therapy for opiate dependence (Woody, Luborsky, McLellan, & O'Brien, 1990; Woody, McLellan, Luborsky, & O'Brien, 1995). One compared SE therapy, CT, and standard drug counseling (DC) for methadone-maintained, opiate-dependent patients (Woody et al., 1983, 1990). Patients in the SE therapy and CT conditions also received individual DC. Treatment was set at a maximum of 6 months. The average patient, however, attended 10–12 sessions of psychotherapy plus an additional 12 sessions of DC. Outcomes measured 7 months after intake demonstrated that both SE therapy and CT yielded significantly more benefits than DC alone on measures of employment, legal problems, psychiatric symptoms, and opiate-positive urine samples (see Table 1 for SE therapy results and Table 2 for a comparison of SE therapy and DC). Additional analyses revealed that the superiority of SE therapy and CT was most pronounced among patients with severe psychiatric symptoms (Woody et al., 1984).

A second study compared SE therapy with DC among psychiatrically symptomatic, opiate-dependent patients in community-based methadone treatment programs (Woody et al., 1995). The study was designed to address two concerns raised about the earlier 1983 study: (a) Would the results generalize from a university-affiliated research clinic to typical community-based drug treatment programs? (b) Did the effects result from having two therapists or counselors compared with only one (DC alone)? In the second study, patients were assigned to either an SE psychotherapist plus a drug counselor or to two drug counselors. Patients treated with SE therapy demonstrated significant changes across treatment on measures of psychiatric symptoms, employment problems, legal problems, and drug use (see Table 1). The between-groups effects comparing SE therapy+DC with DC+DC are presented in Table 2. Although Woody et al. (1995) did not report significance tests between treatments, they found average effect sizes of 0.07 comparing treatments 7 months after intake and .26 at the 6-month follow-up evaluation across all outcome measures. These between-groups effect sizes, presented in Table 2, revealed small effects at 7 months and moderate effects at follow-up favor-

Table 2

Between-groups Effect Sizes Comparing SE Therapy With DC for the Treatment of Opiate Dependence

Measure	Opiate dependence (1990)		Opiate dependence (1995 termination)	Opiate dependence (1995 follow-up)
	ES	p	ES	ES
BDI	−0.38	.01	−0.10	−0.33
SCL-90	−0.27	.01	0.02	−0.21
Maudsley	−0.36	.01	−0.15	−0.64
Employment factor	−0.62	.01	−0.18	−0.87
Drug factor	−0.02	ns	−0.10	−0.39
Legal factor	−0.30	.01	0.33	−0.03
Psychological factor	−0.54	.05	0.07	−0.20

Note. Effect size is defined as the SE mean minus the DC mean divided by the DC standard deviation. *p* values for opiate dependence 1995 sample were not recorded. ES = effect size; BDI = Beck Depression Inventory; Maudsley = Maudsley Neuroticism score; the Employment, Drug, Legal, and Psychological factors are from Addiction Severity Index. SE = supportive–expressive; DC = direct counseling.

ing SE therapy. In addition, Woody et al. reported that both treatment conditions had similar overall proportions of opiate-positive urine samples. However, opiate-positive urine samples over the past 12 weeks of the treatment period increased for DC alone but decreased over this same period for SE therapy+DC. Moreover, patients in SE therapy+DC had fewer cocaine-positive urine samples and required lower doses of methadone. Patients in DC alone lost some of their gains at the 6-month follow-up, whereas the SE therapy+DC patients maintained or continued improving. Thus, controlled outcome data from two studies indicate that SE therapy for opiate dependence (as an adjunct to methadone maintenance) is an efficacious treatment that appears to be superior to DC alone, particularly at follow-up.

SE Therapy for Treating Depression

Although a number of treatments for major depression have been developed, including both medication and psychosocial treatments such as CT and interpersonal therapy, the research (e.g., Elkin et al., 1989) suggests few differences among these treatments. Because dynamic therapy is widely practiced in the community, it is important to determine whether dynamic therapy would be a relatively efficacious treatment for depression as well. If dynamic therapy is at least as effective as other available treatments for depression, therapists who practice dynamic therapy would not be obligated to refer such patients or to be retrained in other treatments. These considerations in mind prompted a revision of SE therapy, tailoring the treatment to major depression.

SE psychotherapy for treating depression (Luborsky, Mark, et al., 1995) postulates that depressive symptoms are a response to the helplessness experienced in interpersonal situations perceived by patients as dangerous. Supportive techniques are used to bolster a positive therapeutic alliance that can decrease the patient's sense of helplessness. Interpretative techniques are used in the context of this positive relationship to help patients explore their maladaptive relationship patterns and the role of their depression in these patterns. Patients are helped to understand their relationship patterns and to find new, more adaptive ways of responding. The termination of the treatment is used to further understand the relationship pattern and to consolidate treatment gains.

Two uncontrolled pilot studies used the SE therapy for depression treatment manual. Luborsky et al. (1996) reported on the combined results of the two pilot studies. One pilot study involved 25 patients diagnosed with some form of chronic depression (e.g., major depression of more than 2 years' duration, major depression plus dysthymia), and the second used 24 patients who met the criteria for current major depression. All patients were treated by a psychiatrist or psychologist with extensive experience using the SE model. Treatment lasted 16–20 sessions. The chronic depression group did not differ significantly from the current major depression group at intake on age, gender, or symptoms.

The results of this investigation are presented in Table 1. All patients showed significant change in symptoms as measured by the Beck Depression Inventory (BDI) and the Hamilton Rating Scale for Depression (HRSD) across the acute treatment phase. In addition, patients maintained treatment gains across the follow-up period. There were no significant differences in symptom change between the chronic depression group and the episodic depression group. Furthermore, stepwise regression analyses, used to evaluate predictors of treatment outcome, showed that intake level of functioning, as well as the presence of a comorbid Axis I diagnosis, significantly predicted symptom change, whereas the chronic versus nonchronic depression variable predicted less than 1% of outcome variance.

Although these studies were uncontrolled, the results raise the possibility that SE therapy may be a useful treatment for depression. Despite the large pre- to posttreatment effect sizes, however, patients on average did not end therapy being completely asymptomatic (the mean HRSD at termination was 6.56, $SD = 5.80$). Further controlled comparisons of SE therapy with other treatments for depression are obviously necessary to understand whether SE therapy can be as beneficial as these other treatments.

SE Therapy for Treating Cocaine Abuse

SE psychotherapy for treating cocaine abuse also has evolved from the general SE model, which focuses on exploring patients' maladaptive relationship patterns in the context of a supportive relationship. The treatment has been adapted to the special needs of cocaine-dependent patients, who often demonstrate an impaired capacity to experience because they have learned to substitute cocaine for emotional experiencing. SE treatment for cocaine addiction therefore must first focus on abstinence from cocaine and attendance at therapy sessions. The therapist attempts to build a positive therapeutic alliance by developing clear, realistic treatment goals and by understanding the role of cocaine use in patients' maladaptive relationship theme. Patients' maladaptive relationship patterns are then used throughout treatment to understand the roadblocks they encountered in their attempts to remain abstinent.

Two studies have been completed involving SE therapy for treating cocaine abuse. The first (Kang et al., 1991) compared three treatments for outpatient cocaine-dependent patients: family therapy, SE therapy, and paraprofessionally led group therapy. For SE therapy, the manual modified for the treatment of drug dependence was implemented (Luborsky et al., 1977). The patient sample was particularly difficult, involving urban cocaine-dependent patients; 72% of them were crack smokers. Unfortunately, the authors did not report comparisons between the treatment conditions, probably because attrition was such a major problem and the overall results were negative. Only 53% of randomized patients attended at least one treatment session, and only 22% completed at least six sessions of treatment. Of those patients who attended three or more treatment sessions, only 25% were abstinent during treatment. The authors concluded that more intensive treatment than once per week is probably needed. Among major problems with that study, however, is that no information was presented on the selection, training, and certification of the therapists in the treatment manuals or on the integrity of the delivery of the treatments through the use of adherence and competence ratings. Whether the poor outcomes were a function of the difficult population, the intensity of treatment, therapist competence, or other factors is unclear. In addition, the study was performed without input from experienced SE supervisors and trainers from the University of Pennsylvania, where manual-guided SE therapy was developed. The study also said little about the relative value of SE therapy per se, because all treatment modalities examined apparently fared poorly.

SE therapy also is one of the treatment modalities in the ongoing multicenter National Institute on Drug Abuse (NIDA) Cocaine Collaborative Treatment Study (Crits-Christoph, Siqueland, Blaine, et al., 1997). Unlike the Kang et al. (1991) study, the NIDA Cocaine Collaborative Treatment Study used a new treatment manual adapting SE therapy to the treatment of cocaine dependence (Mark & Faude, 1995; Mark & Luborsky, 1992). In addition, there was extensive attention to the selection, training, and monitoring (with adherence and competence rating scales) of therapists within the project.

The NIDA Cocaine Collaborative Treatment Study involves five data collection sites plus a coordinating center at the University of Pennsylvania as well as collaborators from NIDA.[1] The design of the project involves four treatment conditions: group drug counseling (GDC) alone, SE therapy+GDC, CT+GDC, and individual

---

[1]The National Institute on Drug Abuse (NIDA) Collaborative Cocaine Treatment Study is a NIDA-funded cooperative agreement involving four clinical sites, a coordinating center, and NIDA staff. The coordinating center at the University of Pennsylvania, Department of Psychiatry, includes the following people: Paul Crits-Christoph, PhD (principal investigator); Lynne Siqueland, PhD (project coordinator); Karla Moras, PhD (assessment unit director); Jesse Chittams, MA (director of data management/ analysis); and Larry Muenz, PhD (statistician). The collaborating scientists at the Treatment Research Branch, Division of Clinical and Research Services at NIDA, include Jack Blaine, MD, and Lisa Simon Onken, PhD. The four participating clinical sites are as follows: University of Pennsylvania, Department of Psychiatry—Lester Luborsky, PhD (principal investigator), Jacques Barber, PhD (co-principal investigator), Delinda Mercer, MA (project director); Brookside Hospital/Harvard Medical School—Arlene Frank, PhD (principal investigator), Stephen F. Butler, PhD (co-principal investigator), Sarah Bishop, MA (project director); McLean/Massachusetts General Hospital–Harvard University Medical School, Department of Psychiatry—Roger D. Weiss, MD (principal investigator), David R. Gastfriend, MD (co-principal investigator), and Lisa M. Najavits, PhD, and Margaret L. Griffin, PhD (project directors); University of Pittsburgh/ Western Psychiatric Institute and Clinic, Department of Psychiatry— Michael E. Thase, MD (principal investigator), Dennis Daley, MSW, and Ishan M. Salloum, MD (co-principal investigators), and Judy Lis, MSN (project director). The Training Unit includes heads of Cognitive Therapy Training Unit: Aaron T. Beck, MD (University of Pennsylvania, Department of Psychiatry) and Bruce Liese, PhD (University of Kansas Medical Center, Department of Family Medicine); heads of Supportive–Expressive Therapy Training Unit: Lester Luborsky, PhD, and David Mark, PhD (University of Pennsylvania, Department of Psychiatry); heads of the Individual Drug Counseling: George Woody, MD (Veterans Administration/ University of Pennsylvania, Department of Psychiatry) and Delinda Mercer, MA; and Group Drug Counseling Unit: Delinda Mercer (head), Dennis Daley, and Gloria Carpenter, MEd (assistant head; Treatment Research Unit—University of Pennsylvania, Department of Psychiatry). The monitoring board includes Larry Beutler, PhD, Jim Klett, PhD, Bruce Rounsaville, MD, and Tracie Shea, PhD. The contributions of John Boren, PhD, NIDA, the project officer for this cooperative agreement, also are gratefully acknowledged.

drug counseling (IDC) plus GDC. Six months of treatment are provided. Further details of the project, including specific patient-treatment matching hypotheses, can be found in Crits-Christoph, Siqueland, Blaine, et al. (1997).

Although the main clinical trial involving 480 patients is still ongoing, some results from the pilot and training phase of the project have been reported. The pilot and training phase was designed to train the therapists in the respective treatment manuals, pilot test the procedures, and provide preliminary data on the usefulness of these treatments in a cocaine-dependent population. Because the design required four training cases per therapist, a total of 313 patients were treated during the pilot and training phase. Of these, 100 were treated with SE therapy by 24 therapists. Data on the relative efficacy of the different treatment conditions during the pilot and training phase were not reported because therapists were in training and not yet consistently delivering the treatments with acceptable levels of adherence and competence (indeed, a number of therapists were dropped from the project because of inadequate levels of adherence and competence). However, data pooled across the three individual treatment modalities suggested that relatively favorable outcomes were obtained. For example, 75% of patients randomized to treatment achieved at least 1 month of abstinence and 51% achieved at least 2 consecutive months of abstinence (Crits-Christoph, Siqueland, Thase, et al., 1997). These outcomes compare favorably with other promising psychosocial treatments for cocaine dependence (e.g., Carroll, Rounsaville, Gordon, et al., 1994; Carroll, Rounsaville, Nich, et al., 1994; Higgins et al., 1993).

Data from the pilot and training phase of the NIDA Cocaine Collaborative Study also were used to examine training effects (i.e., were therapists able to learn to implement the manual-guided treatments)? This study (Crits-Christoph et al., in press) is the largest investigation of training in manual-guided psychotherapies yet performed. The extent to which SE therapy, CT, and IDC therapists displayed learning (increased competence) both within cases (over sessions) and across four training cases was examined. Therapists participated in didactic workshops and received intensive supervision throughout the training phase. The results indicated that, although CT therapists showed steady improvement in ratings of competence both within training cases (over sessions) and over sequential training cases, SE therapists demonstrated on average only a small learning effect within training cases and no carryover of learning to subsequent training cases. Therapists in IDC had results similar to SE therapy (no learning over training cases but some learning within a case).

Although SE therapists did not improve on average over training cases, many of them were performing adequate (although not outstanding) SE therapy throughout. In general, the SE therapists were a highly experienced group. Only about 50% of applicants to the SE therapy condition were selected even to begin the training phase, and those chosen had on average 10 years of postdoctoral psychotherapy experience. Thus, it is unclear whether the lack of a training effect for SE therapy was a function of the difficult patient population for SE therapy, a "ceiling effect" in which therapists were already performing SE therapy as well as might be expected, inadequate training procedures, or the inherent difficulty in learning to perform SE therapy well. Reports from the SE therapy supervisors and trainers in the project suggest that many dynamic therapists have difficulty adequately formulating and interpreting interpersonal themes (CCRT patterns) consistently. It may be that SE therapists are "born" rather than made, but this issue awaits further study.

SE Therapy for Treating Obsessive–Compulsive and Avoidant Personality Disorders

Barber, Morse, Krakauer, Chittams, and Crits-Christoph (1997) evaluated the efficacy of SE therapy for treating patients with obsessive–compulsive disorder (OCD) and avoidant personality disorder (APD). The treatment was modified specifically for Axis II patients, including a longer time of 52 weekly sessions. For patients with APD, therapists focused on the patient's rigid defenses and the interference of avoidant behavior in the formation of an alliance and the elaboration of the CCRT. With patients with OCD, therapists emphasized the identification of patients' emotions rather than getting immersed in the details of their psychotherapy narratives.

Twenty-four patients with APD and 14 patients with OCD were treated with 52 sessions of SE therapy. Barber et al. (1997) reported that both groups of patients showed significant improvements across treatment on measures of personality disorders, depression, anxiety, and interpersonal problems. In addition, only 39% of patients with APD and 15% of patients with OCD met diagnostic criteria for their respective disorders at treatment termination. The pre- to posttreatment effect sizes across a variety of measures are presented in Table 1. Patients diagnosed with OCD revealed significant changes from intake to termination on the Wisconsin Personality Disorders Inventory, $t(21) = 3.57$, $p < .005$, as well as significant changes in slope across treatment on the BAI ($p < .001$), the BDI ($p < .0001$), the Hamilton Anxiety Rating Scale (HARS; $p < .005$), the HRSD ($p < .001$), and the Inventory of Interpersonal Problems (IIP; $p = .02$). Patients diagnosed with APD showed significant slopes on the BAI ($p < .001$), the BDI ($p < .0001$), the HARS ($p < .0001$), the HRSD ($p < .0001$), and the IIP ($p < .001$).

Key Constructs in the Process of SE Therapy

Although these outcome studies of SE therapy have yielded promising results, such studies do not investigate the potential mechanisms of the therapeutic action. Patients may show positive changes from SE therapy for many reasons unrelated to the theoretical model of SE therapy. Studies attempting to validate aspects of the process of treatment can more directly examine more hypothesized mechanisms of change. Studies from the Center for Psychotherapy Research at the University of Pennsylvania on the process of SE therapy have focused primarily on two main patient variables—the therapeutic alliance and the CCRT—reflecting, respectively, the important patient dimensions corresponding to the supportive and expressive components of SE therapy. Studies of the role of the therapist have focused on their ability to formulate and interpret CCRT patterns correctly as well as on studies of therapist adherence and competence in implementing SE therapy. In the next section, we summarize the results of this research.

The Therapeutic Alliance

Many investigators have examined the role of the therapeutic alliance in predicting the outcome of SE psychotherapy. Morgan, Luborsky, Crits-Christoph, Curtis, and Solomon (1982) used the Penn Helping Alliance Rating Scale (PHARS) to evaluate the role of the alliance for the 10 most improved and 10 least improved patients from the Penn Psychotherapy Project (Luborsky et al., 1980). The PHARS consists of 10 items that represent two domains of the alliance: a helpful attitude from the therapist and a collaborative effort between patient and therapist. Two independent expert judges rated the PHARS on two early and two late psychotherapy sessions for each patient. The results indicated that the 10 most improved patients had significantly higher alliances than the 10 least improved patients. The relation between the alliance and outcome was significant even after controlling for pretreatment psychiatric severity.

Luborsky, Crits-Christoph, Alexander, Margolis, and Cohen (1983) further examined the therapeutic alliance for these patients using the Helping Alliance Counting Signs Method. Two independent expert judges located signs of the therapists' helpful attitudes and the collaborative effort between the patient and therapist. Each sign is rated on a 1–5 intensity scale. The session score consists of the total number of signs per session weighted by the intensity. The results revealed moderate agreement between the counting signs method and the PHARS. As with the PHARS, the most improved patients had significantly more signs of the alliance than the least improved patients. The results of these studies are consistent with the theory that the quality of the helping alliance plays an important role in the symptom course across SE psychotherapy.

Luborsky, McLellan, Woody, O'Brien, and Auerbach (1985) examined the role of the therapeutic alliance in treatment outcome for the study of CT, SE psychotherapy, and DC in the treatment of opiate addiction (Woody et al., 1983). The authors reported a significant relation between the helping alliance at Session 3 and treatment outcome, but they did not provide results for individual treatment conditions. Although these results suggest that the alliance is an important factor in treatment outcome, they do not clarify the role of the alliance in SE psychotherapy per se.

Barber, Crits-Christoph, and Luborsky (1996) evaluated the contributions of therapist competence in SE therapy techniques to symptom course, controlling for the therapeutic alliance for 29 patients treated with SE therapy for major depression. These patients were a subset of those included in the investigation by Luborsky et al. (1996), reviewed earlier. Although Barber et al. (1996) did not specifically report the relation of the alliance to symptom course, J. P. Barber (personal communication, May 30, 1997) reported that there was a trend for Session 6 alliance, as measured by the Helping Alliance Questionnaire, to predict subsequent symptom change ($s_r = -.25, p = .10$). However, Session 3 alliance did not significantly predict subsequent symptom course ($s_r = .03, p = .86$). Furthermore, the cross-product of the alliance and competence on expressive techniques scores did not significantly predict subsequent symptom course ($p = .90$).

Several reasons account for the lack of statistically significant results for the alliance predicting outcome in the Barber et al. (1996) study. One is that therapists participating in the study were highly selected and trained, and it appeared as though most patients formed strong alliances with their therapists. Thus, there may have been a restriction of range on the alliance variable that prevented a relationship with outcome from emerging. Furthermore, Barber et al. used a self-report measure of the alliance, whereas previous researchers (e.g., Morgan et al., 1982) have used a clinical-judge rating method. To our knowledge, there is not yet any evidence that the relationship between techniques and outcome varies as a function of the quality of the therapeutic alliance in SE therapy.

The CCRT

Perhaps the central defining feature of SE therapy is the focus on patients' core conflictual relationship themes. Because the CCRT is the central aspect of the treatment model, we have examined the reliability and validity of assessments of CCRTs using two instruments: the traditional CCRT method and a newer offshoot, the Quantitative Assessment of Interpersonal Themes (QUAINT) method. We now present studies using each of these methods.

The traditional CCRT method. This method, originally proposed by Luborsky et al. (1977), identifies the CCRT from the narratives patients tell of their interactions with others. These narratives are termed *relationship episodes* (REs) and are defined by Luborsky and Crits-Christoph (1990) as "a part of a session that occurs as a relatively discrete episode of explicit narration about relationships with others or with the self" (pp. 15–16). A particular RE involves the same people and the same ideas, and it mostly occurs at one point in time. Further details on procedures for locating relationship episodes in transcripts of psychotherapy sessions can be found in Luborsky and Crits-Christoph (1990).

REs are identified by judges who are instructed to identify all of the REs in a transcript. However, only the REs of acceptable quality are retained for coding of the CCRT. The quality of an RE is determined by ratings of the completeness of the interpersonal interaction and the richness of the detail used to describe it. An example of an RE from the study of SE therapy for treating depression discussed earlier is as follows:

> This morning my boyfriend really got on my nerves and I was late and I was irritated and I told him to get ready because I wanted to leave. He asked me what was wrong and it just really made me mad because he knew that I was late and that I had to leave. Then we got into a big argument. He didn't understand why I was getting upset about being late. I felt that he knew that I get upset when I'm late and he was just exploiting it by asking dumb questions. I tried to explain that to him but I didn't feel that he accepted that at all. I told him that I didn't think that he was accepting and he sort of didn't want to talk so I just left. I just don't want to fight with him.

This episode was rated as 5.0 for completeness, representing the clarity with which the patient describes the other person's response, her own response and feelings, and what she wanted from the interpersonal situation.

Once REs have been identified, a second set of independent judges code the CCRT from the REs. Three components of each patient's CCRT pattern are formulated: (a) the patient's main wishes, needs, or intentions toward the other person; (b) the responses of the other person; and (c) the responses of the self. The CCRT judge first identifies each of the main wishes, responses from the other person, and responses of self within each RE for a given patient. The judge then reviews all REs for a patient and rescores the wishes and responses within each RE. The overall CCRT for a patient is then determined by examining which wishes and responses occur most frequently across that patient's REs. The words judges use to describe the main wishes, responses from the other person, and responses of self in the overall CCRT are then coded (by another set of judges) into a common language using a set of "standard categories" described by Barber, Crits-Christoph, and Luborsky (1990). Several researchers (Barber, Luborsky, Crits-Christoph, & Diguer, 1995; Crits-Christoph, Cooper, & Luborsky, 1988; Luborsky & Diguer, 1998) have examined the extent to which CCRT patterns can be reliably inferred in naturalistic psychotherapy data. The results have been remarkably consistent, with kappa coefficients averaging around .65 for judgments of predominant wishes, responses from the other person, and responses of self (the three components of the CCRT) across eight samples.

The validity of the CCRT method was examined by Crits-Christoph and Luborsky (1990), who evaluated change in the pervasiveness of maladaptive relationship patterns across the course of dynamic psychotherapy. Relationship episodes were identified in the early and late sessions for 33 patients treated with 21–149 sessions of psychodynamic psychotherapy. Two independent judges used the tailor-made CCRT method to rate the presence of wishes, responses of the other person, and responses of self in each narrative. The tailor-made themes were then translated to standard categories for each judge. A composite of the two judges' ratings was formed by choosing the wishes and responses that were rated by both judges. The most pervasive wishes and responses were selected for each patient separately across the early and late sessions. A CCRT pervasiveness score was computed by dividing the number of episodes containing the CCRT component by the total number of episodes.

The two judges demonstrated good interjudge agreement on the pervasiveness scores for each of the CCRT components. A two-variable repeated measures analysis of variance was used to evaluate the change in pervasiveness from early to late across the CCRT components. A significant Time × Component interaction suggested that changes across treatment were not consistent across the CCRT components. Paired t tests revealed that negative responses of the other person and negative responses of self decreased significantly across treatment, whereas positive responses of the other person increased. In addition, residual changes on the wish and response of self-components were significantly correlated with symptom change across the treatment as measured by the Hopkins Symptom Checklist. These results are consistent with the hypothesis that change in core relationship themes mediates change in presenting symptoms in SE therapy, and lend some validity to the CCRT method.

A variety of additional studies also have explored the validity of the CCRT method. A central finding is that CCRTs appear to be a function of what the patient brings to therapy, as opposed to a function of the therapist's attempts to elicit patterns, because CCRTs obtained from interviews before therapy were highly consistent with CCRTs scored from subsequent psychotherapy sessions (Barber et al., 1995). In addition, Popp et al. (1996) found that CCRTs derived from psychotherapy narratives were highly similar to CCRTs reported in dreams. It was also found that most patients diagnosed with major depression had the same CCRT pattern (Eckert, Luborsky, Barber, & Crits-Christoph, 1990). Connolly, Crits-Christoph, Shelton, et al. (1997) examined self-understanding of CCRT patterns over the course of SE therapy. The investigators found greater change in self-understanding in SE therapy than in a medication control condition; however, the amount of change in self-understanding was not related to symptom change.

The QUAINT method. The QUAINT method (Crits-Christoph, Demorest, & Connolly, 1990) was developed as a modification of the CCRT method on the basis of criticisms of the traditional way of assessing the CCRT. Specifically, three problems with the CCRT method were addressed: (a) Judges may be biased toward scoring common themes across relationship episodes for each patient if they read these episodes in sequence; (b) previous research on categories of interpersonal behavior should be used for standard categories; and (c) the method yields few quantitative data. These problems were corrected by presenting relationship episodes to judges in random order across patients; implementing the Structural Analysis of Social Behavior (Benjamin, 1974) categories as the system for standard categories; and instructing judges to rate each standard category on a 1–5 scale for each episode on the extent to which that category is present in an episode. This system allows for easier assessment of reliability and provides quantitative scores for examining profiles of themes for patients.

To date, the QUAINT method has been used to examine the

nature of interpersonal patterns. Crits-Christoph et al. (1990) examined QUAINT profiles for one patient across 31 psychotherapy sessions. A cluster analysis of the QUAINT items for each psychotherapy narrative revealed that the patient had multiple interpersonal patterns. The results further revealed that the themes expressed in narratives about the therapist became more similar to those expressed in narratives about significant people in the patient's life by the end of treatment.

Crits-Christoph, Demorest, Muenz, and Baranackie (1994) used the QUAINT method to examine the consistency of CCRTs over relationship episodes. The psychotherapy narratives from 60 male opiate addicts were rated by three independent, advanced graduate student judges. The QUAINT vocabulary consists of 32 wishes, 32 responses from the other person, and 40 responses of self. The judges rated the extent to which each of the 104 items was present in each narrative on a 1–5 scale. Only the 38 items that demonstrated adequate interjudge reliability (intraclass correlation coefficients for three judges pooled ≥.65) were retained for further analysis.

Within each patient, the 38-item QUAINT profiles for each relationship episode were compared using the Pearson product–moment correlation coefficient and the average correlation between narratives computed. A permutational test assessed the statistical significance of the average correlations for each patient. Each patient's narrative profiles were randomly permuted 1,000 times. For each permutation, the random profiles were intercorrelated and the average correlation computed. Each patient's obtained average correlation was compared with the distribution of 1,000 correlations resulting from the random permutations.

The results revealed a modest level of consistency of interpersonal themes across patients. Patients' average correlations ranged from .00 to .44, with a median correlation of .13 (Crits-Christoph et al., 1994). However, 49 of the 60 patients demonstrated significant levels of consistency based on the permutational tests. Although the results revealed low consistency of interpersonal themes on average, patients demonstrated wide variability in the pervasiveness of interpersonal themes and most patients demonstrated greater-than-chance consistency.

The QUAINT method was further used by Connolly et al. (1996)

to examine the consistency between narratives told by patients regarding significant people in their life and the narratives told about their therapists. In that investigation, 35 of the 60 patients examined in the study by Crits-Christoph et al. (1994) were selected because they each related at least one narrative about the therapist. Because results of the Crits-Christoph et al. (1994) study revealed only small consistency of themes across all REs, we rejected the concept that the CCRT pattern applies to all REs. This led us to change the procedure we used for determining each patient's CCRT pattern. Rather than simply relying on the pattern that emerges as being the highest in frequency across all REs, as had been done in previous research using the CCRT, for the Connolly et al. (1996) study we implemented an approach involving cluster analysis of themes for each patient. This method allowed us to identify more clearly the multiple themes that existed for each patient and to examine only wishes and responses that co-occurred with each other in REs.

Connolly et al. (1996) intercorrelated and cluster analyzed the 38-item QUAINT profiles for narratives told about other people for each of 35 patients. The dendrograms for the hierarchical cluster analyses were used to determine subsets of narratives that demonstrated similar interpersonal themes. For each patient, the level of the hierarchy in which all clusters had a median interprofile correlation of at least .30 was selected for further examination. For each cluster, an interpersonal theme was computed by averaging across the REs in that cluster. The main cluster was defined as the one that contained the greatest number of narratives. The average profile for this cluster was used to represent the patient's most pervasive interpersonal theme. All clusters were then examined relative to the narratives about the therapist.

To evaluate the statistical significance of these correlations, permutational tests similar to those implemented by Crits-Christoph et al. (1994) were used. Once again, 1,000 permutations were performed. For each permutation, the random profiles were intercorrelated and cluster analyzed, and the most pervasive interpersonal theme was identified. The most pervasive interpersonal theme, as well as all cluster themes from the random permutations, was correlated with the patient's therapist narrative for each of the 1,000 permutations. The distribution of correlations between the random cluster themes and the therapist theme was used to determine the probabilities of the obtained correlations.

The results revealed that all patients had at least one cluster that contained multiple narratives, supporting the hypothesis that patients demonstrate similar interpersonal themes across at least some relationships in their lives. Most patients had more than one cluster of narratives, suggesting that some patients experience more than one interpersonal theme. Furthermore, for 60% of patients, there was a significant correlation between some cluster and the therapist narrative, whereas for 34% of the patients, there was a significant correlation between the most pervasive interpersonal profile and the therapist theme.

These results indicated that some patients experience interpersonal themes with their therapists that are similar to the patterns evident in relationships with other people but that the theme "transferred" to the relationship with the therapist is not always the most pervasive interpersonal pattern evident in psychotherapy narratives. That only some patients exhibited a strong transference reaction to the therapist suggests that the emphasis in SE therapy on the CCRT pattern outside of treatment, rather than a strong focus on the theme with the therapist as is done in other models of dynamic therapy, both brief and long term, is likely to make the treatment approach more appropriate to a wider range of patients. Limitations of the study, such as the use of early treatment sessions and the nature of the patient population (opiate dependent) restrict the generalizability of the findings and suggest that much additional research is warranted to understand the nature of transference patterns within psychotherapy and SE therapy in particular.

Therapist Actions in SE Therapy

Studies described previously on the alliance and CCRT provide some degree of validation of important constructs in SE therapy. They do not, however, investigate the issue of whether the particular therapist interventions within SE therapy are important determinants of outcome. Perhaps change (in both symptoms and relationship patterns) is a function of the positive relationship with the therapist, a factor common to many if not all forms of psychotherapy. We turn now to studies that have directly examined the role of therapist interventions in SE therapy.

The accuracy of addressing the CCRT. Crits-Christoph et al. (1988) examined the accuracy of therapists' interpretations excerpted from two early treatment sessions of 43 patients who received moderate-length (about 1 year) dynamic therapy. Although this sample was not in manual-guided SE therapy, a post hoc analysis of the treatment sessions revealed that the therapy was similar to SE therapy in many respects (Luborsky, Crits-Christoph, Mintz, & Auerbach, 1988). Luborsky was in fact the clinical supervisor on several cases in the sample.

The accuracy of interpretation was assessed in a multistep process. In the first step, patients' central relationship themes were identified using the CCRT method (Luborsky & Crits-Christoph, 1990). Next, all therapist statements meeting a definition of interpretation were identified and extracted from transcripts. For the RE described previously, the therapist used the following interpretation later in the session: "I think this touches you because you're close with him and you want him to understand you and not have to ask dumb questions. I think it must be very frustrating." In the final step, each interpretation was rated on a 4-point scale assessing the degree to which the therapist addressed each CCRT wish, negative response from the other person, and negative response of self. The assessment of interjudge reliability indicated that accuracy of intervention could be rated reliably (pooled judge intraclass correlations ranged from .76 to .84 for the three CCRT components).

The results indicated that accuracy on a composite measure of main wishes and responses from others was significantly related to outcome (partial $r = .43$ with residual gain on general adjustment), even after controlling for the effects of general errors in technique and the quality of the therapeutic alliance. Therapies characterized by a high focus on the CCRT yielded a symptomatic improvement effect size of 1.5 (Cohen's d) compared with low focus on the CCRT therapies. Accuracy on the negative responses of self was not related to outcome. These results suggest that when therapists accurately focus more on the interpersonal aspects of patient material (i.e., the wishes toward others and their expected or actual responses), rather than on patients' feeling states (i.e., the response of self component of the CCRT), greater progress occurs.

Consistent with the results presented by Barber et al. (1996), the additional hypothesis tested—that accurate interpretations would have their greatest positive impact in the context of a positive therapeutic alliance—was not confirmed. This latter result was surprising, given the common clinical notion in many models of dynamic therapy that the background of a positive alliance is necessary for interpretative work. This sample, however, had a relatively restricted range on the alliance variable (i.e., few highly negative alliances because only patients who completed at least eight sessions were included in the study), which may have prevented a meaningful interaction between alliance and interpretative accuracy from emerging.

In a second study, Crits-Christoph, Barber, and Kurcias (1993) examined the relationship between therapist accuracy and the development of the therapeutic alliance over the course of treatment. They used the original accuracy ratings from the Penn Psychotherapy Project (Crits-Christoph et al., 1988). Accuracy scores and therapeutic alliance scores were available for early treatment sessions. To examine how accuracy related to change in the alliance, it was necessary to transcribe and score the alliance in later sessions. The therapeutic alliance was assessed using a modified version of the Helping Alliance Counting Signs Method (Luborsky et al., 1983) and was scored on the two early- and two late-treatment sessions (approximately 8 months into treatment that lasted 1 year on average). We found that a composite accuracy on the wish and response from other dimensions of the CCRT correlated significantly with the change in the alliance from early to later in treatment. This result was independent of the impact of psychological health–sickness on the alliance. Further analyses suggested that accurate interpretations served both to improve a poor alliance and maintain an initially positive one. Thus, it was concluded that the quality of the relationship with the therapist is not simply a function of what the patient brings to therapy but that it is affected by the technical interventions made by the therapist. Thus, the supportive and expressive aspects of SE therapy are not independent but are likely to affect each other mutually.

Therapist adherence and competence in delivering SE therapy. Barber et al. (1996) examined the relation between adherence and competence in delivering SE therapy and psychotherapy outcome. Twenty-nine patients with a diagnosis of major depression each received 16 weekly sessions of SE psychotherapy. The Penn Adherence-Competence Scale for SE Therapy (Barber & Crits-Christoph, 1996) was rated by two doctoral-level clinicians on Session 3 audiotapes. The scale consists of 45 items that can each be rated for adherence and competence on a 7-point Likert scale. The items form three theoretically derived subscales, including General Therapeutic Techniques, Supportive Techniques, and Expressive Techniques.

The results revealed that competence in the use of expressive (i.e., CCRT-focused) techniques was associated ($r = .53$, $p < .01$) with the outcome of brief dynamic therapy for depression, even after controlling for the amount of improvement before Session 3, initial patient health and sickness, and the quality of the therapeutic alliance. Adherence to supportive techniques, adherence to expressive techniques, and competence in supportive techniques did not significantly predict symptom change across SE psychotherapy. These results indicated that competency of expressive techniques predicted symptom change rather than the mere frequency of expressive techniques.

Summary

This review indicates that SE psychotherapy may be a promising treatment for a variety of disorders. Although outcome data on SE treatment have been examined for the treatment of depression, GAD, cocaine abuse, and opiate dependence, only two controlled studies that we know of have been conducted to date. These controlled studies evaluated the efficacy of SE therapy for opiate dependence compared with DC, with one investigation revealing more positive results than the second. The open trials of SE therapy for the treatment of GAD and depression appear to be promising, but the results cannot be fully interpreted in the absence of a control condition. Although SE therapy may be a promising treatment for a variety of conditions, additional controlled efficacy data are needed to understand the types of patients for which this treatment has clinical utility. Furthermore, it may be that SE therapy, as well as other forms of dynamic therapy, are most useful for presenting problems that do not fit into the *Diagnostic and Statistical Manual of Mental Disorders* classification. Although it is important from a public health viewpoint to examine the usefulness of dynamic therapy for major disorders, the broader value of dynamic psychotherapy for society may rest in terms of the more common, but less severe, problems in everyday living. Naturalistic studies of the effectiveness of psychotherapy (e.g., Seligman, 1996) can contribute to understanding the impact of psychotherapy beyond the public health emphasis on *Diagnostic and Statistical Manual of Mental Disorders* disorders.

Although research on the efficacy of SE therapy has yet to yield compelling findings, research on the process of SE therapy has supported the validity of aspects of the SE model. Findings indicate that the accuracy of, and general quality of, the expressive techniques within SE treatment are related to the outcome of therapy. The accuracy of interventions also is related to the development of the therapeutic alliance.

The process and outcome findings reviewed in this chapter support the SE treatment model, yet it should be noted that most of the findings produced thus far do not specifically support the SE model in comparison with other dynamic therapy approaches. We know of no study, for example, that has indicated that SE therapy is superior to other dynamic therapy approaches. Moreover, most of the findings on the process of therapy are consistent with traditional concepts within the psychoanalytic literature. For example, the importance of the alliance, originally mentioned by Freud (1912/1958c) and later by Greenson (1965) and Zetzel (1958), has been evident in our data as well as many other studies of psychotherapy. Accuracy of interpretation, as emphasized by Fenichel (1945), also has been shown to relate to treatment outcome. Some findings, however, suggest that the particular operationalization of dynamic constructs in SE therapy may have some value. Research indicating that therapist accuracy relative to patient CCRTs predicts outcome implies that the CCRT concept, unique to SE therapy at least in the details of its structure (e.g., wishes, responses from others, responses of self), may be an especially useful way of organizing clinical material into a dynamic formulation. Similarly, findings on the gains in self-understanding of CCRT patterns over the course of brief dynamic therapy lend support to this conceptualization of insight. However, no evidence has yet been found that gains in self-understanding are associated with symptom change as would be hypothesized by both the SE model (Luborsky, 1984) as well as traditional psychoanalytic theories (Freud, 1901–1905/1953). Data suggesting that skillful interpretations of general (i.e., outside of therapy) patterns in SE therapy are related to a positive therapeutic outcome, rather than a strong emphasis on the patient–therapist relationship, as well as data on the lack of transference-to-the-therapist patterns with some patients, also suggest that models such as SE therapy that place less exclusive emphasis on transference patterns with the therapist may have wider applicability.

Despite the extensive set of studies reviewed in this chapter, from a larger perspective it is evident that empirical support for SE therapy is still at an early stage of development. Psychotherapy is inherently difficult to study in a way that leads to definitive conclusions, and many studies are therefore needed to converge on a clear understanding about the relative efficacy and mechanism of a given therapeutic approach. Moreover, the technology of psychotherapy research has changed dramatically within the past 10–15 years, with the introduction of treatment manuals, other techniques to aid in the standardization of treatment (e.g., adherence scales), and clearer specification of patient samples. Thus, it will be many years before real answers are available about the types of patients for whom SE therapy is indicated and how the treatment works. We continue our efforts in examining SE therapy not with the belief that SE therapy will likely be the treatment of choice for all, or even many, of the presenting problems of patients seeking psychotherapy. However, the evidence accumulated to date encourages the belief that dynamic treatments such as SE therapy will have an important, unique ongoing role as a treatment method for some patients needing help.

References

American Psychiatric Association. (1994). *Diagnostic and statistical manual of mental disorders* (4th ed.). Washington, DC: Author.

Barber, J. P., & Crits-Christoph, P. (1995). *Dynamic therapies for psychiatric disorders (Axis I)*. New York: Basic Books.

Barber, J. P., & Crits-Christoph, P. (1996). Development of a therapist adherence/competence rating scale for supportive-expressive dynamic psychotherapy: A preliminary report. *Psychotherapy Research, 6*, 79–92.

Barber, J. P., Crits-Christoph, P., & Luborsky, L. (1990). A guide to the CCRT standard categories and their classification. In L. Luborsky & P. Crits-Christoph (Eds.), *Understanding transference: The CCRT method* (pp. 37–50). New York: Basic Books.

Barber, J. P., Crits-Christoph, P., & Luborsky, L. (1996). Effects of therapist adherence and competence on patient outcome in brief dynamic therapy. *Journal of Consulting and Clinical Psychology, 64*, 619–622.

Barber, J. P., Luborsky, L., Crits-Christoph, P., & Diguer, L. (1995). A comparison of core conflictual relationship themes before psychotherapy and during early sessions. *Journal of Consulting and Clinical Psychology, 63*, 145–148.

Barber, J. P., Morse, J. Q., Krakauer, I. D., Chittams, J., & Crits-Christoph, K. (1997). Change in obsessive-compulsive and avoidant personality disorders following time-limited supportive-expressive therapy. *Psychotherapy, 34*, 133–143.

Beck, A. T., & Emery, G. (1985). *Anxiety disorders and phobias: A cognitive perspective*. New York : Basic Books.

Benjamin, L. S. (1974). Structural analysis of social behavior. *Psychological Review, 81*, 392–425.

Bibring, E. (1954). Psychoanalysis and the dynamic psychotherapies. *Journal of the American Psychoanalytic Association, 2*, 745–770.

Borkovec, T. D. (1994). The nature, functions, and origins of worry. In G. C. L. Davey & F. Tallis (Eds.), *Worrying: Perspective on theory, assessment, and treatment* (pp. 5–34). New York: Wiley.

Borkovec, T. D., Robinson, E., Pruzinsky, T., & DePree, J. A. (1983). Preliminary exploration of worry: Some 39 characteristics and processes. *Behavior Research and Therapy, 21*, 9–16.

Bryk, A. S., & Raudenbush, S. W. (1992). *Hierarchical linear modeling*. Newbury Park, CA: Sage.

Carroll, K. M., Rounsaville, B. J., Gordon, L. T., Nich, C., Jatlow, P., Bisighini, R. M., & Gawin, F. H. (1994). Psychotherapy and pharmacotherapy for ambulatory cocaine abusers. *Archives of General Psychiatry, 51*, 177–187.

Carroll, K. M., Rounsaville, B. J., Nich, C., Gordon, L. T., Wirtz, P. W., & Gawin, F. (1994). One-year follow-up of psychotherapy and pharmacotherapy for cocaine dependence. *Archives of General Psychiatry, 51*, 989–997.

Chambless, D. L., & Gillis, M. M. (1993). Cognitive therapy of anxiety disorders. *Journal of Consulting and Clinical Psychology, 61*, 248–260.

Connolly, M. B., Crits-Christoph, P., Demorest, A., Azarian, K., Muenz, L.,

& Chittams, J. (1996). Varieties of transference patterns in psychotherapy. *Journal of Consulting and Clinical Psychology, 64,* 1213–1221.

Connolly, M. B., Crits-Christoph, P., Shappell, S., Barber, J. P., & Luborsky, L. (1997, June). *The role of transference interpretations in brief supportive-expressive psychotherapy for depression.* Paper presented at the annual meeting of the Society for Psychotherapy Research, Geilo, Norway.

Connolly, M. B., Crits-Christoph, P., Shelton, R., Hollon, S., Kurtz, J., Barber, J. P., Butler, S. F., Baker, S., & Thase, M. E. (1997). *The reliability and validity of a measure of self-understanding of interpersonal patterns.* Manuscript submitted for publication.

Crits-Christoph, P., & Barber, J. P. (1991). *Handbook of short-term dynamic psychotherapy.* New York: Basic Books.

Crits-Christoph, P., Barber, J. P., & Kurcias, J. (1993). The accuracy of therapists' interpretations and the development of the therapeutic alliance. *Psychotherapy Research, 3,* 25–35.

Crits-Christoph, P., Connolly, M. B., Azarian, K., Crits-Christoph, K., & Shappell, S. (1996). An open trial of brief supportive-expressive psychodynamic psychotherapy in the treatment of generalized anxiety disorder. *Psychotherapy, 33,* 418–430.

Crits-Christoph, P., Cooper, A., & Luborsky, L. (1988). The accuracy of therapists' interpretations and the outcome of dynamic psychotherapy. *Journal of Consulting and Clinical Psychology, 56,* 490–495.

Crits-Christoph, P., Crits-Christoph, K., Wolf-Palacio, D., Fichter, M., & Rudick, D. (1995). Brief supportive-expressive psychodynamic therapy for generalized anxiety disorder. In J. P. Barber & P. Crits-Christoph (Eds.), *Dynamic therapies for psychiatric disorders (Axis I)* (pp. 43–83). New York: Basic Books.

Crits-Christoph, P., Demorest, A., & Connolly, M. B. (1990). Quantitative assessment of interpersonal themes over the course of a psychotherapy. *Psychotherapy, 27,* 513–521.

Crits-Christoph, P., Demorest, A., Muenz, L. R., & Baranackie, K. (1994). Consistency of interpersonal themes. *Journal of Personality, 62,* 499–526.

Crits-Christoph, P., Frank, E., Chambless, D. L., Brody, C., & Karp, J. F. (1995). Training in empirically validated treatments: What are clinical psychology students learning? *Professional Psychology: Research and Practice, 26,* 514–522.

Crits-Christoph, P., & Luborsky, L. (1990). Changes in CCRT pervasiveness during psychotherapy. In L. Luborsky & P. Crits-Christoph (Eds.), *Understanding transference: The core conflictual relationship theme method* (pp. 133–146). New York: Basic Books.

Crits-Christoph, P., Siqueland, L., Blaine, J., Frank, A., Luborsky, L., Onken, L. S., Muenz, L., Thase, M., Weiss, R., Gastfriend, D., Woody, G., Barber, J., Butler, S., Daley, D., Bishop, S., Najavits, L., Lis, J., Mercer, D., Griffin, M. L., Moras, K., & Beck, A. T. (1997). The National

Institute on Drug Abuse Collaborative Cocaine Treatment Study: Rationale and methods. *Archives of General Psychiatry, 54,* 721–726.

Crits-Christoph, P., Siqueland, L., Chittams, J., Barber, J., Beck, A. T., Frank, A., Liese, B., Luborsky, L., Mark, D., Mercer, D., Onken, L., Najavits, L., Thase, M., & Woody, G. (in press). Training in cognitive therapy, supportive-expressive therapy, and drug counseling treatments for cocaine abuse: Results from the NIDA Cocaine Collaborative Treatment Study. *Journal of Consulting and Clinical Psychology.*

Crits-Christoph, P., Siqueland, L., Thase, M. E., Weiss, R. D., Chittams, J., Gastfriend, D. R., Frank, A., Woody, G., Luborsky, L., Onken, L. S., Blaine, J., & Muenz, L. (1997). *Psychosocial treatment of cocaine dependence: Improvements in drug use, psychiatric symptoms, and interpersonal problems.* Manuscript submitted for publication.

Eckert, R., Luborsky, L., Barber, J. P., & Crits-Christoph, P. (1990). The narratives and CCRTs of patients with major depression. In L. Luborsky & P. Crits-Christoph (Eds.), *Understanding transference: The CCRT method* (pp. 222–234). New York: Basic Books.

Elkin, I., Shea, T., Watkins, J. T., Imber, S. D., Sotsky, S., Collins, J. F., Glass, D. R., Pilkonis, P. A., Leber, W. R., Docherty, J. P., Fiester, S. J., & Parloff, M. B. (1989). National Institute of Mental Health Treatment of Depression Collaborative Research Program. *Archives of General Psychiatry, 46,* 971–983.

Fenichel, O. (1945). *The psychoanalytic theory of neurosis.* New York: Norton.

Freud, S. (1953). Fragment of an analysis of a case of hysteria. In J. Strachey (Ed. and Trans.), *The standard edition of the complete psychological works of Sigmund Freud* (Vol. 7, pp. 15–122). London: Hogarth Press. (Original work published 1901–1905)

Freud, S. (1958a). The handling of dream interpretation in psychoanalysis. In J. Strachey (Ed. and Trans.), *The standard edition of the complete psychological works of Sigmund Freud* (Vol. 12, pp. 89–96). London: Hogarth Press. (Original work published 1911)

Freud, S. (1958b). The dynamic of transference. In J. Strachey (Ed. and Trans.), *The standard edition of the complete psychological works of Sigmund Freud* (Vol. 12, pp. 97–108). London: Hogarth Press. (Original work published 1912)

Freud, S. (1958c). Recommendations to physicians practicing psychoanalysis. In J. Strachey (Ed. and Trans.), *The standard edition of the complete psychological works of Sigmund Freud* (Vol. 12, pp. 109–120). London: Hogarth Press. (Original work published 1912)

Freud, S. (1958d). On beginning the treatment: Further recommendations on the technique of psychoanalysis. In J. Strachey (Ed. and Trans.), *The standard edition of the complete psychological works of Sigmund Freud* (Vol. 12, pp. 212–244). London: Hogarth Press. (Original work published 1913)

Freud, S. (1958e). Remembering, repeating and working through: Further recommendations on the technique of psychoanalysis. In J. Strachey

(Ed. and Trans.), *The standard edition of the complete psychological works of Sigmund Freud* (Vol. 12, pp. 145–156). London: Hogarth Press. (Original work published 1914)

Freud, S. (1958f). Observations on transference-love: Further recommendations on the technique of psychoanalysis. In J. Strachey (Ed. and Trans.), *The standard edition of the complete psychological works of Sigmund Freud* (Vol. 12, pp. 157–171). London: Hogarth Press. (Original work published 1915)

Greenson, R. (1965). The working alliance and transference neurosis. *Psychoanalytic Quarterly, 34,* 158–181.

Higgins, S. T., Budney, A. J., Bickel, W. K., Hughes, J. R., Foeg, F., & Badger, G. (1993). Achieving cocaine abstinence with a behavioral approach. *American Journal of Psychiatry, 150,* 763–769.

Jensen, J. P., Bergin, A. E., & Greaves, D. W. (1990). The meaning of eclecticism: New survey and analysis of components. *Professional Psychology: Research and Practice, 21,* 124–130.

Kang, S., Kleinman, P. H., Woody, G. E., Millman, R. B., Todd, T. C., Kemp, J., & Lipton, D. S. (1991). Outcomes for cocaine abusers after once-a-week psychosocial therapy. *American Journal of Psychiatry, 148,* 630–635.

Levenson, H., Speed, J., & Budman, S. H. (1995). Therapist's experience, training, and skill in brief therapy: A bicoastal survey. *American Journal of Psychotherapy, 49,* 95–117.

Lichtenstein, J., & Cassidy, J. (1991, April). *The inventory of adult attachment (INVAA): Validation of a new measure.* Paper presented at the Society for Research in Child Development, Seattle, WA.

Lowenstein, R. M. (1951). The problem of interpretation. *Psychoanalytic Quarterly, 20,* 1–14.

Luborsky, L. (1976). Helping alliance in psychotherapy. In J. Claghorn (Ed.), *Successful psychotherapy* (pp. 92–116). New York: Brunner/Mazel.

Luborsky, L. (1984). *Principles of psychoanalytic psychotherapy: A manual for supportive-expressive treatment.* New York: Basic Books.

Luborsky, L. (1990). The convergence of Freud's observations about transference and the CCRT evidence. In L. Luborsky & P. Crits-Christoph (Eds.), *Understanding transference: The core conflictual relationship theme method* (pp. 251–266). New York: Basic Books.

Luborsky, L., & Crits-Christoph, P. (1990). *Understanding transference: The core conflictual relationship theme method.* New York: Basic Books.

Luborsky, L., Crits-Christoph, P., Alexander, L., Margolis, M., & Cohen, M. (1983). Two helping alliance methods for predicting outcomes of psychotherapy: A counting signs vs. a global rating method. *The Journal of Nervous & Mental Disease, 171,* 480–491.

Luborsky, L., Crits-Christoph, P., Mintz, J., & Auerbach, A. (1988). *Who will benefit from psychotherapy? Predicting therapeutic outcomes.* New York: Basic Books.

Luborsky, L., & Diguer, L. (1998). The reliability of the CCRT measure: Results from eight samples. In L. Luborsky & P. Crits-Christoph (Eds.), Understanding transference: The Core Conflictual Relationship Theme method (2nd ed.; pp. 97–107). Washington, DC: American Psychological Association.

Luborsky, L., Diguer, L., Cacciola, J., Barber, J. P., Moras, K., Schmidt, K., & DeRubeis, R. J. (1996). Factors in outcome of short-term dynamic psychotherapy for chronic vs. nonchronic major depression. *Journal of Psychotherapy Practice and Research, 5,* 152–159.

Luborsky, L., Fabian, M., Hall, B. H., Ticho, E., & Ticho, G. (1958). Treatment variables. *Bulletin of the Menninger Clinic, 22,* 126–147.

Luborsky, L., & Mark, D. (1991). Short-term supportive-expressive psychoanalytic psychotherapy. In P. Crits-Christoph & J. P. Barber (Eds.), *Handbook of short-term dynamic psychotherapy* (pp. 110–136). New York: Basic Books.

Luborsky, L., Mark, D., Hole, A. V., Popp, C., Goldsmith, B., & Cacciola, J. (1995). Supportive-expressive dynamic psychotherapy of depression: A time-limited version. In J. P. Barber & P. Crits-Christoph (Eds.), *Dynamic therapies for psychiatric disorders (Axis I)* (pp. 13–42). New York: Basic Books.

Luborsky, L., McLellan, A. T., Woody, G. E., O'Brien, C. P., & Auerbach, A. (1985). Therapist success and its determinants. *Archives of General Psychiatry, 42,* 602–611.

Luborsky, L., Mintz, J., Auerbach, A., Crits-Christoph, P., Bachrach, H., Todd, T., Johnson, M., Cohen, M., & O'Brien, C. (1980). Predicting the outcome of psychotherapy: Findings of the Penn Psychotherapy Project. *Archives of General Psychiatry, 37,* 471–481.

Luborsky, L., Woody, G. E., Hole, A. V., & Velleco, A. (1977). *Treatment manual for supportive-expressive dynamic (psychoanalytically oriented) therapy: Special adaptation for treatment of drug dependence.* Unpublished manuscript.

Luborsky, L., Woody, G. E., Hole, A. V., & Velleco, A. (1995). Supportive-expressive dynamic psychotherapy for treatment of opiate drug dependence. In J. P. Barber & P. Crits-Christoph (Eds.), *Dynamic therapies for psychiatric disorders (Axis I)* (pp. 131–160). New York: Basic Books.

Malan, D. H. (1976). *The frontier of brief psychotherapy: An example of the convergence of research and clinical practice.* New York: Plenum.

Mark, D., & Faude, J. (1995). Supportive-expressive therapy of cocaine abuse. In J. P. Barber & P. Crits-Christoph (Eds.), *Dynamic therapies for psychiatric disorders (Axis I)* (pp. 294–331). New York: Basic Books.

Mark, D., & Luborsky, L. (1992). *A manual for the use of supportive-expressive psychotherapy in the treatment of cocaine abuse.* Unpublished manuscript, Hospital of the University of Pennsylvania, Philadelphia.

Massion, A. O., Warshaw, M. G., & Keller, M. B. (1993). Quality of life and psychiatric morbidity in panic disorder and generalized anxiety disorder. *American Journal of Psychiatry, 150,* 600–607.

Messer, S. B., & Warren, C. S. (1995). *Models of brief psychodynamic therapy: A comparative approach.* New York: Guilford Press.

Molina, S., Roemer, L., Borkovec, M., & Posa, S. (1992, November). *Generalized anxiety disorder in an analogue population: Types of past trauma.* Paper presented at the Association for the Advancement of Behavior Therapy, Boston.

Morgan, R., Luborsky, L., Crits-Christoph, P., Curtis, H., & Solomon, J. (1982). Predicting the outcomes of psychotherapy by the Penn helping alliance rating method. *Archives of General Psychiatry, 39,* 397–402.

Popp, C. A., Diguer, L., Luborsky, L., Faude, J., Johnson, S., Morris, M., Shaffer, N., Shaffler, P., & Schmidt, K. (1996). Repetitive relationship themes in waking narratives and dreams. *Journal of Consulting and Clinical Psychology, 64,* 1073–1078.

Rickels, K., Downing, R. W., Case, G. W., Csanalosi, I., Chung, H., Winokur, A., & Gingrich, R. L., Jr. (1985). Six-week trial with diazepam: Some clinical observations. *Journal of Clinical Psychiatry, 46,* 470–474.

Rickels, K., Schweizer, E., & Lucki, I. (1987). Benzodiazepine side effects. *American Psychiatric Association Annual Review, 6,* 781–801.

Roemer, L., Borkovec, M., Posa, S., & Lyonfields, J. (1991, November). *Generalized anxiety disorder in an analogue population: The role of past trauma.* Paper presented at the Association for the Advancement of Behavior Therapy, New York.

Safran, J. D., & Segal, Z. V. (1990). *Interpersonal process in cognitive therapy.* New York: Basic Books.

Seligman, M. E. P. (1996). Science as an ally of practice. *American Psychologist, 51,* 1072–1079.

Sifneos, P. (1992). *Short-term anxiety-provoking psychotherapy: A treatment manual.* New York: Basic Books.

Stone, L. (1951). Psychoanalysis and brief psychotherapy. *Psychoanalytic Quarterly, 20,* 215–236.

Strupp, H. H., & Binder, J. L. (1984). *Psychotherapy in a new key: A guide to time-limited dynamic psychotherapy.* New York: Basic Books.

Wallerstein, R. S. (1986). *Forty-two lives in treatment: A study of psychoanalysis and psychotherapy.* New York: Guilford Press.

Wallerstein, R. S., Robbins, L., Sargent, H., & Luborsky, L. (1956). The psychotherapy research project of the Menninger Foundation: Rationale, method, and sample use. *Bulletin of the Menninger Clinic, 20,* 221–280.

Wittchen, H.-U., Zhao, S., Kessler, R. C., & Eaton, W. W. (1994). DSM-III-R generalized anxiety disorder in the national comorbidity survey. *Archives of General Psychiatry, 51,* 355–364.

Woody, G. E., Luborsky, L., McLellan, A. T., and O'Brien, C. P. (1990). Corrections and revised analyses for psychotherapy in methadone maintenance programs. *Archives of General Psychiatry, 47,* 788–789.

Woody, G. E., Luborsky, L., McLellan, A. T., O'Brien, C. P., Beck, A. T.,

Blaine, J., Herman, I., & Hole, A. (1983). Psychotherapy for opiate addicts: Does it help? *Archives of General Psychiatry, 40,* 639–645.

Woody, G. E., McLellan, A. T., Luborsky, L., & O'Brien, C. P. (1995). Psychotherapy in community methadone programs: A validation study. *American Journal of Psychiatry, 152,* 1302–1308.

Woody, G. E., McLellan, A. T., Luborsky, L., O'Brien, C. P., Blaine, J., Fox, S., Herman, I., & Beck, A. T. (1984). Psychiatric severity as a predictor of benefits from psychotherapy: The Penn-VA study. *American Journal of Psychiatry, 141,* 1172–1177.

Zetzel, E. (1958). Therapeutic alliance in the analysis of hysteria. In E. Zetzel (Ed.), *The capacity for emotional growth* (pp. 182–196). London: Hogarth Press.

Pronoun Co-occurrence as a Measure of Shared Understanding

Donald P. Spence

O ne of the most important goals of early members of the Royal Society in London in the 17th century was to become reconnected with the natural world. "What was said to be overwhelmingly wrong with existing natural philosophical traditions was that they proceeded not from the evidence of natural reality but from human textual authority" (Shapin, 1996, p. 68). The so-called Book of Nature held the answers, and the job of science was to find ways of opening its pages, deciphering its sentences, and making sense of what was found. Science had, for too long, relied on the teachings of Aristotle, Galen, the Catholic Church, and other authorities to show how the world worked, and the time had come for new investigators to look for themselves.

A similar sentiment can be detected among contemporary psychoanalysts: Many of them feel that the time has come to go back to the Book of Nature and study the psychoanalytic process as it unfolds through the speech of the patient and analyst. A study of this kind must begin, at a minimum, with a transcription of the hour, that is, turning what is on the tape recorder into readable hard copy. In the ideal case, this transcription would include not only the content of the session but also the pauses (measured to the closest millisecond); the interruptions, repetitions, and parallel utterances (when both parties talk at once); the paralinguistic sounds that surround the intelligible words; and, when necessary, the actual sound of the key phrases (prosodics) when the meaning is in doubt (the word *uhm*, e.g., might mean one thing with a rising inflection and something else with a falling inflection). To borrow an example from O'Connell and Kowal (1995), "a greeting might be transcribed simply with the *verbal* content 'hello.' Whether it was said loudly (*prosodics*), laughingly (*paralinguistics*) or with an accompanying gesture (*extralinguistics*) might or might not be included in the transcript" (O'Connell & Kowal, 1995, p. 94; italics in original).

In most of the process studies in psychotherapy or psychoanalysis, the focus has been on content alone. This restriction stems in part from the fact that psychoanalysts have no recognized convention telling them how to code the additional variables. It can be seen that a full understanding of any analytic interchange will necessarily consider the exact rendering of each utterance, its attendant pauses, and the size and shape of the nonlexical markers that are mostly ignored in the usual transcription. This is a task for the future, however. A focus on content alone—the actual words spoken—is progress enough.

To appreciate just how radical this departure is, analysts need only remember that the usual report of an average analytic hour is little more than an extended anecdote told by an interested party. As a result, analysts never know how far they can trust the report and have no clear knowledge of what is being left out. From the start of the case study tradition in psychoanalysis (i.e., from the beginning of Freud's case histories), the emphasis has been on telling a good story as opposed to providing a complete account. Unwitting modifications to this story may be going on all the time as the analyst's memory of the case or a particular session is being unwittingly revised on the way to publication. These changes, largely out of awareness, will slowly and insidiously tilt the understanding of the analytic encounter away from what actually happened, away from the unexpected (and sometimes the patently harmful), and toward the politically and clinically correct.

One result of reducing analysts' reliance on authority in the study of the analytic process is a new awareness of the patient–therapist interchange. Contributing to this new awareness is a significant shift in the view of the mind since the time when Freud began developing his revolutionary technique. The method of free association was first introduced as a substitute for hypnosis. Embedded within this technique was the idea that trance states can lead the way to a more basic truth than what lies on the surface —in other words, deeper is better. Reliance on the archeological metaphor continued long after hypnosis was given up and the analytic process was seen as a way of removing successive layers of deposited memories. The mind was seen as essentially a static object of study, a collection of thoughts and memories to be systematically opened up.

It is probably no accident that Freud seized on the archeological metaphor at precisely the moment when archeology was headline news. During the years when Freud was writing, Schliemann was excavating Troy, Evans was exploring Knossos, and it would be only a short time before Carter discovered the tomb of King Tut. Had he been working in some other period of history, Freud almost certainly would have chosen another guiding metaphor, and precisely because the metaphor was fortuitous should make analysts hesitate before reading too much into it.

Analysts are familiar with the parallels Freud found between conducting psychoanalysis and uncovering ruins. He believed that it was possible to reconstruct earlier happenings in the life of the patient from current memories:

> Just as the archeologist . . . determines the number and position of the columns from depressions in the floor . . . so does the analyst proceed when he draws his inferences from the fragments of memory, from the associations and from the behavior of the subject of the analysis. (Freud, 1937/1950, p. 259)

Archeology proved to be such a guiding metaphor that Freud believed that

> I had no choice but to follow the example of those discoverers whose good fortune it is to bring to the light of day after their long burial the priceless though mutilated relics of antiquity. I have restored what is missing; but, like a conscientious archaeologist, I have not omitted to mention in each case where the authentic parts end and my constructions begin. (Freud, 1905/ 1925, p. 12)

The concept of a buried unconscious, hidden deep within the mind and knowable only through fleeting fluctuations in manifest content is, in part, another outgrowth of archeological language. *Deep* becomes a metaphor for both earlier and more troubled (higher temperatures, perhaps, as in the Earth's core). If, however, deeper ruins are indeed survivors from an earlier era, no evidence warrants the use of this reasoning in matters of the mind. And there is no molten magma inside the brain, pushing toward the surface—that explanation belongs more properly to geology. The flow of associations is unrelated to the flow of lava. Nor is there any evidence that the patient's associations, as they are given, have anything much to do with the way the same material was first laid down (as in geology). Associations that seem to flow according to the primary process or that seem driven by one or more specific drives may in fact be an attempt, on the patients' part, to reinstate the conversational rules that they were brought up with and cannot do without. When these calls to return to normal rules are heeded by the analyst, patients may feel reassured and safe; when they are disregarded, patients may simply try harder to make the analyst respond. These attempts are usually interpreted as transference reactions of various kinds; this diagnosis overlooks the extent to which analysts have all grown up with a normal conversational model and will immediately react to its violation.

Analysts no longer believe that memories are laid down in layers, to be preserved, more or less intact, over the life of the individual. Furthermore, there is growing evidence that the mind is not something to be unpacked, like rock strata, but something that comes alive in conversation and in interaction with others. Analysts are beginning to realize that they "can attribute mind, mental acts and mental processes only to a creature who is or has been engaged in interpersonal relationships" (Cavell, 1988, p. 590). Words or sentences or memories are not stored in the brain as files are stored on the hard disk of a computer. On the contrary, they are activated by the situation people find themselves in as they speak and remember and their meanings are always affected by the context of the moment. In certain relationships, people feel clever and find the right word always on the tip of their tongue; in other settings, they feel stupid and cannot finish their sentences. The same person, the same brain, but the way it shows itself is as much a function of the conversational moment as of the soft tissue inside the skull.

The recent literature on narration makes the same point slightly differently. Story production in a two-person situation is, more often than not, the direct result of the interaction between two speakers, and the study of interactional contexts has become a predominant focus of recent work on narrative (Mishler, 1995). Stories, it would seem, are coproduced, and, even when one speaker is the teller and the other the listener, it is the function of the latter to help the former expand on key points in his or her account, to explain inconsistencies and discrepancies, and to help him or her make public and sharable what has been largely private and solipsistic. One might say that the listener has the function of turning an interior account into something that makes public sense. This task takes a lot of work; only a small minority of people can make sense simply by opening their mouth.

Recent work on conversational analysis (see Drew, 1995) extends this argument one step further by paying close attention to exactly how the two speakers contribute to the maintenance of mutual intelligibility and understanding.

> Participants' analyses of each other's talk are manifest in their responses or next turns: thus the meaning which B attributes to A's prior turn is exhibited in an adjacent next turn. Thus speaker A may inspect B's response to discover whether B properly understood, that is, to check the adequacy or correctness of B's understanding. (Drew, 1995, p. 77)

(I provide an example of this kind of error correction later in this chapter when the patient responds to an intervention by saying "I don't quite see the connection.")

Psychoanalysis as Conversation

What can analysts learn if they view psychoanalysis as a kind of conversation? Because normal face-to-face conventions have been set aside once the patient lies down on the couch, the usual cues for turn taking become irrelevant and analysts can ask, How long does it take the patient to become accustomed to this new set of rules? Do other signals emerge to take their place? Deprived of eye contact and gestural display, it seems likely that pauses and more subtle verbal markers may assume a much more significant function under the new arrangement (where one speaker is invisible). Careful study of these substitutes may indicate that the way the analyst responds to these attempts to continue the conversation may have a significant impact on the patient's sense of safety and sense of familiarity. Such a study might show that if these substitutes are continually disregarded, the patient may feel increasingly misunderstood and even endangered.

If analysts think of the analytic process as a certain kind of conversation, then it follows that a careful study of pronoun use might provide a way to analyze the dialogic relationship more systematically. If a female patient, for example, uses only the pronouns *I* or *me* in her free associations and never refers, directly or indirectly, to the analyst either by name or with the pronoun *you*, then one can assume that she is minimizing the conversational, two-person aspect of the relationship. Consider the following fragment (from Hour 937 from the case of Mrs. C.):

> Uhm, was, I think I was thinking about first, the way [my baby] was today, and particularly this afternoon. I left her crying and uhm, and she had wanted to play. And I think she wanted to have a game of my dressing her, which she's done a lot. And usually, if I'm feeling in a good mood, and we have to go do something, I try to do it in a game form, which she likes to do now. And so she'll keep on resisting being dressed, or maybe she's just in that kind of obstinate mood a lot lately. I don't know which it is, but in any case I try to, to treat it like a game, except sometimes when I'm really feeling tired, I just can't. But then I try to warn her that I just don't want to play that kind of game.

The prominent pronouns here are *I*, *my*, *we*, and *her* (with *we* being used in connection with the baby); strikingly absent are *you* or any other more direct reference to the analyst. Because there are no *yous*, there can be no co-occurrences of *you* and *me*. A careful reading of this passage would suggest that the patient is completely absorbed in the events of the afternoon and thoughts about her baby; the analyst might not even be in the room. One also might speculate that an interpretation made during this segment of the hour would probably stand a low likelihood of being heard because the patient seems so completely absorbed in her baby and the events that had taken place before the hour. Even a comment about these events might not have registered if she is sufficiently self-absorbed; if registered, it might easily be misunderstood.

By contrast, consider the following fragment from the same hour:

> (Pause) Well, I'm not sure I uhm, what you just said makes me think that maybe you've misunderstood me. Because I don't think I thought what I just said until you told me you were cancelling, which was at the end of the hour. So, it wasn't something I was thinking of until after I left here really, or you know, directly when you were telling me and time was up. Unless you mean that I wasn't thinking about the fantasies yesterday, which I know is true. But I think I have the feeling I was beginning to near the end.

Pronouns referring to the analyst tend to be intermixed with pronouns referring to the patient. One may have the impression that the patient is speaking with the analyst very much in mind; she may even be listening for his response to specific aspects of her associations. One also may speculate that, because of the high co-occurrence of *you* and *me*, interventions made during this fragment would stand a high likelihood of being heard (and a good possibility of being agreed with). One also might predict that the analyst, because he feels included in the "conversation," would be strongly tempted to intervene.

This reasoning led to the following predictions:

1. Analytic hours that are characterized by a high rate of co-occurring pronouns (*you* and *me*, *you* and *I*, *my* and

yours, etc.) would contain a higher number of interventions by analysts than hours showing a low rate of co-occurring pronouns. This prediction rests on the assumption that when analysts feel included in the conversation, they will be more likely to speak.

2. Interventions will tend to occur at points during the session when the co-occurrence rate is high.

3. During analytic hours characterized by a high rate of co-occurring pronouns, analysts would make their first response earlier in the session than would be the case with low rate hours. This prediction rests on a similar assumption: If analysts feel included in the conversation, they will more likely speak early than late.

4. Analytic hours characterized by a high rate of co-occurring pronouns also would be characterized by a sense of shared understanding in the conversation. Low co-occurrence hours, on the other hand, would tend to be dominated by misunderstandings and disagreements.

Method of Measuring Co-occurrence

Seventy analytic hours, divided into 7 blocks of 10 contiguous sessions, were selected from the well-studied case of Mrs. C. (detailed descriptions of the case can be found in Dahl, 1988; Jones & Windholz, 1990; Teller & Dahl, 1986). The blocks were taken from each of the 6 years of the case, with 2 blocks of 10 hr taken from the first year and the remaining blocks taken from each of the subsequent years.

For an earlier study of lexical co-occurrence in written American discourse (Spence & Owens, 1990), I developed a computer program (written in C-language) that could quickly count the co-occurrence of any two words in an extended sample of machine-readable prose. The program counted the number of times the first word of the pair was followed by the second within a search space of 1,000 characters. I adapted this program to patient transcripts by adding the condition that searches for co-occurring pairs would always be halted by each new therapist intervention. The total number of co-occurring pairs found per analytic hour was divided by the total number of words spoken by the patient to yield a co-occurrence rate for shared pronouns; this rate is called the *co-occurrence rate of transference pronouns* (CORtrans). Five pairs of pronouns were measured: *you* and *me*, *you* and *I*, *us* and *we*, *us* and *them*, and *my* and *yours*.

Once the 70 hr had been scored for pronoun co-occurrence, I designated the 35 sessions scoring above the median as related hours (showing a higher degree of relationship between the patient and analyst) and the 35 sessions scoring below the median as isolated hours.

The case of Mrs. C. has become a landmark case in the psychoanalytic research literature because it is a complete, naturally terminated, clinically successful, supervised analysis running some 1,100 hr, with the patient being seen five times a week on the couch. It was conducted by an experienced analyst and supervised by an eminent and widely published colleague (supervision normally took place on Monday morning, before the Monday hour). All hours were tape-recorded, but only a small fraction have been transcribed. All proper names and identifying information have been disguised, and a uniform convention has been used to designate the length of pauses and silences. The patient, a married social worker in her late 20s, sought treatment because of lack of sexual responsiveness, difficulty in experiencing pleasurable feelings, and low self-esteem. She was the second of four children from a professional family.

Results

For Hypothesis 1, the correlation between CORtrans (rate of co-occurring pronouns) and the number of interventions across the 70 hr of the case was significant, $r(68) = .30$, $p = .01$, and supported the first hypothesis.

I next computed, for each block of 10 hr, the correlation between CORtrans and the number of interventions per session; these data are plotted in Figure 1. This graph shows that the relation between these two variables becomes increasingly positive over the course of treatment, suggesting that in the latter phases of the analysis, the analyst was becoming increasingly responsive (probably with-

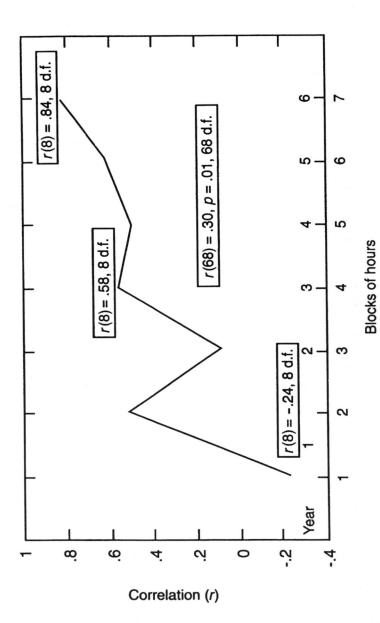

Figure 1.   Relation between CORtrans and interventions—Mrs. C.

out awareness) to the pairing of *you* and *me* and related indexicals. In the final 10 hr (6th year of treatment), the correlation rose to .82 (significant at the .01 level). The rising pattern of correlations over the course of treatment suggests two possible explanations: (a) The analyst was becoming increasingly sensitive to the patterning of pronouns in the patient's associations and was using this pattern as a way of deciding when to speak and (b) the patient was learning that one way to prompt the analyst to enter the conversation was to pepper her associations with frequent pairings of *you* and *me* (both tendencies, of course, may be operating together).

To understand in greater detail the extent to which pronoun co-occurrence was in fact determining analytic activity, I divided each of the last 10 hours (Hours 936–945) into equal-sized segments of approximately 500 words each and scored each segment for CORtrans and the number of interventions. Figure 2 shows these data. Not only was the correlation highly significant, $r(82) = .30$, $p < .005$, but the analyst's interventions tended to track the co-occurrence rate of shared pairs of pronouns.

I next examined one particular interpretation regarding Hypothesis 2: when the analyst pointed out a recurrent pattern of behavior in the patient's associations (Item 62 in Jones' Q-sort; see Jones & Windholz, 1990). This intervention had been reliably scored by Jones and his colleagues in their earlier study. A colleague and I, serving as judges, set out to replicate this evaluation, and our consensus was that the response occurred seven times in the last block of 10 sessions. Figure 3 shows that it was always made when the CORtrans was higher than average, $t(8) = 6.24$, $p = .002$. It would appear that the analyst first formulated the target interpretation and then waited for the moment when the patient was most ready to hear it (i.e., at a moment marked by a high rate of shared pronouns). Note that a rise in CORtrans was a necessary condition only for the interpretation; it was not sufficient to trigger this particular response if it was not appropriate to the clinical material (note that in Hours 937–939, the peaks in CORtrans did not trigger an interpretation). These findings support Hypothesis 2.

Hypothesis 3 predicted that interventions would occur earlier during high co-occurrence hours. I developed a program that measured the amount of time elapsed in the session before the analyst

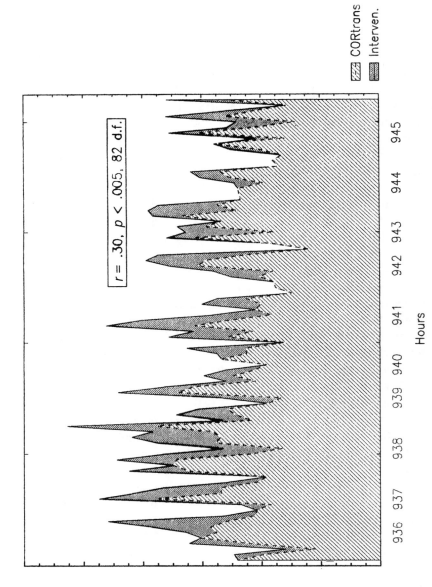

Figure 2. Relation of interventions to CORtrans—Hours 936–945.

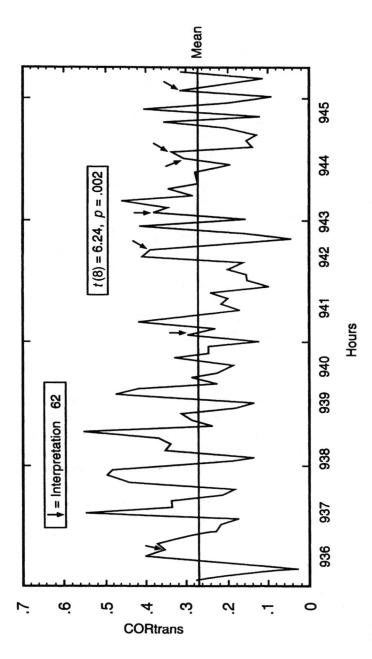

Figure 3. Expressions of Interpretation 62 as a function of CORtrans—Mrs. C.'s therapist identifies a recurrent theme in patient's conduct.

made his first intervention. I could make this estimate because any pause longer than 30 s was noted in the transcript. I scored each of the 70 hr using this measure. The findings are presented in Figure 4. It can be seen that interventions made during high co-occurrence hours tended to occur at an average of slightly more than 6 min after the beginning of the hour, whereas interventions made during low co-occurrence hours tended to occur after an average 12-min delay (about twice as long). The difference was significant, $t(68) = 2.90$, $p = .005$, and suggested that the analyst sensed the increased rate of co-occurring pronouns early in the session. Feeling that he was being included in the conversation, he intervened earlier than when he was feeling left out.

Hypothesis 4 stated that pronoun co-occurrence should reflect the degree of understanding that takes place during the session. Hours characterized by a high rate of co-occurrence also should demonstrate a sense of shared understanding and a more spontaneous give and take. In support of this prediction, I found that the 3 hr with the lowest co-occurrence (Hours 266, 259, and 438) tended to be dominated by misunderstandings and disagreements. In the most isolated hour (Hour 266, CORtrans = 0), the patient (after a 4-min silence) began by talking about her feelings about not finishing a report; switched to thoughts she had on the subway while going to her appointment; discussed a dream about trying to get into an art class; returned to some thoughts she had while teaching; and then shifted to a conversation with a friend about birth control pills, their dangers, and her uncertainty over whether to use nothing or to replace the pills with a diaphragm. The analyst intervened at this point to ask, "That's an art class that you have to get into?"—a surprising nonsequitur.

One can speculate that the analyst may have felt excluded by the absence of co-occurring pronouns and felt less inclined to listen closely; perhaps for this reason, he reverted to an earlier topic. The patient, surprised, responded by saying, "I don't quite see the connection." The analyst answered as follows:

> Well, I don't know that there is. It just strikes me that you tell me the dream, you don't say anything about it, and then say what you've really been thinking about now is, among other things, whether you should learn to use a diaphragm, and

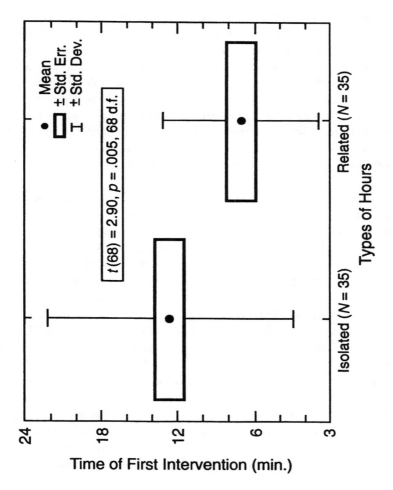

Figure 4. Effect of therapist–patient relationship on time of first intervention—Mrs. C.

whether you need it and why do you need it—which are the
questions of the dream.

The therapist acknowledged the abruptness of the intervention but
then tried to defend it (in a manner not altogether convincing).

In the next most extreme isolated hour (Hour 259, CORtrans =
.006), the patient began with a short silence and then said that two
things occurred to her as she came into the room (note that neither
thought concerned the analyst). The first was connected to doing
some reports that were almost due and finding herself unable to
begin. Throughout the segment she was silent about the nature of
the reports. The second theme concerned her urge to eat when she
returned home and how she often found herself eating while working. After about 3 min of associations, the analyst (not responding
directly but going back to the first topic) asked, "What goes into
the reports?"

Once again, the analyst changed the subject and returned to an
earlier topic. This time there was no confusion, but it was perhaps
symptomatic of the isolated nature of the hour that the analyst did
not track the patient's sequence of topics and that the patient, in
turn, did not disclose the nature or content of the reports she was
describing. One has a sense that she was not revealing as much as
she knew about her thoughts and that the analyst not only felt
excluded but underinformed.

In the third most isolated hour (Hour 438, CORtrans = .014), the
patient had been talking about her new baby and worrying about
whether she was a good mother. After describing a recent experience with the baby's diarrhea and worried that perhaps it was
worse than usual, she said, "And it's almost as if I'm looking for
all sorts of little signs constantly, to indicate there's something
wrong with her, so I won't kill her. Because, I, I'm afraid that otherwise I'll s—, miss them, and I'll kill her by inattention."

The analyst said, "I guess it really is very much as though you're
afraid of that."

The patient paused, sniffed, and said, "And the other thing that's
been, I don't know, I've been back and forth on it for 3 days, is
calling her pediatrician again. I, I actually called him once and
couldn't get him."

In this instance, the analyst made an apparently empathic intervention only to find that the patient seemed unable to stay with her thoughts (her fear) and changed the subject to calling the pediatrician. In the first 2 previous hours, the analyst changed the subject; here, the patient made the change. It would appear that it was particularly difficult during isolated hours for both the patient and analyst to talk about the same thing at the same time.

Also worth noting is how the state of being excluded affected the analyst: It seemed to have made him a poorer listener who often found it difficult to keep abreast of the patient's flow of ideas. One can speculate that isolated hours, because they tend to exclude the analyst from the conversation and cause fewer and more delayed interventions, may actually prevent an empathic immersion in the material and thus interfere with a deeper understanding of the patient's thoughts and feelings. It begins to look as if listening while silent may be significantly different from listening while actively engaged, and both parties may contribute to the change. When the analyst is silent, the patient may feel that she is less interesting and therefore takes less care to make perfect sense; as she becomes more ambiguous and misunderstood, the analyst, in turn, pays less attention and his silence increases. The patient senses his decreased interest and the cycle continues until the end of the hour.

The 3 highest hours, by contrast, conveyed a picture of shared understanding and spontaneous give and take. In the hour with the highest co-occurrence score (Hour 938, CORtrans = .273), the patient began with a fantasy about the analyst. As she was going up the stairs to her session, she imagined that he was following close behind her. "What a joke it would be," she stated, "if you really were coming up behind me, just like I'd been fantasizing. And, and then I was afraid to turn around and see who it was. . . . I didn't know what I'd do if it did turn out to be you."

After the patient added a few more sentences, the analyst brought her back into the fantasy by asking, "Here I am walking behind you. What do you want me to do?"

The patient responds with a sexual thought that led to associations about her husband. The analyst repeated his question about what she wanted, and the patient responded, "sort of a general feeling of your . . . making me feel very special. Uhm, by being a mixture of a lover and a father, you know, who, and, and that's finding me special in two different ways."

In the second highest hour (Hour 433, CORtrans = .242), the patient had just returned from delivering her baby (born in the 3rd year of the analysis). She began the hour after a 4-min silence by saying that she had two things on her mind and that one was connected with the analyst.

The third highest hour (Hour 432, CORtrans = .231) immediately preceded the second; the patient began with a thought she had forgotten the day before and then remembered when she returned home. She realized at that time that she would not be free to come to her regular session (because of the baby) and wondered whether the analyst could change her time.

Each of the 3 hr scoring the highest on pronoun co-occurrence began with a thought about the analyst. Further reading suggested that the patient and analyst were closely attuned, sharing a conversation that flowed easily from one to the other. Questions seemed relevant to the immediately preceding material and were readily understood; there were few if any non sequiturs, and the analyst easily followed the patient's sequence of associations. The patient appeared to be more open and frank in her disclosures and less inclined to give guarded responses or make statements that required a clarifying question.

Discussion

Detailed analysis of hours that showed high and low pronoun co-occurrence suggested that the micromeasure, CORtrans, may be a marker for a more comprehensive macromeasure that could be defined as heightened coherence in the analytic conversation. In other words, by measuring the way in which the patient uses first- and second-person pronouns, one may be able to form an estimate of the degree to which patient and analyst are truly responsive to each other's thoughts and feelings. One can speculate that high CORtrans hours are apparently marked by an increase in the degree to which the patient discloses significant material, an increase in the patient's sense of being understood by the therapist, and an increase in the patient's acceptance of the therapist's interpretations. By measuring CORtrans (a relatively fast, simple, and highly reliable operation), one can estimate the nature of the therapeutic alliance and the extent to which the therapeutic dialogue truly responds to each person's moods and intentions. By scoring for pronoun co-occurrence, one can rapidly and accurately identify those hours in which true dialogue has been established and have the option of subjecting them, at some later time, to a more in-depth clinical appraisal.

One also can begin to understand why, in the most isolated hours, analysts become more cautious, neutral, and nonresponsive in their interventions. If low CORtrans hours make analysts feel excluded, they will wait longer before making an initial intervention (see Figure 4). Patients, more and more aware of the silence, may begin to feel that the analysts are not paying close attention to their associations and, as a result, they may become more superficial in their references. As patients become more ambiguous, analysts may listen even less carefully, with the result that all parties become more separated from the other and less committed to forging a joint dialogue. At the extreme, the analysts' attention may stray from the here-and-now focus of the hour and the chance of non sequiturs begins to increase.

This argument suggests that silent analysts, even if listening with evenly hovering attention, may not be completely attuned to the full range of meanings that are latent in patients' material. Silent listening may allow too much scope for random associations or ruminations on one or more topics that are no longer current; by failing to keep abreast of the changing focus of patients' utterances, analysts may miss the complex mixture of latent and manifest meanings that lend patients' thoughts their special flavor. By lagging behind the current topic, analysts also may give the impression that they are no longer closely attending to the full range of connotations of patients' associations and may, in subtle ways, convey the impression that it no longer matters whether the patients really speak what comes to mind. By seeming to discount the "basic rule" (of saying whatever comes to mind), analysts may encourage patients to be more selective in their choice of topics; to fall silent while deciding what to say next; and, in a variety of ways, to allow more deliberation to intervene between thought and speech.

From the patients' side, one can argue that during the isolated hours, they are more resistant and less interested in collaborating with analysts; as a result, patients minimize the use of second-person pronouns (references to analysts) and create the impression that they are talking only to themselves. The effect on analysts is to make them feel disregarded, excluded, and minimized. No longer part of the conversation, analysts find it more difficult to follow and, as a result, (a) wait longer before speaking; (b) make fewer interventions; and (c) have more trouble tracking patients' associations and run a higher risk of replying with a non sequitur.

When pronoun co-occurrence is high, on the other hand, the conditions are favorable for a mutually productive therapeutic alliance. One may speculate that during these moments, the analysts' timing may be subtly improved and, in both form and content, their interventions may be more sensitive to the linguistic demands of the moment. At its most obvious, this rule might mean that analysts repeat a phrase or metaphor just used by patients; complete an uncompleted thought; and, in other ways, show, by choice of form and content, that patients are being followed attentively.

During high co-occurrence hours, patients may have the sense that they are being understood in a new and more fundamental way. There may be a parallel between this kind of empathic response and what has been called *contingent responsiveness* in developmental research. It has been argued that it is through consistent, predictable repetition of shared patterns of behavior that the infant, in association with the mother, gains a sense of agency and control (see Martin, 1989; Stern, 1974). Some authors have argued that contingent responding in infancy may even lay the groundwork for higher level processes such as empathy and identification (Basch, 1983). With respect to the analytic situation, Emde (1990) argued that "psychoanalysis may be a special form of developmental experience" (p. 901). He suggested that certain kinds of "normative biologically prepared processes are actualized, and they depend on the interactive, emotional availability of the analyst" (Emde, 1990, p. 903).

Something of this kind may have taken place during the latter phases of treatment with Mrs. C. One may speculate that, over the course of the analysis, the analyst became increasingly skilled at adopting the modal stance of free-floating attention and, as a result, became increasingly sensitive to (but not necessarily conscious of) subtle indicators such as pronoun pairings. As he became more sensitive, he may have entered into a more regressive mode of listening. As a result, he was able to respond to the patient in a way that took advantage of an earlier form of communication laid down in the early months of the patient's life. The analyst's new sensitivity allowed this earlier pattern to be "actualized" in treatment (to use Emde's, 1990, language), and the patient may have had the sense that she was being listened to and perhaps even understood in a new, more fundamental manner.

Figure 3 offers a way of understanding some important dimensions of the analyst's contingent response. He identified a recurrent theme in the patient's relationships only at the moment in the session when the co-occurrence rate was above the mean. He may have sensed that it was only at those moments that he stood a better-than-even chance of being heard and understood, whereas the patient, from her side, may have found herself listening more acutely when she had just finished pairing herself and her analyst in her free associations (i.e., including him in her thoughts). Interventions at this time may have given her the feeling that she was being listened to in a way that preconsciously reminded her of a deeper kind of pre-oedipal understanding, perhaps of a time when her needs were empathically sensed and taken care of almost before they were put into words.

As the patient continued to experience the sense of being understood by the analyst's contingent response, one would expect that she, in turn, would develop greater trust, would become more disclosing, and would begin to introduce significant new material. There are the beginnings of an explanation for the rising function graphed in Figure 1. As the analyst began to respond, in the early hours of the case, to the latent theme of shared discourse (as measured by pronoun co-occurrence), the patient began to feel more understood. Not only was the analyst responding to the content of her discourse, but the timing of his response (triggered increasingly often by *you* and *me* pairings) might have been indicating to her that he was attuned to her in a deeper sense as well. As she began to feel understood, she more than likely would have become more disclosing and less resistant, bringing new material into the hour and thus signaling the analyst that he was responding appropriately. He was rewarded by the increase in new material (even though he might not have been conscious of the pronoun pairings) and became more confident in his pattern of responding; this, in turn, encouraged the patient, and Figure 1 shows the result.

Conclusion

Is pronoun co-occurrence a truly analytic variable? I raise this question because, when clinicians are informed about work on pronoun choice, they often say that they never listen for pronoun pairings and that this measure is never mentioned by Freud (not even once!). In fact, it is probably asking the impossible to expect analysts to keep track of pronoun pairings because they almost never listen for individual words; they listen for meanings and almost never track lexical markers. Nevertheless, the data reported here suggest that at some, perhaps preconscious, level, the analyst was sensitive to a change in pronoun pairings. (Whether this awareness extends to other analysts is, of course, a question for future research.)

Further research also is needed to explore the question of cause. Although I have many reasons to believe that changes in pronoun use influenced analyst activity (as in Figure 1), it also could be argued that he became more skilled in the timing and wording of his interventions, thereby creating greater trust in the patient, which moved her to include him more in her associations. Correlations, of course, are almost always silent about cause, and one may find that both effects are true at different times in the treatment. This is an instance in which the data on prosodic, paralinguistic, and extralinguistic usages are sorely needed; such information might even distinguish between moments when pronoun use affects interventions and moments when the opposite is true.

It is also noteworthy that the role of pronoun co-occurrence would not have been discovered if researchers had depended only on the traditional case report. Pronoun frequency, by definition, cannot be captured by subjective report. However, having measured it, researchers now find that it correlates with other, more traditional clinical features and that it may provide an underlying lawfulness for understanding the clinical process, a lawfulness that has thus far eluded clinicians and researchers alike. Attempts to extract the surface meaning of a session have frequently been frustrated by what has been called the *Roshomon effect*, that is, the construal of meanings is always a personal adventure, framed by the context of the moment, and this context can never be perfectly translated or exported (see, e.g., Rubovits-Seitz, 1986). It may turn out, however, that each of the separate ways of understanding a clinical happening, in partial or total disagreement with one another, may all connect with some underlying phenomenon that clinicians cannot put into words (e.g., pronoun co-occurrence) and that, once clinicians discover this underlying substrate, much of the apparent disagreement fades away. For example, further study of this phenomenon might reveal that (a) truly mutative interpretations tend to occur at moments of high pronoun co-occurrence; (b) interventions that patients remember most fondly tend to occur right after they have referred to analysts in conjunction with themselves; or (c) high pronoun co-occurrence marks a moment when analysts start listening more carefully to patients and borrowing one or more of patients' key expressions to use in their interventions. At the other extreme, one might find that serious misunderstandings are more apt to occur during intervals of low co-occurrence and that the onset of serious resistance or a prolonged negative transference might be discovered in a series of zero co-occurrence sessions.

My two central findings—that interventions across the first 6 years of the analysis of Mrs. C. tended to be correlated with pronoun occurrence and that a particular intervention within Sessions 936–945 always occurred when CORtrans was above the mean—suggest that pronoun co-occurrence operates as an important background variable in determining when analysts intervene. Awareness of this influence should caution analysts not to place too much importance on the content of a particular intervention because its impact on patients may depend more on its timing (i.e., its utterance relative to the ongoing co-occurrence rate). From the analyst's side, it would seem that he responded to being included in the patient's associations and that pronoun co-occurrence might have been a more important influence on his interventions than the more obvious content of the patient's associations. In other words, his reasons for a particular intervention may, on close examination, turn out to be less convincing than he thought at the time (i.e., more rationalization than explanation). The critical variable, in many cases, may be the sheer frequency of *you* and *me* pairings, not the manner in which his intervention brought together, or called attention to, a number of thematically related associations by the patient.

It would be a mistake, however, to assume that other variables are not also affecting when and how often analysts intervene. Still largely unstudied is the role of nonlexical features such as inflection, stress, and gesture. With eye contact eliminated as a cue to turn taking and to various shades of meaning (e.g., irony or sarcasm), analysts must become aware of other signals, and it would not be surprising to find that they become increasingly sensitive to slight variations in pitch, pause, and pronunciation. Careful study of these variables also might show a lawful relation to content and frequency of intervention.

Analysts also need to remember that the correlation between CORtrans and interventions is far from perfect, an indication that a productive hour can easily occur in the absence of high co-occurrence. One can assume that even when the content of a session seems unrelated to them, analysts might still feel valued and included, and analysts need to explore such hours to determine how they differ from more banal sessions. Pacing may make a difference here, along with choice of language. When content is being continually withheld (as in Hour 259), analysts will naturally feel excluded; if, on the other hand, key terms are systematically explained as patients continue to associate, analysts might feel more included. Also important is what might be called *ease of fit*. If the central character in the monologue bears an obvious resemblance to the analysts, it becomes easier for them to feel involved and talked to, even when never mentioned by name.

More generally, the use of pronoun co-occurrence (and similar kinds of measures) provides a way to learn from other disciplines and gives researchers in other fields a way of learning from psychoanalysis. Careful study of the literature on eye contact in face-to-face conversation would probably suggest other hypotheses to explore because pronoun pairing can be thought of as a kind of verbal eye contact. By grounding clinical observations on more reliable and easily countable measures, analysts invite collaboration from other fields and move to reduce the isolation that, for better or worse, has long haunted psychoanalysis. In the next few years, there should be a sharp rise in the number of clinical studies that are augmented by some kind of objective measure that will help to reduce some of the interfering and counterproductive subjectivity of the impossible profession.

References

Basch, M. F. (1983). Empathic understanding: A review of the concept and some theoretical considerations. *Journal of the American Psychoanalytic Association, 31,* 101–126.

Cavell, M. (1988). Solipsism and community: Two concepts of mind in psychoanalysis. *Psychoanalysis and Contemporary Thought, 11,* 587–613.

Dahl, H. (1988). Frames of mind. In H. Dahl, H. Kachele, & H. Thoma (Eds.), *Psychoanalytic process research strategies* (pp. 51–66). Berlin: Springer.

Drew, P. (1995). Conversation analysis. In J. A. Smith, R. Harre, & L. Van Langenhove (Eds.), *Rethinking methods in psychology* (pp. 64–79). Thousand Oaks, CA: Sage.

Emde, R. N. (1990). Mobilizing fundamental modes of development: Empathic availability and therapeutic action. *Journal of the American Psychoanalytic Association, 38,* 881–913.

Freud, S. (1925). Fragment of an analysis of a case of hysteria. In J. Strachey (Ed. and Trans.), *The standard edition of the complete psychological works of Sigmund Freud* (Vol. 7, pp. 7–122). London: Hogarth Press. (Original work published 1905)

Freud, S. (1950). Constructions in analysis. In J. Strachey (Ed. and Trans.), *The standard edition of the complete psychological works of Sigmund Freud* (Vol. 23, pp. 257–269). London: Hogarth Press. (Original work published 1937)

Jones, E. E., & Windholz, M. (1990). The psychoanalytic case study: Toward a method for systematic inquiry. *Journal of the American Psychoanalytic Association, 38,* 985–1015.

Martin, J. A. (1989). Personal and interpersonal components of responsiveness. In M. M. Bornstein (Ed.), *Maternal responsiveness: Characteristics and consequences* (pp. 5–14). San Francisco: Jossey-Bass.

Mishler, E. G. (1995). Narrative accounts in clinical and research interviews. In B.-L. Gunnarsson, P. Linell, & B. Nordberg (Eds.), *The construction of professional discourse.* New York: Longman.

O'Connell, D. C., & Kowal, S. (1995). Basic principles of transcription. In J. A. Smith, R. Harre, & L. Van Langenhove (Eds.), *Rethinking methods in psychology* (pp. 93–105). Thousand Oaks, CA: Sage.

Rubovits-Seitz, P. (1986). Clinical interpretation, hermeneutics, and problem of validation. *Psychoanalysis and Contemporary Thought, 9,* 3–42.

Shapin, S. (1996). *The scientific revolution.* Chicago: University of Chicago Press.

Spence, D. P., & Owens, K. C. (1990). Lexical co-occurrence and association strength. *Journal of Psycholinguistic Research, 19,* 317–330.

Stern, D. N. (1974). Mother and infant at play: The dyadic interaction involving facial, vocal and gaze behaviors. In M. Lewis & L. A. Rosenblum (Eds.), *The effect of the infant on its caregiver* (pp. 187–214). New York: Wiley.

Teller, V., & Dahl, H. (1986). The microstructure of free association. *Journal of the American Psychoanalytic Association, 34,* 763–798.

Chapter 6

The Voyage of *el Rubaiyat* to the Discovery of FRAMES

Hartvig Dahl

Hölzer and Dahl (1996) began their account of "How to Find FRAMES" as follows:

> A psychotherapeutic "talking cure" relies essentially on a patient's storytelling. Thus, the principle of free association as the "basic rule" of psychoanalysis is to sample stories that are characteristic or typical of a person's emotional experiences. FRAMES as defined and described by Dahl and Teller (1994) are *Fundamental Repetitive And Maladaptive Emotion Structures* that capture the plots of these stories.[1] These plots reoccur again and again with different people in different situations under different circumstances. And it is the repetition of these plots in and

---

[1] See also Dahl (1988); Teller and Dahl (1981, 1986).

out of the therapeutic situation that makes possible inferences about what clinicians call a patient's basic psychodynamics. Their maladaptive character lies mainly in their invariance. Their tendency to recur over and over makes for a typically inflexible, neurotic patient. (p. 177; italics added)

A Story

In 1988 Strupp, Schacht, and Henry proclaimed a hallowed goal: *"The principle of P-T-O Congruence proposes that the intelligibility of psychotherapy research is a function of the similarity, isomorphism, or congruence among how we conceptualize and measure the clinical problem (P), the process of therapeutic change (T), and the clinical outcome (O)"* (p. 7; italics in original). This chapter is the story of my own often blind, but always exciting voyage in search of that goal I could not articulate.

I have one small piece of evidence that a harbinger of my voyage occurred in the spring of 1941 when I was a freshman at Jamestown College in Jamestown, North Dakota. I have been especially reminded of it because in recent times I was inducted into that school's Alumni Hall of Fame. I thought it was astonishing that the Board of Trustees of this small, private, church-sponsored college would even consider the esoteric accomplishments of a big-city research psychoanalyst from Gotham. But during my freshman English course, my professor, Marion Jackson, required each of us to write a research paper on any topic at all. The only requirement was that it be properly researched and well written. It turned out that there were almost no references in the college library for my chosen topic, "The Thinking Processes of the Sub-Conscious Mind." So, because my father was a railroad man and could get me free passes, I took a trip to the University of Minnesota, where I used the library and unearthed the French school of the turn of the century and completely missed any references to Freud, who was unknown to me then—hence "sub-conscious" instead of "unconscious."

After college and medical school, hungry for adventure, I interned at the famous Gorgas Hospital in the Panama Canal Zone. It was there that an intern from Kansas, Harry Hunter, and I rebuilt a tiny boat modeled on the African Queen and christened it *el*

Rubaiyat. On Good Friday, 1947, we set off for an island in the Pacific Ocean 12 miles offshore. At 5:00 p.m. we were swamped in a short squall and our boat overturned. We clung to the barnacled hull overnight and at sunrise, by jettisoning our 16 horsepower Johnson outboard engine, we were able to right the boat so we could sit on the inner bottom of the hull in the warm salt water up to our necks and expose our heads to the tropical sun. By sundown Saturday, none of the many ships that passed, nor the planes that flew over, had seen us.

Then I had my first experience of confirming what I later believed was one of Freud's great insights: the phenomenon of fulfilling a deep wish by hallucinating the experience of satisfaction (Freud, 1900/1953). After sunset, for what later seemed like hours, I stood at the water fountain in my ward at Gorgas drinking utterly delicious ice-cold water and contentedly watching the nurses and patients go about their business. Then silence—nothing. The next thing I knew I was lying on my back, unable to move, in a darkened bunk. A seaman saw my eyes open and told me that I was on the *U.S.S. Recovery*, a Coast Guard vessel that, on its last crisscrossing on the shore side of a well-known current headed toward Asia, had spotted us a half mile away, 70 miles offshore—on Easter Sunday afternoon.

The next morning in Gorgas Hospital, the superintendent came to see us after I had absorbed 8 liters of IV saline and worried about the white mush that passed for my skin. He simply said, "You must have been saved for something important."[2] This is the story of what I now imagine I was saved for. It is the story of a long voyage that led to Virginia Teller's and my discovery of a new way to represent the plots of the stories that patients tell when they lie on the couch and are told to say everything that comes to mind.

---

[2]As the reader will learn, beginning this report with a personal story is not as inappropriate as might at first appear. FRAMES are the plots of stories and, as clinicians will readily grasp, the narrator may be the last to understand their real significance. Events such as *daring, excitement, rescue, salvation,* and *arrogance* are the stuff of fables, folktales, and, yes, even of FRAMES.

Background

Of course, nobody can say everything that comes to mind, as Anna Freud (1936/1946, p. 15) well knew. It is the giving of the rule that is important, because it puts patients in such conflict that they cannot avoid expressing the variety of both their wishes and their defenses, and "free" means the freedom to be multiply constrained. Indeed, I agree with Ernest Jones (1953) when he wrote, "The devising of this method was one of the two great deeds of Freud's scientific life, the other being his self-analysis through which he learned to explore the child's early sexual life" (p. 241).

But in his self-analysis, Sigmund Freud discovered something much more important than the details of his early sexual life. He uncovered his own versions of the erotic attractions and jealous hatreds that he later proposed as an ubiquitous story of childhood. Moreover, his genius lay in his ability to recognize equivalent stories, both when they were heavily disguised—as in his own or his patients' dreams—*and* when they were the stuff of ancient legends like Sophocles' story of Oedipus Rex. Freud was able to extract the essential events of the plot and to recognize some of these events as symbolic equivalents of others. Not many little boys actually kill their fathers and marry their mothers, but Freud extracted the essential emotions of the plot: fear, jealousy, love, and guilt. By now the world has generally accepted the truth of Freud's astute generalization. He succeeded brilliantly in what Simon (1981) described as the task of science, that is, "to make use of the world's redundancy to describe that world simply" (p. 222). Freud captured the redundancy of the central emotions in a universal human story. And as we shall see, emotions proved to be the key to a new procedure for finding and representing FRAMES.

Simon (1981) also emphasized that how one represents a problem or a solution is all-important:

> That representation makes a difference is a long-familiar point. We all believe that arithmetic has become easier since Arabic numerals and place notation replaced Roman numerals, although I know of no theoretic treatment that explains why.
> That representation makes a difference is evident for a different reason. . . . [A]ll mathematical derivation can be viewed sim-

ply as change in representation, making evident what was previously true but obscure.
    This view can be extended to all of problem solving—solving
a problem simply means representing it so as to make the solution transparent. (p. 153)

I would add this: Complex problem solving involves a lot of free
association, of seemingly haphazard trials and errors, of twists and
turns that only in retrospect fit into a true picture of the discovery
process. It also requires careful recording of the steps, writing it
down, as it were. If the now well-known and widely studied psychoanalytic case of Mrs. C. had not been fully tape-recorded and
if many sessions had not been carefully transcribed, Teller would
not have found two crucial sentences in the transcript of hour 5—
and FRAMES, I am quite sure, would still be waiting to be discovered.[3] Nor would FRAMES be represented as they are now
were it not for benefactors and mentors who prepared me to recognize the new representations. Discoveries do not occur in a vac-
uum. So I believe it is important to understand some crucial precursors.

Emotions

In retrospect, the single most important requirement was a rational
classification system for emotions and a coherent theory of their
functions. In Masling's 1983 volume, I summarized two emotion
studies (Dahl, 1983): (a) an empirical classification of some 370
emotion labels (Dahl & Stengel, 1978) and (b) a new psychoanalytic
model of motivation postulating emotions as appetites and messages (Dahl, 1978). Except in Germany[4] these studies have been
widely ignored by the psychoanalytic community.
    The theory included three more or less radical propositions. First,
emotions share the central properties of *somatic appetites*—such as

---

[3]An additional partial bibliography of Mrs. C. studies is included at the
end of the main reference list.
[4]The volume *How to Classify Emotions for Psychotherapy Research* (Dahl,
Hölzer, & Berry, 1992) was published by the University of Ulm.

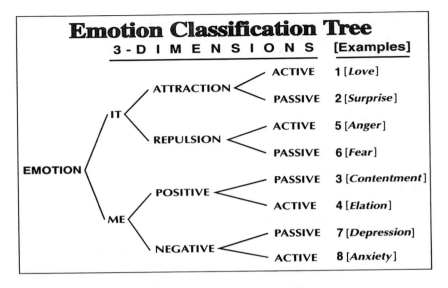

Figure 1. A 3-dimensional tree derived from Dahl & Stengel's (1978) emotion classification study. The examples shown were all empirically classified with a chance $p < 10^{-9}$.

thirst, hunger, and sex—rather than those of the psychoanalytic concept of *drives*. Second, emotions with objects, *IT emotions*, function essentially as appetitive *wishes* about those objects, while emotions that index an inner state, *ME emotions*, function as *beliefs* about the state of fulfillment or nonfulfillment of the wishes about the objects.[5] Third, the IT and ME emotions together form the core of an information feedback system that provides basic information about our most fundamental motives and their outcomes. The classification tree for emotions is shown in Figure 1. The schema in Figure 2 includes the eight main (plus eight transitional) categories, together with their arbitrary code numbers, their abstract definitions, examples of words empirically classified in them, and a statement of their functions as wishes or beliefs. Three variations of the theoretical information feedback model are displayed in Fig-

---

[5]Klein (1967) proposed an idea very similar to this when he rejected an energic drive discharge model and substituted the concept of satisfaction or nonsatisfaction of wishes.

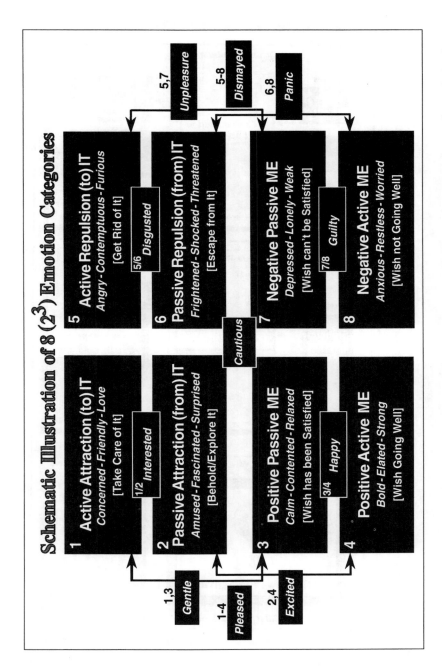

Figure 2. Eight main (plus 8 transition) emotion categories together with their arbitrary code numbers, their abstract definitions, typical examples of empirically classified emotion labels, and a statement of their generic functions as wishes or beliefs.

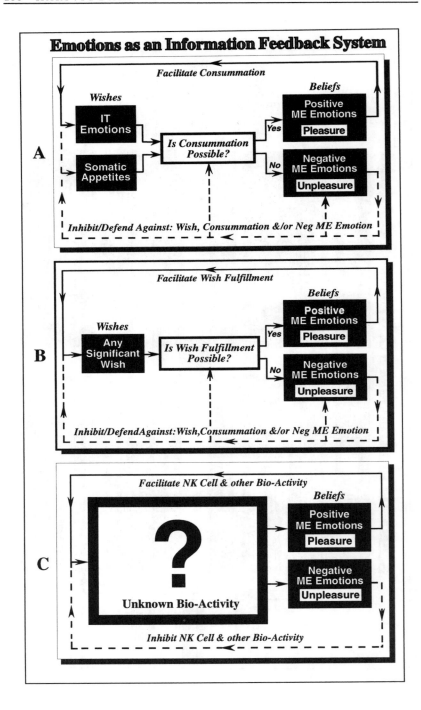

Emotions as an Information Feedback System

A

Facilitate Consummation

Wishes

IT Emotions

Somatic Appetites

Is Consummation Possible?

Yes

No

Beliefs

Positive ME Emotions — Pleasure

Negative ME Emotions — Unpleasure

Inhibit/Defend Against: Wish, Consummation &/or Neg ME Emotion

B

Facilitate Wish Fulfillment

Wishes

Any Significant Wish

Is Wish Fulfillment Possible?

Yes

No

Beliefs

Positive ME Emotions — Pleasure

Negative ME Emotions — Unpleasure

Inhibit/Defend Against: Wish, Consummation &/or Neg ME Emotion

C

Facilitate NK Cell & other Bio-Activity

?

Unknown Bio-Activity

Beliefs

Positive ME Emotions — Pleasure

Negative ME Emotions — Unpleasure

Inhibit NK Cell & other Bio-Activity

ure 3 (see panels A, B, and C). What all three figures implicitly claim is that the ME emotions are basic information about the state of our appetites, of our other wishes, and of our biological equilibria.[6]

Sharir (1991) empirically tested a cardinal prediction of the emotion theory, namely, that IT emotions (wishes) followed by Negative (NEG) ME emotions (beliefs that the wishes cannot be or are not likely to be fulfilled) are much more likely to be accompanied by or immediately followed by defenses than are IT emotions to be followed by Positive (POS) ME emotions (beliefs that the wishes are being or are likely to be fulfilled)—in short, the hypothesis that defenses are provoked by NEG ME emotions. She used the videotapes of three therapy sessions (early, middle, and late) from each of 26 short-term psychotherapy cases and had raters independently classify the emotions (according to Dahl & Stengel, 1978) and defenses (according to Vaillant, 1977) in each 2-minute segment. The mean Cohen's Kappa reliability measure for three different pairs of emotion raters was .73 ± .04.[7] Using sophisticated time-series analyses, she tested the hypothesis that defenses more closely follow NEG ME emotions than POS ME emotions. The re-

---

[6]I cannot review here the growing literature on the effect of reduced Negative (NEG) ME emotions on immune functions (O'Leary, 1990), NK (natural killer) cell activity in women with breast cancer (Levy, Herberman, Lippman, & D'Angelo, 1991), and prolonged survivals in cancer patients who received psychotherapy compared with controls (Spiegel, 1996).

[7]In classifying particular emotion expressions in transcripts, Silberschatz (1978) reported mean alpha coefficient reliabilities of .83 ± .04, and Seidman (1988) reported mean alpha coefficients of .76 ± .05.

Figure 3. (A) Representation of Dahl's theory of emotions as an Information Feedback System. Emotions with objects (IT emotions, e.g., love, surprise, anger, fear) function as appetitive wishes about objects. If the wish can be consummated, the result is a Positive ME emotion (e.g., contentment, joy). If the wish cannot be consummated, the result is a Negative ME emotion (e.g., anxiety, depression). (B) ME emotions provide feedback information about the status of satisfaction of any significant wishes. (C) ME emotions also provide feedback that affects the activity of NK cells and other immunological processes.

low NEG ME emotions than POS ME emotions. The results strongly supported the theory's prediction ($p < .001$).

An important advantage of these emotion categories and this theory is that they permit systematic explanations of much clinical knowledge about classical symptom and character diagnostic categories and about addictions and—surprisingly—include Luborsky's (1990) three main Core Conflictual Relationship Theme (CCRT) categories, albeit represented differently. Luborsky's three categories are Core wishes, Response of the other (RO), and Response of the Self (RS). In Figure 3, panels A and B, *wishes* correspond to Luborsky's core wishes. The RO corresponds to the question "Is consummation possible?" and the RS is the answer expressing the beliefs about the outcome of the core wishes. More recently I have also elaborated on the theoretically important relationships between emotions and defenses (Dahl, 1995).

Meanwhile, in addition to recordings and transcripts of Mrs. C., I had collected samples of 14 other partially recorded psychoanalytic (or long-term psychotherapy) cases. At Downstate Medical Center, Norbert Freedman, who was director of the psychology department and head of the Doctor of Medical Science program, permitted me to find a linguist to join our research group. I put a want ad in the *New York Times* requesting a linguist with computer background who was interested in doing psychoanalytic research.

Teller did not see the 1975 ad, but someone who knew her told her that she should apply. Skeptically, she did and was awarded what turned out to be two 2-year fellowships connected with Downstate's Research Training Program for Psychiatrists. She helped finish a book, *Word Frequencies of Spoken American English* (Dahl, 1979), a document based on one million words of speech taken from 15 hours of transcripts from each of the 15 different recorded cases that I had collected. And she joined Rubinstein (1978) and me in our ongoing study of clinical inference. It was in the course of these investigations that we discovered FRAMES.

In retrospect, it is possible to see the role played by each of the studies on which I reported earlier (in Masling, 1983) in preparing the soil for what proved to be Teller's linguistic seed. The ability of computer content analyses to represent the course of an unsuccessful analysis and the power of everyday factor analyses of word counts to reveal three clinically compelling word clusters persuaded me that there were indeed regularities and truths to be found with "objective" methods. And if any further motivation were needed, it was provided by our finding the strong biases that clinicians have in favor of evidence each has discovered for himself or herself (Dahl, 1983). While unsurprising in hindsight, these biases were nonetheless chastening and reinforced my belief that we desperately needed many more rigorous discovery and validation procedures if we were to have any hope of establishing a basic science foundation for psychoanalysis. My theory of emotions and a reliable and intuitively satisfying system for their classification are only now, as we shall see, proving their worth. It should be entirely clear how thoroughly I disagree with Eissler's (1969) astonishing claim that "the psychoanalytic situation has already given forth everything it contains" (p. 469).

The Search for Order

But beyond these earlier studies has been the pervasive influence of developments in the field of cognitive science since the first meeting of the Cognitive Science Society in 1979 at the University of California, San Diego. Of those in a long list who have most influenced me, none have captured the essence of the problem better than Simon (1981) in his account of how to find order in the enormous complexity of adaptive systems such as ourselves. Because he wrote so clearly, I quote him again:

> A man, viewed as a behaving system, is quite simple. The apparent complexity of his behavior over time is largely a reflection of the complexity of the environment in which he finds himself. . . . Behavior is adapted to goals, hence is artificial, hence reveals only those characteristics of the behaving system that limit adaptation. (p. 95)

This is a truly profound idea, and when I first heard him say this in 1979, I was immediately reminded of a 20-year project led by Barker (1968) of the University of Kansas. Barker and Wright were social psychologists who set up a branch of their department in Oskaloosa, Kansas, in order to exhaustively describe social settings of that small midwestern town. For example, they cataloged in minute detail the things people did and said in literally more than 200 places such as churches, drugstores, grain elevators, garages, restaurants, schools, scout meetings, and grocery stores. In the end, they were disappointed that they could predict only 50% of people's behavior by knowing where they were! Their disappointment is understandable only in their own terms; in my terms, they had simply documented (ahead of time) Simon's profound truth.

At the same 1979 meeting, Minsky (see Minsky, 1975) got to the core of a central problem in getting machines to understand the world in ways that people simply take for granted, a key issue in artificial intelligence. Here is his famous two-sentence illustration: "Mary was invited to Jack's party. She wondered if he would like a kite." What people in our culture have little trouble understanding is that this is a children's birthday party. Mary is wondering what gift to give and, usually, only children think of kites as appropriate. In the end, Minsky invented the term *frames* to refer to generalized *plots* of stories, with common sense supplying the expected default values for missing elements. In other words, he focused on the role of common sense in our knowledge of the plots—that is, the structures—of stories.

A related profound influence came from both Simon and Bertrand Russell, but Russell (1948), for me, best expressed the central idea, namely, that "structure" is the heart of the matter. Let me use his example. Imagine Beethoven's writing the score of the Fifth Concerto for Pianoforte. Picture, if you can, the structure of this magnificent work in his brain. Of course you cannot, but you will agree that in some way unknown to us, the structure was in fact represented in Beethoven's neurons. Then picture an orchestra and a pianist with these scores and a conductor with memories of these scores, each member playing a small piece of the total structure. Now the structure in Beethoven's head appears as complex sound waves carried in analog representation in the air of the auditorium. Add the members of the audience and each of their private representations of this same complex structure. Now look at the microphone and envision the electromagnetic waves carrying this identical structure through what we used to call the "ether" to machines that convert these back to sound waves in the air to audiences listening on their radios. Again, each listener reproduces in his or her brain the same structure and "hears" the same music. There is no easy concrete way to capture this simplicity and complexity. It can be represented only abstractly, but we all understand it. That is a truly amazing demonstration of the orderliness waiting to be discovered.

The Discovery of FRAMES

Now we come to the orderliness that Teller and I found in the transcript of Hour 5 (Anonymous, 1988) of Mrs. C. Here is the seed, the first two sentences of paragraph 20 as they originally appeared in the transcript:

> And yesterday I had been thinking about calling the parents— and yesterday—just to let them know that, if the children were kind of upset at what I was doing, the reason for it would be this, and that they, if they wanted to support it, they could by explaining that there were lots of boys to be friends with at the school and that type of thing. And—but I hadn't called them and I saw one of the mothers at the dismissal when she came to pick up her boy.

One day, while Teller, Rubinstein, and I were studying this transcript as part of our continuing investigation into the nature of psychoanalytic inference,[8] Teller said that these two sentences were peculiar, linguistically. I passed this by, but after about 6 months, I could not bear not understanding the puzzle any longer. All the details of Teller's analysis of these sentences are described in Teller and Dahl (1981, 1986). Here I will show only the change in punctuation that made apparent that what originally appeared to be one event actually involved four events:

> **And yesterday**—*I had been thinking about calling the parents*— **and yesterday**—just to let them know that, if the children were kind of upset at what I was doing, the reason for it would be

---

[8] A long inquiry which, in the end, yielded little.

<u>this</u>, and that they, if they wanted to support it, they could by explaining that there were lots of boys to be friends with at the school and that type of thing. **And**—*but I hadn't called them*— **and I saw one of the mothers at the dismissal when she came to pick up her boy.**

It turned out that the story of what happened "yesterday" was contained in just 613 words in three paragraphs, 18 through 20.[9] The bold text refers literally to yesterday's event. The italicized text refers to a phone call the patient had been thinking of making before yesterday but hadn't yet made. The underlined part gives details of a request she made to the parents and the rest describes what the parents could do in return. We then focused on understanding the entire three paragraphs. After long study, and particularly because we were actively looking for repetitive events, we made several lists of events that occurred more than once in this 5-minute segment:

Support

1. Wanted approval from her husband
2. Wanted support from the parents

Delays (avoided certain acts)

1. In telling the analyst about the episode
2. In telling her husband
3. In calling the parents
4. In talking to the mother at dismissal

Conflicts

1. Over the boys' being too much together
2. Over trying to separate the boys
3. Over her annoyance with the boys
4. Over inappropriately confronting a mother
5. Over her husband's lack of response

---

[9]These paragraphs appear in Teller and Dahl (1986, pp. 768–769).

Hostility

1. Overt anger at her husband
2. Covert hostile action toward the mother
3. Did not tell the analyst about the episode

But these lists were unsatisfying. We had found repetition, but the lists seemed unconnected with each other. What would one do next, add items to each list and add new lists? "Where was the structure?" was the implicit but unasked question, until one day it occurred to both of us that we were dealing, not with unrelated lists, but with two or three stories constructed much like some Chinese menus: an item from each list! And after our discovery, but not before, it was immediately obvious that we had identified plots of stories—what Minsky had described in other terms—hence our choice of his word, *frames*.[10] And most important, we discovered that what we called a Prototype Frame (a simple, complete story structure) could be reenacted (instantiated) with different persons in different settings, especially in interaction with the analyst. Indeed, instantiations with the analyst provide powerful and compelling demonstrations of how to represent what clinicians call *transference*. Later we will examine in detail the role of transference at a moment of change in Mrs. C.

The next figures show three of our early FRAMES from Hour 5 (Mrs. C). Figure 4 shows the structure of the first two FRAMES we found, Delay and Support, and Exhibit 1 shows examples of the manifest data that justified each event of the Support Prototype.[11] Figure 5 shows the original Critical/Friendly Prototype. Figure 6 represents an interaction between the Support and Delay FRAMES in an Instantiation (repetition) in which these plots are enacted with the analyst in the transference (Dahl, 1988; Teller, 1988; Dahl

---

[10] I converted this to the acronym (**F**undamental **R**epetitive **A**nd **M**aladaptive **E**motion **S**tructures) much later, after we began representing each event as an expression of an emotion.

[11] Teller and Dahl (1986) and Dahl and Teller (1994) described in some detail these early procedures for constructing the FRAMES.

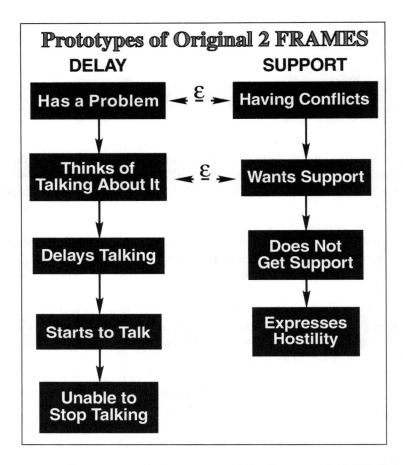

Figure 4.   The events of the Prototypes of the first two FRAMES, Delay and Support, which were identified in paragraphs 18–20. The double arrows with ∈ indicate that the two events in the different FRAMES are members of the same set.

& Teller, 1994; Teller & Dahl, 1981, 1986, 1993). In addition to Delay, Support, and Critical/Friendly, we found two other FRAMES in Hour 5: Control [Acts Inhibited ⇒ Acts Aggressive ⇒ Tries to Control] and Togetherness [Being Close Together ⇒ Dismayed/Dissatisfied ⇒ Tries to Separate]. In addition to these five Prototypes, we found 19 Instantiations, 4 with the analyst (see Table 1).

The Instantiations with the analyst are manifestly transference

Exhibit 1

Documentation of the Supporting Evidence for Each Event in the Support FRAME Prototype

---

1. JUSTIFICATION for **HAVING CONFLICTS**
   Statements about "the thing I did":
   ¶18 ... *either confirmation that I'd done the right thing or a suggestion on what would be a right thing because I wasn't sure. I was upset about something I'd done.*
   ¶18 ... *that wasn't that bad a thing to do.*
2. JUSTIFICATION for **WANTS SUPPORT**
   ¶18 *I was talking to him wanting either confirmation that I'd done the right thing or a suggestion on what would be a right thing.*
   ¶18 *I didn't want him just to listen to me say it. I wanted him to actually react to it, and either suggest another course of action, or, or approval that, well, I guess that in the circumstances that wasn't that bad a thing to do.*
   ASSUMPTION: Spoken approval is one kind of support.
3. JUSTIFICATION for **DOES NOT GET SUPPORT**
   ¶18 *And, and he just didn't say anything, except sort of mutter under his breath.*
4. JUSTIFICATION for **EXPRESSES HOSTILITY**
   ¶18 *And so I got furious at him.*
   WARRANTS FOR INDUCTIVE GENERALIZATION
   ¶18 *I probably do the same thing with David* [husband].
   ¶18 *Last night in particular, I was talking with him ...*
   ¶18 *... and (sniff) I imagine in a way it's the same kind of thing that my father always is doing.*

---

enactments. It did indeed appear that we had found what Simon foresaw, that is, "those characteristics of the behaving system that limit adaptation"—the repetitive and maladaptive behavior structures. Moreover, Dahl (1988) demonstrated that each Prototype implicitly constitutes a prediction that it will repeat and therefore is equivalent to an empirically testable clinical hypothesis.

Problems

But problems remained. First and foremost were the implicit, but not then clearly recognized, difficulties associated with using man-

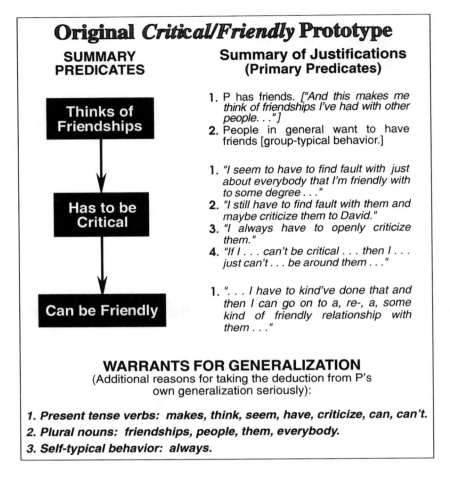

Figure 5. The Prototype of the original Critical/Friendly FRAME structure derived from ¶48 of Hour 5 (Anonymous, 1988).

ifest patient statements as the source of evidence. These posed a minimal problem in identifying Prototypes; for Instantiations, however, what constituted equivalent statements was a matter of differing and sometimes conflicting interpretations of the meanings. To solve this problem, Leeds and Bucci (1984) proposed a rigorous but time-consuming—and ultimately frustrating—systematic procedure for finding FRAMES. The method did not work with analytic transcripts (Leeds, 1988) but succeeded in Davies'

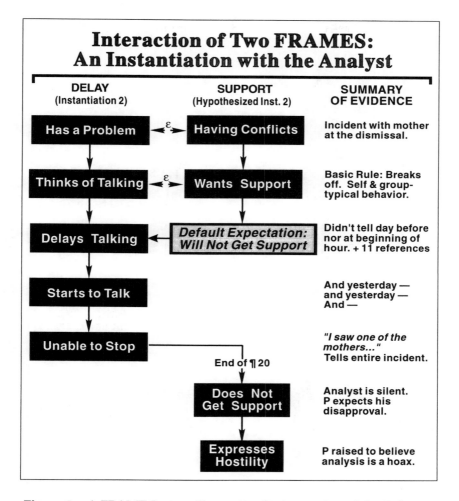

**Interaction of Two FRAMES:
An Instantiation with the Analyst**

DELAY (Instantiation 2)	SUPPORT (Hypothesized Inst. 2)	SUMMARY OF EVIDENCE
Has a Problem ◄ε► Having Conflicts		Incident with mother at the dismissal.
Thinks of Talking ◄ε► Wants Support		Basic Rule: Breaks off. Self & group-typical behavior.
Delays Talking ◄ Default Expectation: Will Not Get Support		Didn't tell day before nor at beginning of hour. + 11 references
Starts to Talk		And yesterday — and yesterday — And —
Unable to Stop	End of ¶ 20	"I saw one of the mothers..." Tells entire incident.
	Does Not Get Support	Analyst is silent. P expects his disapproval.
	Expresses Hostility	P raised to believe analysis is a hoax.

Figure 6.   A FRAME System illustrating the interaction of the Delay and Support FRAMES in an Instantiation with the analyst.

(1988) study of the behavior of 3-year-olds. She found repetitive patterns of interactions of each of 12 children with 3 other persons (mother and 2 children) that were different for each child.

It was possible, however, to understand the source of the failure and the success. To solve the problem of categorizing an indeterminate set of behaviors, the method that Leeds and Davies used required a predetermined set whose identification reliabilities

Table 1

The 5 Prototype and 19 Instantiation FRAMES

Instance	FRAMES	Object	E_1	E_2	E_3	E_4	E_5
Prototype	**Control**	**In a Course**	**56**	**56**	**56**		
I_1	Control	Hus & Tel	12/13	14	12–14		
I_2	Control	Parents	20	21/22	21		
I_3	Control	H & Money	57/58	58	58		
I_4	Control	Assistant	1	2/4	3/9		
I_5	Control	By father	15	15	15		
Prototype	**Critical/Friendly**	**Anybody**	**48**	**48**	**48**		
I_1	Critical/Friendly	Assistant	1	2	1/3		
I_2	Critical/Friendly	*Analyst	47/48	52	61/62		
Prototype	**Delay**	**Boys/Pars**	**19/20**	**20**	**20**	**20**	**20**
I_1	Delay	Husband	19/20	18	18	18	—
I_2	Delay	*Analyst	18–20	18	18–20	19/20	20
I_3	Delay	BuyClothes	60/62	62	60	60	60
I_4	Delay	Telephone	15	—	15	15	15
I_5	Delay	By father	15	—	15	15	
Prototype	**Support**	**Husband**	**18**	**18**	**18**	**18**	
I_1	Support	Boys/Pars	18–20	20	20	20	
I_2	Support	*Analyst	18–20	20	46	52	
I_3	Support	By father	16/17	17	17	17	
Prototype	**Togetherness**	**Boys**	**19**	**19**	**19/20**		
I_1	Togetherness	Professor	55	55	—		
I_2	Togetherness	*Analyst	53/54	53–56	56		
I_3	Togetherness	Father	13/16	16/17	13		
I_4	Togetherness	By father	16	16/17	16		

Note. Objects and paragraph numbers are shown where the evidence for each event was found. E_n = Event sequence with the paragraph numbers where the evidence was found; I_n = Instantiation number. Dashes indicate no evidence found for the event.

could be readily assessed. The range of categories was totally inadequate to capture the range of behaviors and states of the adult analytic case, but it covered a much larger share of the behaviors of the 3-year-old children. Stern (1985), from a developmental point of view, offered a related notion of Representations of Interactions that are Generalized (RIGs), which he described as follows:

> Lived episodes immediately become the specific episodes for memory, and with repetition they become generalized episodes . . . that is, representations of interactions that have been generalized, or RIGs. . . . It is important to remember that RIGs are flexible structures that average several actual instances and form a prototype to represent them all. A RIG is something that has never happened before exactly that way, yet it takes into account nothing that did not actually happen once. (p. 110)

Here it must be emphasized that much later follow-ups would be necessary to determine whether the repetitive patterns exhibited by Davies' 3-year-olds were and would remain flexible and adaptive or whether they would develop the rigid, repetitive, and maladaptive character of FRAMES.

Solutions

Hölzer (1991) in Ulm, Germany solved the behavior category problem that plagued Leeds by recognizing that almost all the events in FRAMES already discovered were expressions of emotions. He therefore proposed using emotion classifications to identify and categorize the texts. This had two major consequences. First, the extraordinary redundancy of emotions in typical texts allowed him to find an event that Teller and I had missed in the Critical/ Friendly FRAME structure. This then led to the insight that the new FRAME structure had two alternative outcomes, not one outcome as we had originally claimed. Second, now the categories of expressed emotions provided the basic FRAME events and their sequence was, as before, determined by the story structure.

Hölzer also suggested revising the method of mapping the text that Teller and I had used in 1981 and 1986 to construct what we then called a category map in which the columns represented the topics that the patient talked about and the row entries were the paragraph and sentence numbers that included the text. Hölzer proposed substituting objects (usually persons) for topics. Thus, an Object Map is a table in which each column represents successive objects (people) about whom the patient talks, and each row entry (keeping the text sequence in order) specifies the paragraph and sentence numbers of the beginning and end of talk about each object. For finding FRAMES, this map serves a function similar to Luborsky's Relationship Episodes in finding CCRTs, that is, to identify segments of the text that are good candidates for finding prototype (and later, instantiated) FRAMES. Figure 7 is the object map of Hour 5.

The switch to emotion categories and object maps led to a 5-step procedure for finding FRAMES (Hölzer & Dahl, 1996). Step 1 is to establish criteria for selecting the sessions. Step 2 is to classify the emotions in each session. Step 3 is to construct an Object Map for each session and highlight cells with sufficient text to offer opportunity for finding Prototypes or Instantiations. Step 4 consists of (a) examining likely stories, (b) listing the sequence of classified emotions (events), and (c) noting the different categories of emotions found. Step 5 involves determining the plot of the story and arranging the discrete emotion categories in the proper order followed by the mechanical process of constructing a diagram to reflect the plot (see Figure 8). But how do we know the proper sequence? Mainly from a commonsense reading, as Minsky claimed.

There is wide agreement in the literature on what constitute the basic plot elements of any story (e.g., Dyer, 1983; Lehnert, 1982; Rumelhart, 1977; Stein, 1982). According to Lehnert, these are (a) a specific protagonist capable of wishing and believing, (b) the protagonist's wishes and beliefs, (c) actions carried out by the protagonist in the service of the wishes, and (d) information about the outcome: satisfaction or nonsatisfaction of the wishes. It should be obvious how these four elements correspond to the functions of my emotion theory categories. Moreover, these components define what would be the clearest kind of Prototype, that is, one that explicitly includes all of the four elements. In an Instantiation, if one event is missing, one may substitute, as a default value, the event from the Prototype as a tentative hypothesis.

This new procedure was first applied to the text of paragraph

48 in Hour 5. Teller and Dahl's original, largely commonsensical and intuitive method for finding FRAMES had, in the case of the Critical/Friendly FRAME, overlooked the patient's expression of *feeling inferior*—an event identified as a result of Hölzer's insight that the events in the plots are systematically represented in expressions of emotion. Each emotion expression is underlined and followed by its category code in the text of ¶48:[12]

> ¶48   And this makes me think of uhm, (stomach rumble) *friendships I've had with other people* [1] and, *something that I don't like to admit* [7], because *I don't approve of it* [1SN → 5AS] (nervous chuckle), so *I can't imagine anybody else would* [1SN], but *I seem to have to find fault with just about everybody* [5A] that *I'm friendly with to some degree* [1] *whether it's just a small degree or a larger degree* [1]. And, even though in a way *I might feel inferior to them* [7], and *I imagine I feel inferior to a lot of people* [7], *I still have to find fault with them* [5A] and *maybe criticize them to David* [5A], I don't know. *I always have to openly criticize them* [5A], but in any case *I have to kind've done that* [5A] and then I can go on to a re-, a, *some kind of friendly relationship with them* [1]. And *until I've done that* [5A] I *can't really accept them as somebody that I want to be at all close to in any way at all* [1N]. And, and if I can't, *if I find I can't be critical of them in some aspect* [5AN], then *I just can't seem to be around them at all* [1AN]. I, I, I don't know, it's more than sort of being, well, *it's not being in awe of them* [2N]. *It's just feeling very uncomfortable,* [7/8] I guess, with them.

Figure 8 shows the new Critical/Friendly FRAMES, constructed according to the new method, which dramatically reveals the two different outcomes. First the classified emotions are simply listed in the order in which they appear in the text of the transcript. After the different categories are noted, the story content is examined, the plot formulated, and the emotion categories arranged to correspond. This shows that the original FRAME structure omitted a significant event, namely, the patient's expression of feeling inferior. The new method made clear the need to represent two different endings to the FRAME, one in which the patient was able to

---

[12]The emotion category numbers are arbitrary (see Figures 1 and 2 and Dahl, Hölzer, & Berry, 1992). Additional category codes: A = consummatory act; N = negation; S = toward self.

Assistant	Other Teacher	Boys	Other Girl	Super-visor	Other Woman	Other People	Self	Husband	Parent	Father	Mother	Two Boys in School	Their Mother(s)	Students' Parents	Analyst	Husb.'s Analyst	Pro-fessor
1,1-3																	
1,4-2,5	1,4-2,5																
2,6-10																	
3,1-4		3,1-4															
4,1-2																	
		4,2-2															
4,3-3																	
5,1-2			5,1-2														
5,3-7,3																	
				8,1-1													
8,1-3																	
					8,4-4												
8,4-9,1																	
		9,2-5															
9,6-10,2																	
						11,1-1											
							11,1-12,2										
								12,2-2									
							12,3-3									
								12,4-13,1									
									13,1-1								
								13,2-14,8									
							15,1-4										
									15,5-5								
										15,5-6	15,5-6						
										16,1-2							
										16,3-6	16,3-6						
										16,7-17,7							
								18,1-9									
										18,9-9							

												19,1-6					
												20,1-2	20,1-2				
														20,3-3			
													20,4-8				
							20,8-21,1										
														21,2-26,1			
															28,1-40,4		
													40,4-6				
															42,1-46,3		
								46,4-5									
															46,5-7		
								47,1-2									
								47,3-4								47,3-4	
															47,4-5		
						48,1-7											
															50,1-54,1		
																	55,1-6
						56,1-9											
															57,1-1		
								57,1-1									
							57,2-4										
								58,1-6									
							59,1-60,7										
															61,1-2		
						62,1-8											

Figure 7. An Object Map of Hour 5 of Mrs. C. A glance at the columns indicates who the main objects being talked about are and whether the analyst is among them. Blackened cells are prime candidates for places to find FRAMES.

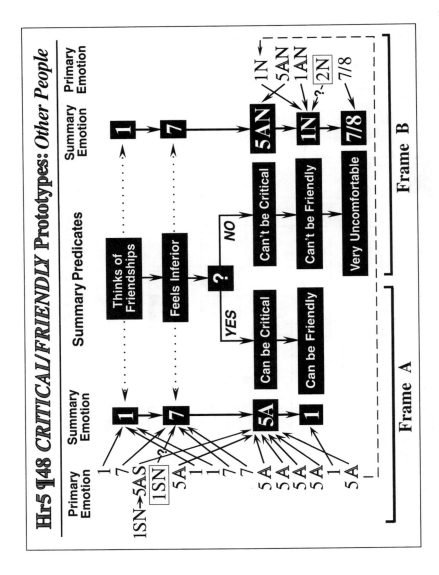

Figure 8. The new method for finding FRAMES has been applied to a reconstruction of the Critical/Friendly FRAMES from ¶48 of Hour 5.

be critical and then friendly, and the other in which she could not be critical and ended up being "very uncomfortable." What this new structure supports is the clinical hypothesis that the patient could overcome or undo her inferior feelings if and only if she could be critical.

Siegel and Sammons (1997) proposed computing the reliability of formulating plots by computing a percent agreement that reflects how similarly the raters assign each emotion code to a particular sequence in the particular FRAME structure.[13] On eight early, middle, and late hours of Mrs. C., the mean agreements between two raters was 74% (range 57–84) on a total of 323 events. Note that now the events are represented as emotion categories (with summary predicates along for the ride). No longer is the FRAME structure defined by the linguistic predicates, but rather by the sequence of specific emotion expressions. This makes finding and matching Instantiations a more rigorous, defined process.

Although each Prototype FRAME structure constitutes a prediction that it will occur again—which can be empirically tested by searching for Instantiations—this is not the only kind of prediction that arises from detailed examination of the manifest content of what patients say. A perceptive reader of ¶48 will note that it contains two other implicit and testable predictions. The first is that there should be more critical than friendly expressions, because the patient cannot always be critical and can be friendly only if she can be critical. Thus, being critical is a necessary but not a sufficient condition for being friendly. L. Horowitz (1977) noted this and tested that prediction using all the manifest Critical or Friendly statements taken from the analyst's detailed process notes for the first 100 hours of the same analysis. As shown in Figure 9, the number of Critical expressions was significantly greater ($t = 2.49$, $df = 9$, $p < .05$) than the Friendly expressions over 10 blocks of 10 hours each.

---

[13]For example, in Figure 8, each rater assigns each emotion code to one of the sequences in the FRAME structure. Thus, if each rater assigned the order 1, 7, 5A, 1 for the "yes" branch and the order 1, 7, 5AN, 1N, 7/8 for the "no" branch, then the agreement would be 100%. If one rater reversed the sequence of one event compared with the other rater, then they would disagree on two events and their agreement would be 78%.

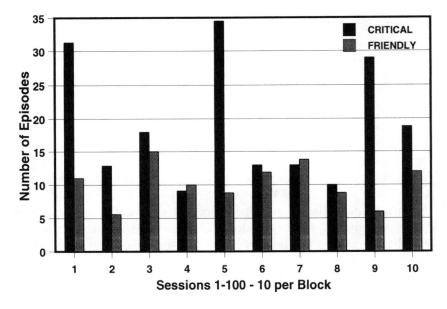

Figure 9.   A plot of the number of Critical and Friendly expressions over 10 blocks of 10 hours of detailed analyst process notes from a study by L. Horowitz (1977).

The second implicit prediction was that Critical expressions should precede Friendly expressions. Figure 10 is a plot of Horowitz's rated directness of Critical and Friendly expressions across the same blocks of 10 sessions. Although highly correlated because the directness of each expression increased over time, the correlation is insignificant ($r_{cf \cdot t} = .01$) when time is partialed out. However, as shown in Figure 11, when Critical expressions in the first block are plotted against Friendly expressions in the second block, and so forth, then the "lag" correlation, after partialing out time, is $r_{c(f+1) \cdot t} = .89$, $df = 6$, $p < .005$, a result that strongly supports the second prediction.

This new procedure has now rediscovered all of the previously identified Prototype FRAMES in Mrs. C. An ongoing research project is systematically identifying FRAMES and defenses in a total of 23 Mrs. C sessions distributed throughout her analysis as well as in early, middle, and late sessions from each of 14 other

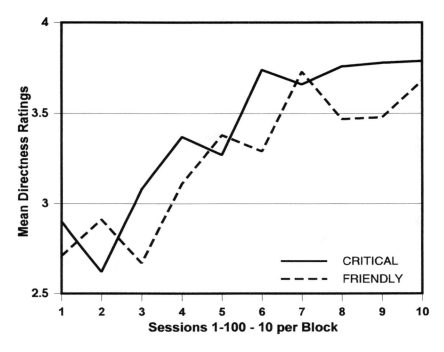

Figure 10.   A plot of the rated directness of the Critical and Friendly expressions across 10 blocks of 10 sessions each.

psychoanalytic cases. Thus far, FRAMES have been easily identified in 18 psychoanalytic and dynamic psychotherapeutic cases.

Luborsky, Popp, and Barber (1994) compared FRAMES with six other "transference-related measures"[14] that were used to assess the patient's pathology from a lengthy initial evaluation interview (Smithfield Interview, 1994). Two separate methods—paired comparison judge's ratings and cluster analyses—both showed that, of

[14]Core Conflictual Relationship Theme (CCRT; Luborsky, Popp, Luborsky, & Mark, 1994); Structural Analysis of Social Behavior–Cyclic Maladaptive Pattern (SASB-CMP; Schacht & Henry, 1994); Consensual Response Psychodynamic Formulation (CRPF; L. Horowitz & Rosenberg, 1994); Ideographic Conflict Formulation (ICF; Perry, 1994); Configurational Analysis (CA; M. Horowitz, 1994); Plan Formulation (PF; Weiss, Sampson, & Mount Zion Psychotherapy Research Group, 1986).

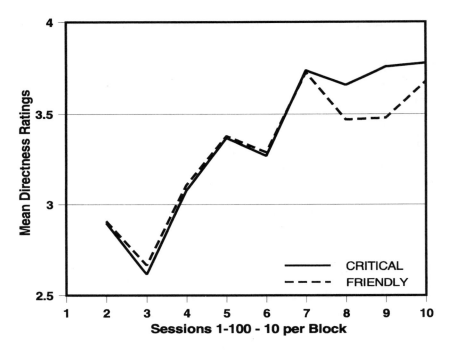

Figure 11. A "lag" plot of the Critical expressions in the first block against the Friendly expressions in the second block, and so on.

the seven measures, CCRTs, SASBs, and FRAMES were most similar to each other in their ability to represent the pathology.

It should be apparent by now that FRAMES do indeed measure "the clinical problem" (i.e., the patient's pathology). But they can also represent structures in a variety of other texts. To illustrate, I will show FRAMES found in (a) a reported nightmare of a hospitalized patient, (b) a note Karl Menninger sent me when I was a psychiatry resident in Topeka, (c) a therapist's interpretation, and not surprisingly, (d) the legend of Oedipus Rex.

The nightmare of a hospitalized woman was reported at the beginning of the 20th recorded therapy session and on the eve of the patient's discharge from the hospital.

¶1   {1} Well Tuesday night I had a (pause)—Tuesday night I saw you (pause). {2} That night I had a really bad night [6] (pause). {3} I went to sleep at 12—after 12 (pause) and I, and I was having a nightmare [6] (pause). {4} And I, I, you know, like for a while I didn't realize I was. {5} And then you do and you want to wake up and you keep saying to yourself you have to wake up [6A] because then you'll know it's only a dream (pause). {6} And I couldn't, you know, (pause). {7} By the time I did which was at 12 to 3 I ran out of that room (pause) completely terrified [6]—so (pause) no coordination. {8} I knocked things off the dresser [6A] really panic-stricken [6–8]. {9} And I went up to the desk and, and Mr. LBT was there and I couldn't talk (pause) and perspiration was just running off me [6–8] (pause). {10} And ah, ah, he gave me a cigarette. {11} I couldn't hold the cigarette [7] so he lit it and I was a mess (pause). {12} From 20 after 3 I stayed up. {13} I refused to even go in the room [6A] (pause). {14} I used the bathroom in the quiet room so I could have the lights on [6A] in the room because my roommate was asleep (pause).

¶2   {1} Now (pause) uhm not only was I upset [8] at the fact of that I had dreamed, I was upset [8] because I was so upset [8], you know. {2} Like I was thinking to myself in fact I had mentioned it to he and Mr. QXN that (pause) had I been home (pause) when this had happened. {3} And it has happened before (pause) and I wake up like that, you know. {4} And I'm by myself I panic [6–8] that much more here, like fine I ran out to the desk and there's people just sitting there waiting for you, you know (pause). {5} Ah I have gone so far as to call a friend at 3:30 in the morning [6A] which is a hell of a time to wake somebody up to tell them that you're terrified [6] (pause), you know, ah and it kind of threw me [8]. {6} And I was very moody and quiet yesterday [7, 8] because I felt that (pause) wow if, if I'm like this here it's OK, but what am I going to do if I am so frightened [6] and I'm home alone (pause)?

¶3   {1} See now in, in the dream I was killing this girl [5A]. {2} I don't remember the beginning because, you know, when you wake up you just remember what was happening at the immediate end (pause). {3} Huh, but I know she had blonde hair (pause) and she was cute and, you know, I was smashing her head in [5A] (pause). {4} And of course like the first couple of times (pause) that I went to hit her [5A] she was like (pause) pleading with me [7], you know, not to huh. {5} And there were, there were a lot of people outside of the room. {6} And the door, I had locked the door and they were all yelling [5A], you know, (pause) for me to let them in and, you know, kicking on the door [5A] and what not. {7} And, and they didn't get in in time (pause) for when, when they did break the door in [5A] (pause) I was covered with blood [5AS], you know. {8} Like her hair was all knotted together [5A]. {9} It was really sick [5A]. {10}

And (pause) when they came over to, to the bed to see what I had done I remember that I had turned around and I was screaming at them [5A] that "you see I told you I would huh and they didn't believe me and I hope you're all satisfied now [5A]." {11} (Pause) And that's when I ran out of the room [6A], you know,—

Figure 12 shows the FRAME structure of the nightmare story. The sequence of emotions in the text dramatically illustrates that the patient did not tell the story in chronological order. The logical beginning, namely her killing a girl, is told at the end, whereas she related her terrified response at the beginning. Throughout, she referred to feeling upset. But there is not much room for doubt about the logical order of the story.

When I was a resident in psychiatry, Karl Menninger sent me a note on his private notepad stationery after a class session in which I had accepted his offer to present my description of a patient (see Dahl, 1995 for a full account of the incident). I began, "The patient was a warm and friendly. . . ." He interrupted me with, "What do you mean, warm?" I replied, "I think you know what I mean, Dr. Karl." After a full minute of looking down at his desk and saying absolutely nothing, he changed the subject. When I returned to my ward after lunch, the following note in his own handwriting was waiting for me (I have added emotion codes):

Dear Dr. Dahl—
    I sincerely apologize [1A] for losing my temper [5A] and speaking so sharply to you [5A] today. There is no way for you to know [5A] how much I want to get certain ideas across in a too short period. As one of the more alert and responsive students [1A], you surprised me so [2] with your reaction that I was thrown off balance. I don't mean to justify myself or neutralize this apology [1A] with this explanation.
    I know you are working hard [1A] and trying to cooperate and improve [5A]. You've been a distinct help to me in the course [1A]. I'd be very sorry [1A] to think I did anything to discourage [5A] or hurt you permanently [5A].

                    KAM

Figure 13 shows the FRAME structure of this brief note. I will leave it to those who knew KAM to decide how accurately this structure captures a central personality characteristic.

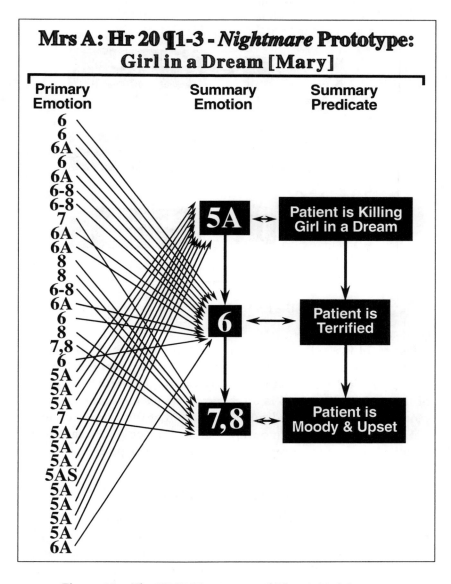

Figure 12.   The FRAME structure of Mrs. A.'s nightmare.

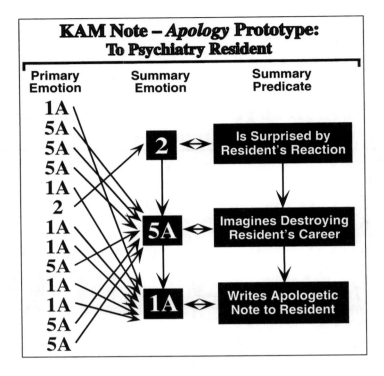

Figure 13.   The FRAME structure of KAM's note.

Figure 14 is a self-explanatory FRAME structure of an analyst's intervention. It is meant only to illustrate the potential for comparing the FRAME structures, if any, of an intervention with those of the patient. Figure 15 is a schematic representation of the basic plot of the legend of Oedipus Rex. Note that this construction did not follow the procedure outlined above; for obvious reasons, the emotion events are extrapolated from the larger plot.

Claims for FRAMES

My basic claim is that FRAMES are prime candidates for Strupp et al.'s (1988) problem-treatment-outcome (PTO) congruence measure. They portray essential elements of a patient's pathology (P), or the "clinical problem." To put it in coarse language, they capture the same dumb things that people do over and over, with different

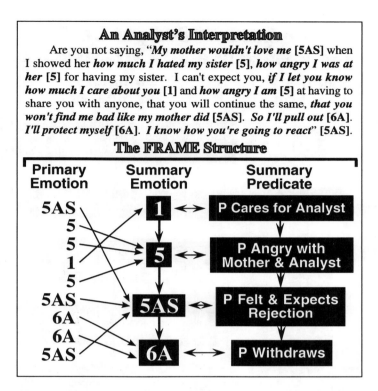

An Analyst's Interpretation

Are you not saying, "*My mother wouldn't love me* [5AS] when I showed her *how much I hated my sister* [5], *how angry I was at her* [5] for having my sister. I can't expect you, *if I let you know how much I care about you* [1] and *how angry I am* [5] at having to share you with anyone, that you will continue the same, *that you won't find me bad like my mother did* [5AS]. *So I'll pull out* [6A]. *I'll protect myself* [6A]. *I know how you're going to react*" [5AS].

The FRAME Structure

Primary Emotion	Summary Emotion	Summary Predicate
5AS	**1** ↔	P Cares for Analyst
5		
5	**5** ↔	P Angry with Mother & Analyst
1		
5		
5AS	**5AS** ↔	P Felt & Expects Rejection
6A		
6A	**6A** ↔	P Withdraws
5AS		

Figure 14. The FRAME structure of an analyst's interpretation.

people, in different situations, at different times—the heart of repetitive, maladaptive behaviors. The specific structure and content of a Prototype implicitly constitutes a hypothesis that the same sequence of events will occur again. Thus, documented Instantiations serve to confirm this prediction and provide evidence for its validity. Failure to find repetitions is presumptive evidence against the validity of the particular Prototype. Moreover, a FRAME structure significantly constrains what can be considered as evidence, since events in an Instantiation must be classifiable as the same emotion categories (with supplementary summary predicates) and the logical sequence of the categories (the *plot*) must be the same as that in the Prototype.

In addition, FRAMES can be found not only in narratives (therapy transcripts, personal notes, therapist's interpretations, fables,

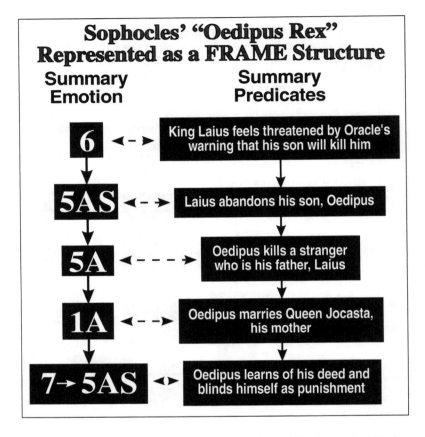

Figure 15.   A FRAME structure representation of the legend of Oedipus Rex.

etc.), but also in the observed behavior of children (Davies, 1988), which in principle opens up an entirely new way to study the developmental origins of maladaptive behavior. And, in contrast to some other measures of pathology (P), FRAMES capture the *specific* maladaptive structures of each person, that is, the plots fit the person instead of the person fitting a universal plot, as in Luborsky's CCRT with its invariant sequence: Wish ⇒ RO ⇒ RS. If a CCRT is used to assess change (T) or outcome (O), it must be done by showing that the content of these three categories changes, rather than their structure.

FRAMES are also clear candidates for measuring clinical outcome (O). If they continue to recur and do not change, then the treatment did not accomplish clearly defined goals and would be considered a failure. On the other hand, if the FRAMES do change, then the nature of those changes will measure the degree of success or failure. In a recent pilot study, Siegel and Sammons (1997) examined 11 sessions of Mrs. C. scattered throughout the treatment. Their central finding about outcome was that in the middle and late hours, none of the FRAMES in Hour 5 were found unchanged. By the end of the analysis, the most recurrent early FRAME structure, Support, had undergone distinct changes. The first two events, Having Problems [7, 8] and Wanting Support [1AS] continued to recur, but the most striking fact is the variety of subsequent events. For example, the patient might be troubled and not get support but nothing follows—or she might get support and that ends it—or she might get support and then feel satisfied—or support might seem equivocal and that ends it. In the next to the last hour of the analysis, the patient's problem was feeling sad at terminating, next she felt supported by the analyst, but then she felt sad again at losing him. This fresh variety indexes a new arsenal of adaptations to replace the rigid, inflexible repetitions of the original FRAME structure. So, in principle, FRAMES offer a precise and congruent assessment of the outcome (O).

This leaves the measure of the process of therapeutic change (T). How do we measure the process of change and the therapist's contribution, if any, to the change? Fortunately, we now have findings from the pilot project showing multiple Instantiations of FRAMES with both the husband and the analyst that highlight, in situ, a moment of change and the analyst's contribution to it at the end of the fourth year of analysis. Moreover, Jones and Windholz (1990), in their report of a 100-item Q-sort analysis of six 10-hour segments of Mrs. C. distributed over the 6 years, singled out the fourth year. They wrote, "In the fourth year . . . there is evidence for the emergence of a transference neurosis. Q-descriptors signified a remarkable heightening of Mrs. C.'s resistances and symptoms, as well as an increase of disturbing affect during the analytic hours, especially defiance, guilt, and the emergence of intense hostility toward the analyst" (p. 1010). Jones and Windholz's findings are important because they offer an independent pointer to the

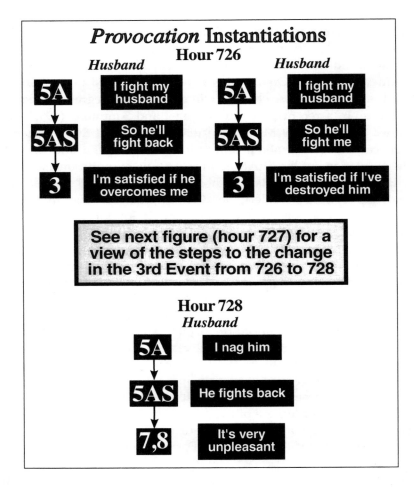

Figure 16. Three Instantiations with the husband of the Provocation FRAMES in Hours 726 and 728.

same period of the analysis that I will now focus on, the last 3 hours before a vacation at the end of the fourth year of the analysis when the patient gives many examples[15] of the emergence of a new FRAME structure that I have named "Provocation."

Figure 16 shows three Instantiations of the Provocation FRAME

---

[15]Found by Siegel and Sammons (1997) in the pilot study.

structure that the patient enacted with her husband in Hours 726 and 728. Note that the three FRAMES have the same structure except for the third event, which changes from [3], indicating satisfaction in Hour 726, to [7, 8] indicating unpleasure in Hour 728. As I indicated above, the summary predicates add information about the content of the events. In the first FRAME instantiation, she provoked her husband and was satisfied if the second wish [5AS] (to be overcome) was fulfilled; in the second, she ended up satisfied if her first wish [5A] (to destroy him) was fulfilled. But something changed by Hour 728; what was satisfying in 726 was unpleasant in 728. What happened in Hour 727 shows the precursors (if not the causes) of the change.

Figure 17 shows three Instantiations with the analyst and one with a man in a mystery story. Early in the session, the patient recalled an interpretation the analyst had made during Hour 726 to the effect that she regularly provoked fights both with him and with her husband. Note that the first two enactments with the analyst in this hour did not include the third event, that is, [3]. Here again, the summary predicates add to our knowledge, and after acknowledging provoking the analyst [5A], the patient implored him to "break through my resistance," that is, attack her [5AS]. And shortly after that she exclaimed, "Doesn't this drive you crazy?" The analyst's initial interpretation was to laugh out loud and ask if that was as transparent to her as it was to him. She first acknowledged her wish to drive him crazy, that is, provoke him, and then wanted to deny it.

Before the second Instantiation, the analyst made a longer interpretation, the substance of which was, "It's your whole way to . . . frustrate me totally." And then the patient repeated the first event and without waiting for a response to her provocation [5A], attacked herself [5AS] by acknowledging that what she was doing was not in her best interests. At that point, the analyst's interpretation reiterated the third event: "Nonetheless, it's very satisfying to you [3]."[16] The patient then recalled[17] a mystery novel she had

---

[16]Here, the therapist's intervention supplied the missing event in the FRAME structure. Alternatively, an intervention might reconstruct and refer to all the events in a FRAME structure (see Figure 14).

[17]Or, as analysts would say, "associated to."

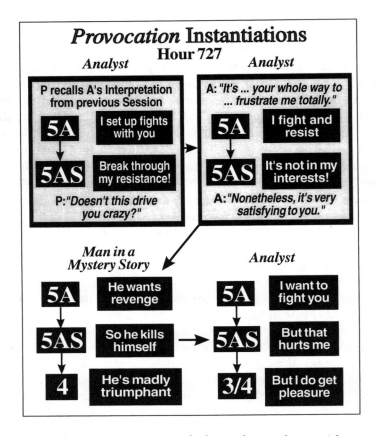

Figure 17. Three Instantiations with the analyst and one with a man in a mystery story of the Provocation FRAMES in Hour 727. The arrows show the sequence of their occurrence. In the highlighted FRAMES, note that the third event is missing. It is replaced in the first by a patient comment and in the second by the analyst's interpretation.

been reading in which the main character, in effect, repeated exactly the same FRAME structure. He wanted revenge [5A] on someone else, got it by killing himself [5AS], and—absurdly—was then madly triumphant [4]! Shortly after this, the patient then reenacted her third Instantiation with the analyst, but this time she acknowledged the pleasure [3/4] she got from it despite the fact that it hurt her own interests.

In the next session, Hour 728, the patient described her provocation of her husband and of his fighting back again, but the third event had changed to feeling very unpleasant [7, 8]. So, clinically, the question at that point was whether this change would continue. Would she decide to stop resisting, accede to her husband's request that she change, and finally give up fighting the proxy battle in the transference with the analyst? What is important here is that the FRAMES method allows us in principle to empirically and rigorously test two hypotheses: (a) Would unpleasure, [7, 8], continue to replace pleasure, [3, 4], as the third event in the Provocation FRAMES? And (b) Would the Provocation FRAMES themselves change in other ways or simply disappear? I say "in principle" because unfortunately, we do not have transcripts of the sessions following the summer vacation after Hour 728. What we do know is that this FRAME did not appear in Hour 766 nor in any of the later sessions that we have examined.

Nonetheless, again we have independent evidence that clear changes occurred during the fifth and sixth years of the analysis from Jones and Windholz (1990):

> Our data from the later period . . . suggest a resolution of transference resistances, signaled in part by the patient's greater openness about her desires, feelings, and fantasies, including sexual desires and a need for intimacy. There was, as well, a significant alleviation of the patient's long-standing feelings of inadequacy, guilt, and anxiety. (p. 1011)

The change in a crucial event of the Provocation FRAME structure from Hour 726 to 728 offers a cogent demonstration of the power of FRAMES to measure the essential characteristics of resolving a transference neurosis by working it through in the enactments with the analyst, that is, to measure the process of therapeutic change (T). Of course, one example cannot prove a cause-and-effect relationship between the analyst's contributions and the patient's different ending in her enactment with her husband in 728. If there were not independent evidence of changes beginning early in the fifth year and if this and her other FRAMES had not disappeared or significantly changed by the end of the analysis, the example would not be very persuasive. What this example does show, I believe, is that FRAMES are strong candidates to provide PTO congruence. They can measure pathology (P), measure both the therapist's and the patient's contributions to the therapeutic process (T), and assess outcome (O).

Finally, it is instructive to compare this systematic, reliable, empirically testable demonstration of change in the FRAMES with a previous *clinical* description of the same change (Dahl, 1991). Near the end of the first hour of the analysis, the patient referred to a very attractive, but aggressive and competitive girl at a party and exclaimed, "Wouldn't it be nice if I could be that free?" In answer to the question "Free to do what?" I wrote:

> ... to disagree, to criticize, to be antagonistic, to fight, in short, to be as aggressive and demanding and as uncaring for the consequences as she had described her own parents in hour 1! ... [Her] Task in the analysis, to say everything (and anything) out loud, perfectly matched her own Goal to be free, and far from being an onerous order that she had to obey,[18] was implicit permission to end up saying, "Doesn't this drive you crazy?" [and] ... to enjoy saying it, to enjoy feeling that the analyst was stuck with her and could not abandon her, as she repeatedly feared her parents could do.

Only after she recognized the limits of these adaptations could she begin to change. Nonetheless, however persuasive in this instance, the clinical account potentially suffers from well-known clinical biases, such as those reported by Dahl (1983), and, more importantly, by the lack of systematic procedures to assess its accuracy. This is where FRAMES can come to the rescue.

The Refrain

At the 20th anniversary celebration of my collaboration with the Department of Psychotherapy at the University of Ulm, Horst Kächele read aloud the last paragraph of my first report of the computer content analysis (Dahl, 1972). It seems fitting to repeat it here:

---

[18]See Caston (1986).

I know this must seem fanciful after so brief an exposure to these quite primitive and tentative demonstrations of a few of the possibilities. Nonetheless, I believe that what I have suggested is essential to attract to psychoanalysis the kind of imaginative and research-oriented candidates that our field needs. And even if in the end these approaches fail, we will have had an exciting time along the way. (p. 256)

It was then that Kächele also announced that that paper had inspired the establishment of the now famous Ulm TextBank of recorded psychoanalytic psychotherapy and psychoanalytic cases.

So why have I chosen the metaphor of *el Rubaiyat* in my title? Because I think it captures many of the characteristics of the voyage of psychoanalysis from Freud's first gropings in the Project for a Scientific Psychology at the end of the 19th century to the current preoccupation of the field with adapting to HMOs and the enormous changes in psychiatry and psychology near the end of the 20th century. For much of the century, the great puzzle was the nature of *unconscious* thinking. Now the big mental puzzle is the nature of *consciousness*.

Our own scientific problem has been to understand the process of psychoanalysis itself. And here we are now adrift in a very large ocean. All the early scientists, mostly European refugees, are gone. The generation trained after World War II with National Institute of Mental Health (NIMH) fellowships and grant support is reaching retirement age. But this time there will be no *U.S.S. Recovery* to help; NIMH money for this kind of research is largely gone. Although there is now renewed assurance of perhaps $200,000 per year for the many necessary areas of research, this amount is extraordinarily modest given the needs. Galatzer-Levy (1997) wrote, "American psychoanalysis is supporting approximately 5 percent of the research that needs to be done. Currently we are paying for our failure to invest adequately in research when psychoanalysis was at its zenith" (p. 26).

More significant is the state of researchers and their research. There is little cooperation among the dozen or so groups doing this kind of research. All are trying to push their own procedures and theories—each, if you will, in their own private *Rubaiyat*. And this chapter is another such example. But perhaps my pessimism is ill-founded. Maybe, just maybe, if a few finally succeed in demonstrating rigorous, clinically meaningful PTO congruent measures, we can persuade others that among us there are serious scientists. If that happens, a generous lookout might notice.

References

Anonymous (1988). The specimen hour. In H. Dahl, H. Kächele, & H. Thomä (Eds.), *Psychoanalytic process research strategies* (pp. 15–28). New York: Springer-Verlag.

Barker, R. (1968). *Ecological psychology.* Stanford, CA: Stanford University Press.

Caston, J. (1986). The reliability of the diagnosis of the patient's unconscious plan. In J. Weiss, H. Sampson, & the Mount Zion Psychotherapy Research Group (Eds.), *The psychoanalytic process: Theory, clinical observations, and empirical research* (pp. 241–255). New York: Guilford Press.

Dahl, H. (1972). A quantitative study of a psychoanalysis. In R. Holt & E. Peterfreund (Eds.), *Psychoanalysis and contemporary science* (pp. 237–257). New York: Macmillan.

Dahl, H. (1978). A new psychoanalytic model of motivation: Emotions as appetites and messages. *Psychoanalysis and Contemporary Thought, 1,* 375–408.

Dahl, H. (1979). *Word frequencies of spoken American English.* Essex, CT: Verbatim.

Dahl, H. (1983). On the definition and measurement of wishes. In J. Masling (Ed.), *Empirical studies of psychoanalytical theories* (Vol. 1, pp. 39–67). Hillsdale NJ: Erlbaum.

Dahl, H. (1988). Frames of mind. In H. Dahl, H. Kächele, & H. Thomä (Eds.), *Psychoanalytic process research strategies* (pp. 51–66). New York: Springer-Verlag.

Dahl, H. (1991). The key to understanding change: Emotions as appetitive wishes and beliefs about their fulfillment. In J. Safran & L. Greenberg (Eds.), *Emotion, psychotherapy and change* (pp. 130–165). New York: Guilford Press.

Dahl, H. (1995). An information feedback theory of emotions and defenses. In H. Conte & R. Plutchik (Eds.), *Ego defenses: Theory and measurement* (pp. 98–119). New York: Wiley.

Dahl, H., Hölzer, M., & Berry, J. (1992). *How to classify emotions for psychotherapy research.* Ulm, Germany: University of Ulm Press.

Dahl, H., & Stengel, B. (1978). A classification of emotion words: A modification and partial test of de Rivera's decision theory of emotions. *Psychoanalysis and Contemporary Thought, 1,* 269–312.

Dahl, H., & Teller, V. (1994). The characteristics, identification and applications of FRAMES. *Psychotherapy Research, 4,* 252–274.

Davies, J. (1988). *The development of emotional and interpersonal structures in three-year-old children.* Doctoral dissertation, Derner Institute for Advanced Psychological Studies, Adelphi University, Garden City, NY.

Dyer, M. (1983). *In-depth understanding: A computer model of integrated processing for narrative comprehension.* Cambridge, MA: M.I.T. Press.

Eissler, K. (1969). Irreverent remarks about the present and the future of psychoanalysis. *International Journal of Psychoanalysis, 50,* 461–471.

Freud, A. (1946). *The ego and the mechanisms of defence.* Madison, CT: International Universities Press. (Original work published 1936)

Freud, S. (1953). The interpretation of dreams. In J. Strachey (Ed. and Trans.), *The standard edition of the complete psychological works of Sigmund Freud* (Vol. 5). London: Hogarth Press. (Original work published 1900)

Galatzer-Levy, R. (1997). The fund for psychoanalytic research: How grants are made. *The American Psychoanalyst, 31*(3), 24–26.

Hölzer, M. (1991, July). *"Frames of Mind" as structured sequences of emotions.* Paper presented at the 22nd meeting of the Society for Psychotherapy Research, Lyon, France.

Hölzer, M., & Dahl, H. (1996). How to find FRAMES. *Psychotherapy Research, 6,* 177–197.

Horowitz, L. (1977). Two classes of concomitant change in a psychotherapy. In N. Freedman & S. Grand (Eds.), *Communicative structures and psychic structures* (pp. 419–440). New York: Plenum.

Horowitz, L., & Rosenberg, S. (1994). The consensual response psychodynamic formulation: Part 1: Method and research results. *Psychotherapy Research, 4,* 222–233.

Horowitz, M. (1994). Configurational analysis and the use of role–relationship models to understand transference. *Psychotherapy Research, 4,* 184–196.

Jones, E. (1953). *The life and work of Sigmund Freud: The formative years and the great discoveries* (Vol. 1). New York: Basic Books.

Jones, E., & Windholz, M. (1990). The psychoanalytic case study: Toward a method for systematic inquiry. *Journal of the American Psychoanalytic Association, 38,* 985–1015.

Klein, G. (1967). Peremptory ideation: Structure and force in motivated ideas. In R. Holt (Ed.), *Motives and thought: Psychoanalytic essays in honor of David Rapaport.* Madison, CT: International Universities Press.

Leeds, J. (1988). *Repetition, science and psychoanalysis: Theoretical considerations and an empirical study.* Unpublished doctoral dissertation, Derner Institute, Adelphi University, Garden City, NY.

Leeds, J., & Bucci, W. (1984). *A reliable method for the detection of repetitive structures in a transcript of an analytic session.* Unpublished manuscript.

Lehnert, W. G. (1982). Plot units: A narrative summarization strategy. In W. G. Lehnert & M. Ringle (Eds.), *Strategies for natural language processing*. Hillsdale: Erlbaum.

Levy, S., Herberman, R., Lippman, M., & D'Angelo, T. (1991). Immunological and psychosocial predictors of disease recurrence in patients with early-stage breast cancer. *Behavioral Medicine, 17,* 67–75.

Luborsky, L. (1990). A guide to the CCRT method. In L. Luborsky & P. Crits-Christoph (Eds.), *Understanding transference: The Core Conflictual Relationship Theme method* (pp. 15–36). New York: Basic Books.

Luborsky, L., Popp, C., & Barber, J. (1994). Common and special factors in different transference-related measures. *Psychotherapy Research, 4,* 277–286.

Luborsky, L., Popp, C., Luborsky, E., & Mark, D. (1994). The Core Conflictual Relationship Theme. *Psychotherapy Research, 4,* 172–183.

Masling, J. (Ed.). (1983). *Empirical studies of psychoanalytical theories* (Vol. 1). Hillsdale NJ: Erlbaum.

Minsky, M. (1975). A framework for representing knowledge. In P. Winston (Ed.), *The psychology of computer vision* (pp. 211–277). New York: McGraw-Hill.

O'Leary, A. (1990). Stress, emotion, and human immune function. *Psychological Bulletin, 108,* 363–382.

Perry, C. (1994). Assessing psychodynamic patterns using the idiographic conflict formulation method. *Psychotherapy Research, 4,* 239–252.

Rubinstein, B. (1978, June). *A new procedure for investigating the nature of clinical inference.* Appendix, paper presented at the Society for Psychotherapy Research Workshop, Toronto, Ontario.

Rumelhart, D. E. (1977). Understanding and summarizing brief stories. In D. LaBerge & S. J. Samuels (Eds.), *Basic processes in reading: Perception and comprehension* (pp. 265–305). Hillsdale, NJ: Erlbaum.

Russell, B. (1948). *Human knowledge: Its scope and limits.* New York: Simon & Schuster.

Schacht, T., & Henry, W. (1994). Modeling recurrent patterns of interpersonal relationship with structural analysis of social behavior: The SASB-CMP. *Psychotherapy Research, 4,* 208–221.

Seidman, D. (1988). *Quantifying the relationship patterns of neurotic and borderline patients in initial interviews.* Unpublished doctoral dissertation, Columbia University Teacher's College, New York, NY.

Sharir, I. (1991). *The relationship between emotions and defenses in the psychotherapy process.* Unpublished doctoral dissertation, New York University, New York, NY.

Siegel, P., & Sammons, M. (1997, June). *FRAMES: Their construction, reliabilities, and validities.* Panel presentation at annual meeting of the Society for Psychotherapy Research, Geilo, Norway.

Silberschatz, G. (1978). *Effects of the therapist's neutrality on the patient's feelings and behavior in the psychoanalytic situation.* Unpublished doctoral dissertation, New York University, New York, NY.

Simon, H. (1981). *The sciences of the artificial* (2nd ed.). Cambridge, MA: The M.I.T. Press.

Smithfield Interview (1994). *Psychotherapy Research, 4,* 155–171.

Spiegel, D. (1996). Cancer and depression. *British Journal of Psychiatry, 168,* 109–116.

Stein, N. (1982). What's in a story: Interpreting the interpretations of story grammars. *Discourse Processes, 5,* 319–335.

Stern, D. (1985). *The interpersonal world of the infant.* New York: Basic Books.

Strupp, H., Schacht, T., & Henry, W. (1988). Problem-treatment-outcome congruence: A principle whose time has come. In H. Dahl, H. Kächele, & H. Thomä (Eds.), *Psychoanalytic process research strategies* (pp. 1–14). New York: Springer-Verlag.

Teller, V. (1988). Artificial intelligence as a basic science for psychoanalytic research. In H. Dahl, H. Kächele, & H. Thomä (Eds.), *Psychoanalytic process research strategies* (pp. 163–177). New York: Springer-Verlag.

Teller, V., & Dahl, H. (1981). The framework for a model of psychoanalytic inference. *Proceedings of the Seventh International Joint Conference on Artificial Intelligence, 1,* 394–400.

Teller, V., & Dahl, H. (1986). The microstructure of free association. *Journal of the American Psychoanalytic Association, 34,* 763–798.

Teller, V., & Dahl, H. (1993). What psychoanalysis needs is more empirical research. *Journal of the American Psychoanalytic Association, 41,* 31–49.

Vaillant, G. (1977). *Adaptation to life.* Boston: Little, Brown.

Weiss, J., Sampson, H., & the Mount Zion Psychotherapy Research Group. (1986). The psychoanalytic process: Theory, clinical observations, and empirical research. New York: Guilford Press.

Selected Additional References to Mrs. C.

Bucci, W. (1988). Converging evidence for emotional structures: Theory and method. In H. Dahl, H. Kächele, & H. Thomä (Eds.), *Psychoanalytic process research strategies* (pp. 29–49). New York: Springer-Verlag.

Bucci, W. (1997). Empirical studies of the analytic process. In *Psychoanalysis and cognitive science: A multiple code theory* (pp. 275–304). New York: Guilford Press.

Bush, M., & Gassner, S. (1986). The immediate effect of the analyst's termination interventions on the patient's resistance to termination. In J. Weiss & H. Sampson (Eds.), *The psychoanalytic process: Theory, clinical observation and empirical research* (pp. 299–320). New York: Guilford Press.

Caston, J., Goldman, R., & McClure, M. (1986). The immediate effects of psychoanalytic interventions. In J. Weiss & H. Sampson (Eds.), *The psychoanalytic process: Theory, clinical observation and empirical research* (pp. 277–298). New York: Guilford Press.

Curtis, J., Ransohoff, P., Sampson, F., Brumer, S., & Bronstein, A. (1986). Expressing warded-off contents in behavior. In J. Weiss & H. Sampson (Eds.), *The psychoanalytic process: Theory, clinical observation and empirical research* (pp. 187–205). New York: Guilford Press.

Dahl, H., & Teller, V. (1991). Characteristics and identification of FRAMES (Tech. Rep. CS-TR 91-11). New York: Hunter College, City University of New York.

Gassner, S., Sampson, H., Brumer, S., & Weiss, J. (1986). The emergence of warded-off contents. In J. Weiss & H. Sampson (Eds.), *The psychoanalytic process: Theory, clinical observation and empirical research* (pp. 171–186). New York: Guilford Press.

Hoffman, I., & Gill, M. (1988). A scheme for coding the patient's experience of the relationship with the therapist (PERT): Some applications, extensions, and comparisons. In H. Dahl, H. Kächele, and H. Thomä (Eds.), *Psychoanalytic process research strategies* (pp. 67–98). New York: Springer-Verlag.

Horowitz, L., Sampson, H., Siegelman, E. Y., Weiss, J., & Goodfriend, S. (1978). Two classes of concomitant change in psychotherapy. *Journal of Consulting and Clinical Psychology, 46,* 556–561.

Luborsky, L. (1988). A comparison of three transference related measures applied to the specimen hour. In H. Dahl, H. Kächele, and H. Thomä (Eds.), *Psychoanalytic process research strategies* (pp. 109–115). New York: Springer-Verlag.

Luborsky, L., & Crits-Christoph, P. (1988). The assessment of transference by the CCRT method. In H. Dahl, H. Kächele, and H. Thomä (Eds.), *Psychoanalytic process research strategies* (pp. 99–108). New York: Springer-Verlag.

Shilkret, C., Isaacs, M., Drucker, C., & Curtis, J. (1986). The acquisition of insight. In J. Weiss & H. Sampson (Eds.), *The psychoanalytic process: Theory, clinical observation and empirical research* (pp. 206–217). New York: Guilford Press.

Silberschatz, G. (1986). Testing pathogenic beliefs. In J. Weiss & H. Sampson (Eds.), *The psychoanalytic process: Theory, clinical observation and empirical research* (pp. 256–266). New York: Guilford Press.

Silberschatz, G., Curtis, J., Fretter, P., & Kelly, T. (1988). Testing hypotheses of psychotherapeutic change processes. In H. Dahl, H. Kächele, and H. Thomä (Eds.), *Psychoanalytic process research strategies* (pp. 129–145). New York: Springer-Verlag.

Silberschatz, G., Sampson, H., & Weiss, J. (1986). Testing pathogenic beliefs versus seeking transference gratifications. In J. Weiss & H. Sampson (Eds.), *The psychoanalytic process: Theory, clinical observation and empirical research* (pp. 267–276). New York: Guilford Press.

Spence, D., Dahl, H., & Jones, E. (1993). Impact of interpretation upon associative freedom. *Journal of Clinical and Consulting Psychology, 61,* 395–402.

Spence, D., Mayes, L., & Dahl, H. (1994). Monitoring the analytic surface. *Journal of the American Psychoanalytic Association, 42,* 43–64.

Teller, V., & Dahl, H. (1984). Recurrent structures in psychoanalytic discourse: Candidates for pattern-directed inference (Tech. Rep. CS-TR 84-01). New York: Hunter College, City University of New York.

Teller, V., & Dahl, H. (1995). What psychoanalysis needs is more empirical research. In T. Shapiro & R. Emde (Eds.), *Research in psychoanalysis: Process, development and outcome* (pp. 31–49). Madison, CT: International Universities Press.

Weiss, J., Gassner, S., & Bush, M. (1986). Mrs. C. In J. Weiss & H. Sampson (Eds.), *The psychoanalytic process: Theory, clinical observation and empirical research* (pp. 155–164). New York: Guilford Press.

Chapter 7

Therapist Interventions and Patient Progress in Brief Psychodynamic Therapy:
Single-Case Design

Stanley B. Messer and Stephen J. Holland

In this chapter we describe a research program that was designed to explore the relationship between therapist interventions and patient (or client) responses in brief psychodynamically oriented psychotherapy. Note that we did not study psychoanalysis per se but brief psychotherapy that is based on the application of psychoanalytic or psychodynamic principles. As such, the therapies were insight based and broadly exploratory within the framework of a psychodynamic focus. This has the advantage of ecological validity because it represents the more typical current mode of practice, but it is at the expense of the kind of depth that psychoanalysis can offer. In presenting the research, we emphasize not only the results attained but also the process by which they were gathered. In this way we hope to remain true to both the difficulties and excitement of carrying out such a project and to demonstrate how this kind of research can be conducted in less-than-optimal circumstances with the hope that others will follow suit.

The Rutgers Psychotherapy Research Group (RPRG) consisted of graduate students from both the PsyD and PhD clinical psychology programs at Rutgers University, which included Stephen J. Holland. Stanley B. Messer headed the project. We were able to obtain some modest funds (about $7,000) from an internal Rutgers source, with few illusions about attaining funding for this kind of project from a national granting institute. We enlisted staff psychologists at the Rutgers College Counseling Center to audiotape cases that we all considered suitable for brief psychodynamic therapy (BPT) and that lasted, by design, about 15 sessions. The tapes were carefully transcribed by paid typists or students, providing an archive from which different kinds of cases could be drawn for study. We interviewed the clients before and after therapy and at 1-year follow-up, completed outcome forms and scales, and had clients and therapists do the same. In this way we were able to make an informed judgment about the relative success of the cases, which was important in validating our psychotherapy progress scale, which we describe below.

We had originally planned to conduct a randomized clinical trial of one of the BPT models (e.g., those of Mann, Malan, etc.; see Messer & Warren, 1995), but it quickly became clear that to do so would require a large budget and a setting that could accommodate such a trial, neither of which was available. Thus, of necessity, even if not by design, we switched to a single-subject research design. In doing so, we came to appreciate the virtues of this method of empirical study, which we now briefly describe.

Quantitative Single-Case Design

Single-case research is a type of intrasubject research in which there is an aggregation of data across cases; generality is established through replication, one case at a time (Hilliard, 1993). Intrasubject research design is concerned with the temporal unfolding of variables within individual participants and involves repeated measurement or observation of a variable over time. Quantitative techniques of analysis are used, such as time series analysis, sequential

analysis, or growth curve analysis, for analyzing the temporal unfolding of variables. These are applied to single cases without ma-
nipulating the variables studied. The quantitative analysis of single
cases requires either ongoing access to the case so that one can
administer questionnaires, or the availability of complete transcripts of sessions. The temporal unfolding of change is crucial in
intrasubject research because it would make no more sense to sample one point in time in an intrasubject study than it would to
sample one participant in an intersubject study.

The emphasis on time in intrasubject research also has important
implications for the unit of statistical analysis used. In intrasubject
research, the proper unit of analysis is a point in time, just as in
intersubject research the unit of analysis is the individual (Hilliard,
1993). As Spence, Dahl, and Jones (1993) stated, from the viewpoint of statistical inference, single-case studies can be seen as providing data samples from a distribution or population that is defined by the individual being studied.

Single-subject design also has gained currency with the acknowledgment that group studies pose their own problems of generalizability. Data averaged across a group do not necessarily tell researchers about the performance of individuals; the average may
in fact reflect a performance not achieved by any individual within
the group. Thus, the question of whether group data can be generalized to individuals must be verified by examining data from
individual cases.

Quantitative single-subject research can be undertaken either for
the purpose of hypothesis testing (confirmatory analysis) or hypothesis generation (exploratory analysis). In his review and cat-
egorization of this kind of research, Hilliard (1993) encouraged investigators to engage in theory-based, question-driven, single-case
research, which is precisely the method used in our project. The
most prominent current example of single-case quantitative study
in the psychoanalytic realm is the case of Mrs. C. (Jones & Windholz, 1990; Spence et al., 1993; Weiss & Sampson, 1986; see also
chapters in this book). There is increasing recognition that, although control cannot be perfect in single-case research, threats to
internal validity can be minimized, objective measures can be used,
generalizability can be studied using replication, and hypotheses
can be tested.

The initial goal of the project was to study psychodynamic therapy as it is taught and practiced, that is, how well therapists track clients' constantly shifting needs and how clients progress or stagnate in response. We chose two therapist variables to study, both of which are considered to be central in BPT: (a) the extent to which the therapist adheres to a psychodynamic focus and (b) the quality of the therapist's interventions. We also chose one client variable —the extent to which clients progressed or stagnated in therapy —to examine in connection with these two therapist variables. Before presenting the measures used and results attained, we describe some features of BPT that constitute the backdrop and broader context of this project.

Brief Psychodynamic Psychotherapy

What are the major features of brief *psychodynamic* therapy? Although any effort to specify its span of sessions is somewhat arbitrary, it can be said to range from 1 to 40 sessions, with 10–25 being typical. A time limit is usually established from the start, which places into motion a series of expectancies that has an effect on both the content of the material that clients bring to therapy and on the length of time they may be willing to remain. The major concepts of psychoanalytic theory are used to understand clients, such as the continuity of normality and psychopathology, waking and dream life, and childhood and adulthood. The major techniques of psychoanalytic therapy are used, such as clarification, interpretation, and confrontation of defenses, impulses, and interpersonal patterns. Unlike the practice in some traditional models of therapy, therapists tend to be relatively active in engaging clients in dialogue.

In BPT, a focus is set that is formulated in psychodynamic terms, such as the presence of pathogenic beliefs, conflicts, maladaptive interpersonal patterns, or negative feelings about oneself. The point is that not all of clients' difficulties can be taken up in a short time period; rather, there is a narrowing and focusing of the work. Goals are often set after the first few interviews (which may or may not be communicated directly to clients) that serve to guide the therapy. These might include a partial or even full resolution of a conflict, a changed interpersonal pattern, or greater ease with recognition and expression of feeling as well as symptom reduction and an enhanced sense of well-being.

There also are criteria for client suitability for this modality (which are observed as much in the breach as in the practice currently because of the pressure brought by managed care to offer all clients only brief therapy). They include clients' ability to engage fairly rapidly and to disengage without being traumatized; the presence of significant ego strength, such as the ability to tolerate frustration; the willingness to participate actively in the treatment (good motivation); and psychological mindedness, or the capacity for insight. Excluded are those with more serious psychiatric disorders such as psychosis, major depression, and substance abuse as well as the more severe personality disorders.

There is extensive research supporting the value of BPT (e.g., Koss & Shiang, 1994), at least as measured in global terms. For example, the dose–effect studies (which track the percentage of clients improved or symptoms alleviated as a function of the number of sessions) suggest that time-limited therapy is helpful to a majority of clients (e.g., 60% improved by 13 sessions and 75% by 26 sessions; Howard, Kopta, Krause, & Orlinsky, 1986). (For a more complete review of the research literature on BPT, see Messer & Warren, 1995.)

There are several models of BPT. Those that derive primarily from drive and ego psychology tend to be focused on formulations that emphasize aggressive, sexual, and dependent impulses and defenses against them as well as oedipal conflicts (e.g., the brief therapies of Malan, Davanloo, and Sifneos). Others are based largely on object relations and interpersonal perspectives, which formulate problems in terms of (a) maladaptive interpersonal patterns (e.g., Levenson & Strupp, 1997); (b) client wishes, the responses of others, and the subsequent response of the self (Luborsky, 1997); (c) pathogenic beliefs and the way they are manifested relative to the therapist (Curtis & Silberschatz, 1997); and (d) schemas and role relationships (M. J. Horowitz & Eells, 1997). In addition to incorporating some of these theoretical approaches, Mann (1991) described a time-limited, 12-session therapy that also includes concepts from self psychology, particularly the use of empathy to heal clients' chronically endured pain. We now turn to those elements of BPT that were incorporated into our research design.

The Psychodynamic Focus

One of the important recent developments in psychoanalytic empirical research has been the effort to systematize case formulation such that scientific standards of reliability and validity could be met (Barber & Crits-Christoph, 1993). There are now several such approaches to case study. One, the Core Conflictual Relationship Theme method, extracts interpersonal relationship patterns from psychotherapy transcripts (Luborsky & Crits-Christoph, 1990), including patients' wishes or needs, the expected or actual responses of others, and the response of the self. A second, the idiographic conflict formulation method (Perry, 1997), assesses wishes, fears, the ways in which patients handle the ensuing conflicts including symptoms and inhibitions, and patients' best level of adaptation to the conflicts.

A third, the consensual response method (Horowitz & Rosenberg, 1994), has judges rate semistructured interviews broken into thought units. The units that have similar meaning across several judges are identified and integrated into a single narrative. Other approaches are the cyclical maladaptive pattern (Schacht & Henry, 1994), configuration analysis (M. J. Horowitz & Eells, 1997), plan analysis (Caspar, 1997), and the plan formulation method (PFM; Curtis & Silberschatz, 1997).

To measure therapists' adherence to a focus, the RPRG chose to use the Mt. Zion PFM in part because the Mt. Zion Psychotherapy Research Group (now known as the San Francisco Psychotherapy Research Group) conducted its research primarily using a single-subject design. The PFM is a procedure for developing reliable psychodynamic formulations on the basis of the material in the first two or three sessions of a case. Patients are said to enter therapy with a plan, partly conscious and partly unconscious, for overcoming their problems with the therapists' help (Curtis & Silberschatz, 1986). Four aspects of patients' expectations of, or beliefs about, the self or others are generated by the method: goals, obstacles (or pathogenic beliefs), tests, and insights, which together constitute the plan.

To elaborate, these include (a) goals, conscious or unconscious, that patients would like to achieve to rid themselves of their suffering; (b) obstacles, those irrational, pathogenic beliefs that prevent patients from becoming free to achieve their goals; (c) tests, the enactment within the therapeutic situation of patients' central conflicts in their effort to get the therapist to disconfirm their pathogenic beliefs; and (d) insights, which are said to help modify the pathogenic beliefs and attain the goals. Once the plan is developed, therapist interventions can be rated for the degree to which they adhere to it using the Plan Compatibility of Intervention Scale, described below.

Cognitive–Dynamic Theory

We found that the literature produced by the Mt. Zion research group did not by itself provide enough information to allow us to construct a plan. Furthermore, the diversity of psychoanalytic theoretical orientations among our group's raters led to low and disappointing interjudge reliability. Because the Mt. Zion group had just begun offering workshops in their method, five members of our research group accepted the invitation to attend. While studying protocols under the tutelage of the Mt. Zion researchers, we frequently disagreed about the "correct" formulation of the cases we were jointly examining. The Mt. Zion researchers' way of viewing the cases was based on Weiss's (1990) cognitive–dynamic theory, which emphasizes two chief motives: separation guilt and survivor guilt. "Separation guilt may develop in a child who wishes to become more independent of a parent but who infers that were he to do so, he would hurt the parent" (Weiss & Sampson, 1986, p. 49). Therefore, such people might be reluctant to separate from their parents lest the latter be harmed.

Survivor guilt is "the guilt of persons who assume they have fared better than their parents or siblings" (Weiss & Sampson, 1986, p. 52), a belief that can prevent them from succeeding too well. In both instances, in other words, people believe that they have harmed others and are to blame for others' unhappiness. According to Weissian theory, these are pathogenic beliefs limiting their independence, life ambitions, or both. Weiss's ideas were based on Freud's later works on ego psychology, in which a larger role is given to children's inferences on the basis of their actual experiences.

Object Relations Theory

The RPRG, on the other hand, considered the same patients' problems to be based not on separation guilt but on unresolved, immature dependency wishes and consequent separation anxiety. This view, derived from an object relations perspective, especially that of Fairbairn (1946/1954), posits three stages of dependence: infantile, transitional, and mature. The infantile stage is characterized by "an attitude of oral incorporation towards, and an attitude of primary emotional identification with the object" (Fairbairn, 1946/1954, p. 145). In other words, there is a taking rather than a giving mode of interaction and a need to be too closely tied to the significant other. Mature dependency, by contrast, "is characterized by a capacity on the part of a differentiated individual for cooperative relationships with differentiated objects" (Fairbairn, 1946/1954, p. 145). Fairbairn emphasized that this is not an attitude of independence but one of "evenly matched giving and taking between two differentiated individuals who are mutually dependent, and between whom there is no disparity of dependence. Further, the relationship is characterized by an absence of primary identification and an absence of incorporation" (Fairbairn, 1946/1954, p. 145). The transitional stage is one of conflict and defense, of trying to deal with the earlier internalized objects—trying to get rid of them but at the same time not wanting to lose them.

In brief, the RPRG viewed separation difficulties, especially those of the patients we were studying jointly, as being caused primarily by unresolved, immature dependency wishes and anxiety rather than by guilt over separation or success. The difference between the two groups' outlooks led us to test whether adherence to a plan based on object relations theory would produce better predictions of in-session patient progress than adherence to a plan based on cognitive–dynamic theory. The first step, however, was to test empirically whether the Mt. Zion group and the RPRG would indeed formulate the same cases differently on the basis of their respective theoretical leanings and whether the PFM could be used in a different setting with good reliability and stability.

For her doctoral dissertation, Collins (1989) presented the initial transcribed interviews of two cases, one each from the archives of the Mt. Zion group and the RPRG, to both groups of researchers to create items for the plans relevant to the particular cases as required by the PFM procedure (see chap. 8 in this book). Intraclass correlations for the pooled judges' item ratings in each of the four segments of each of the two plans that were created separately by the RPRG and Mt. Zion group were high, ranging from .81 to .95 (Collins & Messer, 1991). This was a considerable improvement over the RPRG's initial efforts to achieve reliability and pointed to the importance of theoretical like-mindedness among judges in achieving good reliability (Messer, 1991). Furthermore, the stability of the ratings over a 3-month period ranged from .94 to .98, the first such test of the PFM's staying power.

The next question was whether the Mt. Zion and RPRG panels of judges would derive similar or different formulations of the two cases. The items constructed by both groups were pooled for each case and presented to both panels of judges. The results were striking: Each panel rated its own items much more highly than the items derived by the other group for the same two cases (see Figure 1; Collins & Messer, 1991). In other words, there was a Panel × Plan interaction, especially for the plan segments containing the obstructions and insight items, which are those most highly influenced by theory. Inspection of the items included in each plan revealed that the RPRG rated highly those items attributing the clients' difficulties to unresolved dependency wishes and rated lower those items related to separation or survivor guilt; the converse was true for the Mt. Zion group. That is, the Mt. Zion plan reflected its cognitive–dynamic emphasis, whereas the RPRG plan reflected its object relations emphasis.

The Epistemological Issue of "Accuracy" of the Focus

That two independent research groups using the same method produced two different dynamic assessments of the same participants

Case A   Case B

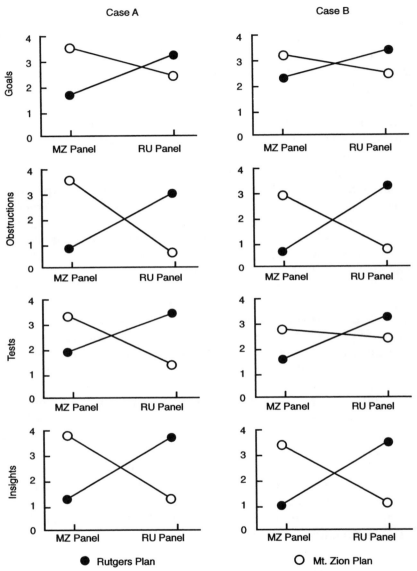

● Rutgers Plan   ○ Mt. Zion Plan

Figure 1.   Plan formulation method. Two-way interactions (Plan ×
Panel) of scores of Rutgers (RU) and Mt. Zion (MZ) judging panels on
Rutgers and Mt. Zion plan items. From "Extending the Plan
Formulation Method to an Object Relations Perspective: Reliability,
Stability, and Adaptability," by W. D. Collins and S. B. Messer, 1991,
Psychological Assessment: A Journal of Consulting and Clinical Psychology, 3,
pp. 75–81. Copyright 1991 by the American Psychological Association.

raises interesting epistemological questions (Messer, 1991). Does the case formulation derive largely from the patient's verbalizations, or is it more reliant on theory, which resides in the mind of the formulator? Does one discover the correct or accurate dynamic formulation as traditional psychoanalytic thinking suggests (e.g., Glover, 1931), or does one construct dynamic formulations on the basis of some mix of observation and theory, as others might claim (e.g., the authors listed in Messer, Sass, & Woolfolk, 1988; Schafer, 1992; Spence, 1982)?

The epistemological question, framed most broadly, is whether there is such a thing as objective knowledge in the social and psychological spheres. Freud believed, as did most of his contemporaries and followers, that there are actual events, memories, and meanings to be discovered. One could dig deeply into layers of the psyche and unearth important relics of the individual's past history that continued to affect the present in the form of symptoms and other behaviors. Interpretations that tallied with what was "real" were said to alleviate symptoms.

Once it became clear that there was no ready cause and effect, one-to-one relationship between specific interpretations and symptom remission, the door was open to the idea that more than one theory or meaning system could be "accurate" or curative. Within a postmodernist or constructivist approach, psychoanalytic accounts are not an unearthing of truth, but instead constitute a narrative unfolding that produces coherence and unity in the description of people's lives (Ricoeur, 1981). "What we discover in psychoanalysis are not pieces of personal history so much as meanings, filtered through memory and through language—that is, through the conversation of analyst and patient" (Woolfolk, Sass, & Messer, 1988, p. 10). The analyst's stories are retellings of the patient's stories (Edelson, 1992).

> The repeated revisions and elaborations of the stories told by both participants lead ideally to a shared, co-authored story that . . . [is] more complex, comprehensive, and complete. They bring to light previously hidden, implicit and conflicted elements that are present in a variety of single or partial stories [resulting in] what Edelson calls a "master story." (Messer & Wolitzky, 1997, p. 35)

However, alternate theoretical models with their different etiological emphases can shape different stories or, in the present language, different plans.

Having available two reliable but different plans (foci, or "stories"), we could now test (a) whether therapist interventions that adhered to a plan or focus would aid the therapeutic process and (b) whether therapist interventions that adhered to an object relations focus (or story) were more or less helpful than those that adhered to a cognitive–dynamic focus (or story).

Measures of Therapist and Patient Variables

Therapist Variables

Therapist adherence to the plan. To assess the extent to which the content of therapists' interventions were compatible with either plan, we used the Plan Compatibility of Intervention Scale (PCIS; Curtis, Silberschatz, Sampson, Weiss, & Rosenberg, 1988). It is a Likert scale ranging from −3 (*strongly antiplan*) to 3 (*strongly proplan*).

Quality of therapist interventions. As mentioned earlier, we also were interested in the relationship between the quality of therapist interventions and client progress. To explore the former required a measure of the extent to which therapists' interventions were responsive to patients' moment-to-moment needs. As part of her doctoral dissertation, Tishby (1991) developed the Rutgers Therapy Process Scale (RTPS) with the help of the RPRG. Although a number of process scales already existed, none was designed to capture the continuously evolving quality of all therapist interventions in individual cases.

An additional feature of our single-case research and the instruments we designed was to consider the context in which therapists' interventions and patient responses were made. The scale tapped three overlapping and interactive dimensions. One was *attunement to the patient* in both dynamic content and affective tone. It reflected the therapist's ability to stay close to patients' themes and current difficulties. A second aspect, *therapist competence*, emphasized the manner in which therapists' understanding was communicated. It assessed the skillful application of psychodynamic technique, including proper timing of interventions, addressing the therapeutic relationship, and the style and phrasing of interventions. *Interpersonal manner*, the third aspect, referred to the way in which therapists related to patients, including being accepting and supportive, inviting patients to collaborate, and striking a balance between observing and participating in the process.

The raters had to decide the following: Does this intervention facilitate the therapeutic process, and is it responsive to patients' needs at the moment or does it hinder the process? Each therapist turn-at-talk was given a single RTPS score using a Likert scale ranging from −3 (*impeding progress or nonresponsive*) to 3 (*facilitating progress or highly responsive*). Raters were given general guidelines and scoring examples for each point on the scale.

The Patient Variable

Turning to the patient variable, our research group searched in vain for a scale to measure shifts in patient process in response to therapist interventions. None of the existing scales, such as the Experiencing Scale (Klein, Mathieu-Coughlan, Gendlin, & Kiesler, 1986) or the Vanderbilt Psychotherapy Process Scale (Suh, Strupp, & O'Malley, 1986), was considered suitable for one or more reasons: They were not designed to measure progress as it is conceptualized within psychodynamic therapy; they measured only a single dimension of patient progress; they did not measure patient stagnation; and they were not designed to assess progress and stagnation on a moment-to-moment basis.

The Rutgers Psychotherapy Progress and Stagnation Scale (RPPSS), developed as part of Spillman's (1991) dissertation with the RPRG's participation, considers eight aspects of progress and stagnation on the basis of a review of the psychoanalytic literature. Each patient's turn-at-talk is assigned a single global score on a 7-point Likert scale ranging from −3 (*strong stagnation*) to 3 (*strong progress*). The scale can be found in Messer, Tishby, and Spillman (1992). A revised version, called the *Rutgers Psychotherapy Progress Scale* (RPPS), is discussed later in this chapter.

Relating Therapist Interventions
to Patient Progress

The PCIS, RTPS, and RPPSS were used in two complete cases of BPT selected by mutual agreement of the RPRG and Mt. Zion group. One case (identified as Case 3-29), selected from a pool of patients treated at the Rutgers College Counseling Center, was a college junior, aged 20, who came to therapy because of mild depression and difficulty concentrating on her work. The other (identified as Diane), selected from a group of patients treated at the Mt. Zion Hospital and Medical Center in San Francisco, suffered from moderate depression and inhibitions about getting started in her profession. Both therapists had several years of postgraduate experience conducting psychotherapy.

For all three scales, raters read the first two sessions of each case to become familiar with the patient's history and initial presentation. In an effort to maximize reliability, after rating the third session the raters discussed the results to resolve any differences in their understanding and scoring of the dimensions. The raters then applied the scales independently to each therapist's or patient's turn at talking from Session 4 until the end of the therapy (15 or 16 sessions). Four raters were used for each scale.

In rating the RTPS and the PCIS, raters read both therapists' and patients' turn at talking. Each therapist's turn at talking was assigned a score on the therapist variables (RTPS and PCIS) before the rater read the patient's response. The patient's response was then read, followed by the next therapist's turn at talking, which would then be rated. By contrast, when scoring the patient variable on the RPPSS, the therapists' turns at talking were deleted from the transcripts, leaving raters with access only to the patients' turn at talking. Each patient's turn at talking was scored before the next one was read (Messer et al., 1992). Although it was recognized that deleting therapists' turns at talking meant some loss of context, it was deemed important to make this compromise so that raters would not be unduly influenced in rating the patient's progress or stagnation by their impression of the quality of the therapist's intervention that preceded it.

The first question asked was whether the scales could be rated reliably. For each scale, intraclass correlations were calculated for every session to assess the reliability of the mean of the scores assigned by the four raters. The intraclass correlation for the RPPSS for each session ranged from .58 to .86, with a mean of .73 for each case. For the RTPS, the mean intraclass correlation for Case 3-29 was .89 and .79 for Diane. For the PCIS, the mean intraclass correlation was .89 for Case 3-29 and .76 for Diane. (It was lower for Diane because the Mt. Zion group used fewer interventions that were relevant to an object relations plan.) Hence, the question of whether the scales were reliable was answered affirmatively.

The second question was whether adherence to the RPRG object relations plan and quality of therapist process would predict patient progress. Initial data analysis using each turn at talking indicated that patients' tendency to continue functioning at the same level of progress was stronger than the effects of therapist intervention, which, although significant, were modest in size. When the scales were correlated by aggregating the data over sessions on a session-by-session basis, we found that the significant correlations were not evenly distributed throughout the sessions. This led us to divide each session into two (to have enough data points) and each case into early, middle, and late phases of therapy, as is commonly used to describe many BPT models (e.g., Mann, Malan, and Sifneos).

The results showed significant relationships between plan compatibility of therapist interventions (the PCIS) and patient progress (the RPPSS) in the early and middle phases of therapy for both cases and between goodness of therapist process (the RTPS) and patient progress in the middle phase. Marmar (1990) and others have described these two phases as defining a focus and working through a focal conflict, which helps explain why the relationship between the therapist dynamic content variable (the plan or focus) and patient progress was strongest at these phases of therapy. Similarly, we view the therapist process variable as becoming most important when the focal conflict is being worked on, namely in the middle phase. We concluded that one cannot necessarily expect individual therapist interventions to have a major impact immediately in the next patient's turn at talking, but, when such data are aggregated in larger units, they indicate a positive impact of interventions that adhere to a focus and are good in process.

The next question was whether interventions compatible with the RPRG object relations plan would predict patient progress better than interventions compatible with the Mt. Zion cognitive–dynamic plan. As far as we know, this was the first study to compare the utility of two different theoretical formulations of the same case. Tishby and Messer (1995) applied the PCIS using the Mt. Zion plan to all therapist interventions in the same two patients described earlier. This scale was then correlated with patient progress on the RPPSS, and the correlations were compared with those found between the Rutgers PCIS and the RPPSS. Correlations were computed for the early, middle, and late phases of therapy. For Diane, interventions compatible with the RPRG plan predicted patient progress better than interventions compatible with the Mt. Zion plan in all three phases of therapy. For Case 3-29, the Rutgers PCIS predicted patient progress better in all but the final phase of therapy. In fact, the Mt. Zion plan was negatively correlated with the RPPSS for all three phases of Diane's therapy and for two of the three phases of Case 3-29's therapy.

Tishby and Messer (1995) concluded that the evidence supported the hypothesis that therapist interventions compatible with the object relations plan, emphasizing dependency issues, helped more than those compatible with the Mt. Zion cognitive–dynamic plan, emphasizing issues of guilt over causing harm to, or separating from, others. Thus, the RPRG plan appears to have been the more "accurate" or resonant formulation for the two patients studied. However, two factors may have influenced the results: First, interventions according to the Mt. Zion plan were rated by RPRG judges, who may have scored it differently than would have the Mt. Zion judges. Second, in their studies, the Mt. Zion group typically focus on interpretations alone or patient "tests" of the therapist, whereas we scored every therapist's turn at talking. The results may have been different had we rated only interpretations or key tests (see Silberschatz & Curtis, 1990).

The Rutgers Psychotherapy Progress Scale

Although the Rutgers Psychotherapy Progress Scale (RPPS) served the purpose of providing a global measure of patient progress, the problems with it led Roberts (1994) and Holland (1994) and the RPRG to make major revisions, resulting in the creation of the RPPS. The old scale required the rater to keep in mind eight different variables; the new one called for eight different judgments about a variety of aspects of in-session progress that would ultimately allow a more fine-grained approach to tracking progress.

The old scale assessed both progress and stagnation, but researchers found it difficult to rate degrees of stagnation and rarely used the lower numbers that indicated greater degrees of stagnation. Hence, the new scale collapsed stagnation, or lack of progress, into one point at one end of the 5-point scale, with the other 4 points gauging the degree of progress.

The old scale was designed to take into account every patient's turn at talking, which resulted in too much "noise"; that is, there were many patient statements that were brief, conveyed little of importance, and hence were difficult to score. Instead, the new scale used ratings based on sequential, 5-min blocks of the transcript, which gave raters more material on which to base their score and lessened the work considerably.

Because of the design of the initial study, it was important to remove therapist interventions to avoid biasing raters in making their judgments. In the present study using the RPPS, raters were given both therapist and patient material to read that preserved the full context. Raters were instructed to use the context by keeping in mind, for example, the patient's particular defensive style in determining whether a response was indicative of progress or stagnation.

Finally, we sharpened the criteria for each component of the scale and provided case examples from the transcripts for the 0–4 scoring points. The result was a 44-page manual containing scoring guidelines, scale point descriptions, and clinical examples that serve as anchors for each scale point.[1] We tried to produce a scale that did not divide each aspect into smaller components, stemming from our belief that too much of the meaning of complex constructs

---

[1]A copy of the Rutgers Psychotherapy Progress Scale and scoring manual may be obtained from Health and Psychosocial Instruments, P.O. Box 110287, Pittsburgh, Pennsylvania 15232-0787.

is lost in such an endeavor. Rather than being tied to a specific school, the scale is broadly psychodynamic in its conceptualization, which allows it to be used to compare progress in different types of psychodynamic therapy. It was designed to be used as a measure of intermediate outcome that could identify in-session changes in patient progress. We now provide brief descriptions of the newly revised scale items.

Scale Values

The following are the scale points: 0 = not present, 1 = slightly present, 2 = moderately present, 3 = very present, and 4 = extremely present.

Scale Items

Significant material refers to the expression of significant current events and memories that are related to important (frequently interpersonal) issues in the patients' lives, especially issues that they have brought to therapy.

Development of insight is new understanding on the part of the patients related to the issues that they are presenting in therapy.

Focus on emotion is the degree to which patients focus on and explore their emotional experience. The emotions discussed may have taken place in the past or are present during the session.

Direct reference to the therapist and therapy refers to patients' statements that involve the expression of feelings, fantasies, or thoughts about, or attitudes toward, the therapist, therapy, or both.

New behavior in the session is the emergence in the therapy session of a new way of behaving or a new way of interacting with the therapist.

Collaboration is the degree to which responses indicate that patients are working spontaneously, collaboratively, and actively on the task of therapy and the degree to which they appear to be actively involved and engaged in the treatment process.

Clarity and vividness of communication refers to the degree to which patients are communicating in a manner that is clear, understandable, vivid, and evocative.

Focus on the self is the degree to which patients are focusing directly on themselves, including their feelings, motivations, and actions relative to others, and are taking responsibility for them.

Raters must continually monitor the context in which clients' statements appear so that they can determine whether the material shows an increase or decrease in the various indicators of progress. The following is an example from the manual of the item "focus on the self," as just defined.

Criteria

Focus on the patient's own experience.   The more patients focus on their own feelings, reactions, motivations, and actions in describing an interaction or situation, the higher the rating for this item. For example, patients who discuss fights that they used to witness their parents having would receive a low rating unless they directly discussed how those fights affected them and what they did in reaction to them.

Taking responsibility.   To receive a high rating, patients must not only describe their personal experience but also take responsibility for that experience. For example, a patient who relates in detail her feelings about a fight with her boyfriend would not receive as high a rating on "focus on the self" as she would if she also explored her role in the fight, why the fight touched off in her the particular emotional reaction that it did, and the motivations involved in her own actions.

Additional Guidelines

Raters are asked to pay close attention to the specific wording of responses in assessing the degree of self-reference. For example, "I want people to understand me" is a better response than "What makes people understand each other . . . ."

The following includes scale point case examples as scored by actual raters ("yk" = you know, and a dot [.] represents a second of silence). More such examples are provided in the manual.

Scale Points

0 = *not focused on the self.*   Patients discuss events or other material that do not directly involve them and without making clear any relevance of the material to the self.

1 = *slightly focused on the self.*   Patients discuss events and others in a way that shows only an implied relevance to the self.

Example: One of my brothers has like severe problems dealing with other people and the other brother is like just totally out for himself.

2 = *moderately focused on the self.*   Patients describe themselves, or how they typically act, in a certain situation or describe the roles they play.

Example: Um, I just, I would just do what they wanted me to do, I mean I just did that all along, I just always, you know (yk), tried to get good grades. I think in high school I did more of what I wanted to do . . . but still like . . . I still, yk, it became . . . even little judgments at home, yk, like when to come in and stuff—I didn't argue about it . . . and I never tested them, I never came in late (sigh).

3 = *very focused on the self.*   Patients "own" their feelings or actions and take more responsibility for who they are or for their part in some interaction or dynamic.

Example: My mom does wife things. She lives vicariously almost, yk, in her husband and her children. Trying to find some fulfillment for herself in us. . . . I find myself like tending towards like doing things for Paul [her boyfriend] and stuff . . . and I can't do that. I have to do it for myself and not expect anything.

4 = *extremely focused on the self.*   Patients accept responsibility for who they are and their actions. Patients are reflective and explore their motivations, reactions, choice of significant others or certain situations, and so on. Statements may take the form of "Why is it that I take this attitude with her?"

Example: I see now that I don't do much to assert myself when I'm on a date, that I just go along with him and just, like, hope that he likes me. But then I get mad that he doesn't treat me better and—it's confusing because I also see how I get mad at me when this happens. . . . It's like then I feel bad and like that maybe I deserve how I'm treated. Yk, I don't think I try to be more—yk, assert myself more because I don't want to be disliked and maybe dumped . . . (sigh), but I also somehow feel that I deserve not to be liked and so when I get treated bad it feels like it was supposed to happen.

The challenge of the current scale was to set criteria that would allow a reliable rating of complex constructs without reducing them to such narrow units that the meaning gets lost. As it has been constructed, the RPPS represents a midpoint between scales that tap constructs using several items requiring a low level of inference, such as the Vanderbilt Psychotherapy Process Scale (Suh et al., 1986), and scales that consist of a single rating, such as the original RPPSS or the Experiencing Scale (Klein et al., 1986). To achieve adequate reliability with this kind of scale, several raters (three or more) are typically required.

Reliability and Validity of the RPPS

Quantitative Analysis

Transcripts of two BPT cases that were conducted by an experienced therapist and that differed in outcome were chosen from our archive for study. The patients were 21- and 30-year-old women with anxiety and relationship difficulties. Each session of these 13- and 16-session therapies was divided into 10, roughly equal 5-min blocks of material. There were two sets of raters, each scoring every other block of material in order, on either the RPPS or on three subscales of the Vanderbilt Psychotherapy Process Scale—Patient Participation, Patient Exploration, and Patient Hostility—totaling 21 items. A composite score, Patient Involvement, was calculated by subtracting the z score for Patient Hostility from the z score for Patient Participation. Patient Participation, Patient Exploration, and Patient Involvement all have been found to be positively correlated with outcome, whereas Patient Hostility has been found to be negatively correlated with outcome (O'Malley, Suh, & Strupp, 1983; Suh et al., 1986).

Reliability. The interrater reliability for the RPPS Total Score was .80 for Case 2-45 and .74 for Case 2-9. Thus, raters were able to apply the scale with adequate reliability. The item, "new behavior," however, had poor reliability for Case 2-9.

Internal consistency. All items except "reference to the therapist and therapy" were significantly related to the total score.

Predictive validity. Six of the eight items and the total score were significantly higher for the patient with the better outcome.

Concurrent validity. The eight items of the RPPS and its total score were correlated with the four subscales of the Vanderbilt scale. Twenty-three of the 36 correlations were significant, and 6 others approached significance, providing good support for the convergent and discriminant validity of the RPPS. The two items that did not correlate well with the Vanderbilt scale were "new behavior" and "reference to the therapist and therapy." We recommended that "new behavior" be dropped because raters had difficulty applying the item as intended, which led to low reliability and validity (Holland, Roberts, & Messer, 1998).

Qualitative Analysis

"Reference to therapist and therapy" posed an interesting problem. It had the highest reliability of any item on the scale, but, unexpectedly, it correlated negatively with other scale items and with the Vanderbilt subscales that correlated with good outcome. It also had a higher average score for the patient with the poorer outcome. This finding was not consistent with a central tenet of psychoanalytic therapy, namely that focusing on patients' transferential feelings should lead to in-session progress.

We conducted a qualitative analysis to better understand this anomalous finding. All blocks rated above zero on this item were read, along with preceding and subsequent blocks. We found that neither client spontaneously made reference to the therapist or the therapy and that the therapist initiated such discussions only when there was manifest resistance (Holland et al., 1998). Although the therapist's style was consistent with traditional approaches to psychoanalytic psychotherapy, it was not consistent with current brief psychodynamic approaches that emphasize active transference interpretation, which had influenced our thinking in constructing this item. Because there was client resistance present in blocks in which "reference to the therapist and therapy" was scored, judges generally assigned lower-than-average ratings for the other RPPS and Vanderbilt items, resulting in the negative correlations between this item and the other measures of in-session progress.

In addition, because Case 2-9 showed considerably more resistance, the therapist had to deal with it more frequently than for Case 2-45, leading to higher ratings for this item in the poorer outcome case (Case 2-9). The following is a typical sequence for Case 2-9 (Session 5, Block 1):

THERAPIST: It seems that you don't know how to start (pause).

CLIENT: Yeah (pause). I'm afraid to start it I guess (pause).

THERAPIST: If that were the case, you'd be afraid of what?

THERAPIST: Uh (pause). I don't know (pause), uh, what you would say to whatever I said, I guess (silence).

THERAPIST: Like what?

CLIENT: Mmm (silence). I don't know, maybe that I'd be criticized for it, or whatever (silence).

THERAPIST: So if I were to tell you what to talk about, that would sort of take you off the hook.

CLIENT: Yeah, I guess, 'cause I don't know what you expect or whatever (silence).

Note that such discussions of Case 2-9's anxieties about opening up in therapy led to discussions of similar anxieties she had in other situations and to greater openness on her part. Inspection of the data revealed that the blocks immediately following transference discussions typically had higher-than-average ratings for the other RPPS and Vanderbilt scale indicators of progress. A good example of this sequence occurred in Session 8. In Block 1, the client started (as usual) by saying that she did not know what to talk about or what the therapist expected. She went on to say that she had been noticing that she blocked herself from being spontaneous in a number of other situations. This was followed by a long discussion of her experience in the day-care program where she worked, in which she had trouble interacting freely with the children. She also expressed anger at the teachers for not giving her enough guidance. This experience was then linked by the therapist to her having grown up with an alcoholic father who, she felt, rarely made clear what was expected of her. The client's subsequent associations supported this interpretation.

The discussion of transference issues in Block 1 of this session and in other places appeared to have played a facilitative role for this patient. If one had looked only at the gross differences between the cases in the scores for "reference to the therapist and therapy" and at the correlations between "reference to the therapist and therapy" and the other variables, one might have mistakenly concluded that such discussions of the transference were harmful. We suggested that this item continue to be rated with the rest of the scale but examined separately before including it in the total score (Holland et al., 1998). In conducting this close reading of the material, we came to appreciate how single-subject research lends itself to fine-grained qualitative and quantitative analysis of data that can clarify the overall statistical findings in an important way.

In brief, there is good preliminary support for a six- (and possibly seven-) item version of the RPPS. Its most appropriate use is in microanalytic process research such as sequential analysis, or analysis of significant change events, in assessing in-session patient progress in psychodynamic psychotherapy.

Methodological and Clinical Implications of the Research

There are three methodological features of this research project that we want to highlight. The first is the fruitfulness of single-case design, which, in this project, included (a) single-case quantitative analysis in which patients' turns-at-talk or a block of psychotherapy material constituted the unit of analysis and (b) confirmatory case study. Although this particular single-case design does not constitute an experiment in which variables are manipulated, thus limiting conclusions about causality, it does include the testing of hypotheses that are subject to disconfirmation. Another feature of single-case design that we used and that we recommend to others is studying more than one case at a time. Doing so increases the likelihood of the results being generalizable and permits a comparison between two cases with different outcomes.

A second methodological feature that is important is the use of

context. The concepts measured by the scales are complex and require an understanding of the patient and the course of therapy.
These are unlikely to be obtained from 10-min samples taken from
sessions and scored in scrambled order. For example, to judge
whether a statement by a patient represents insight or resistance
requires knowledge of the patient's characteristic defenses, which
comes from a familiarity with the presenting issues and what has
come before the scoring point. Our belief in the importance of context, however, requires empirical testing.

A third methodological feature, and one we encourage other researchers to use, is combining quantitative and qualitative analysis.
By examining each instance of reference to the therapy or therapist,
we came to understand what triggered such discussion (i.e., resistance) and the salutary effect its exploration had on subsequent
blocks of material. This kind of supplementary analysis can help
to make sense of purely quantitative data. The sequential scoring
of full transcripts of single cases made this possible in a way that
large-sample, traditional research could not.

The results of this project have implications for practicing clinicians. One is the importance of recognizing the decisive role of
theory in the way that clinicians formulate cases. Recall that two
groups of researchers arrived at much different formulations of the
same case on the basis of their different theoretical approaches. It
behooves therapists to keep track of their own theoretical biases
and to consider the value that a different understanding and approach may have, especially when therapy is not proceeding
smoothly.

In this connection, it appears that not just any formulation can
be expected to produce patient progress. That patients showed
more in-session progress when therapist interventions were compatible with one but not the other plan suggests that there may be
validity to the concept of "accuracy" of formulation. Clearly, much
more research is required before firm conclusions can be reached
on this controversial issue.

Our research attests to the value of therapists making interventions compatible with a well-formulated focus in BPT. In addition,
the results confirm the importance of what is commonly thought
of as good therapist process, which included attunement to patients in both dynamic content and affective tone, competent ap-

plication of psychodynamic technique, and an accepting and supportive interpersonal manner.

Finally, that the RPPS showed good initial reliability and validity suggests that the variables it includes could be profitably kept in mind by therapists in gauging their patients' in-session progress. In fact, while working on the development and testing of this scale, we and members of our research team found ourselves thinking in just this way. That is, knowledge of the RPPS helped us to focus on and consider whether our interventions were leading to progress or stagnation in the psychotherapies that we were conducting.

References

Barber, J. P., & Crits-Christoph, P. (1993). Advances in measures of psychodynamic formulations. *Journal of Consulting and Clinical Psychology*, 61, 574–585.

Caspar, F. (1997). Plan analysis. In T. D. Eells (Ed.), *Handbook of psychotherapy case formulation* (pp. 260–288). New York: Guilford Press.

Collins, W. D. (1989). *The reliability, stability, and theoretical adaptability of the Plan Diagnosis Method*. Unpublished doctoral dissertation, Rutgers University, New Brunswick, NJ.

Collins, W. D., & Messer, S. B. (1991). Extending the plan formulation method to an object relations perspective: Reliability, stability, and adaptability. *Psychological Assessment: A Journal of Consulting and Clinical Psychology*, 3, 75–81.

Curtis, J. T., & Silberschatz, G. (1986). Clinical implications of research on brief dynamic psychotherapy: I. Formulating the patients' problems and goals. *Psychoanalytic Psychology*, 3, 13–25.

Curtis, J. T., & Silberschatz, G. (1997). The Plan Formulation Method. In T. D. Eells (Ed.), *Handbook of psychotherapy case formulation* (pp. 116–136). New York: Guilford Press.

Curtis, J. T., Silberschatz, G., Sampson, H., Weiss, J., & Rosenberg, S. (1988). Developing reliable psychodynamic case formulations: An illustration of the Plan Diagnosis Method. *Psychotherapy*, 25, 256–265.

Edelson, M. (1992). Telling and enacting stories in psychoanalysis. In J. Barron, M. Eagle, & D. M. Wolitzky (Eds.), *Interface of psychoanalysis and psychology* (pp. 99–124). Washington, DC: American Psychological Association.

Fairbairn, W. R. D. (1954). Object relations and dynamic structure. In
    W. R. D. Fairbairn (Ed.), *An object relations theory of the personality* (pp.
    137–151). New York: Library of the Behavioral Sciences. (Original
    work published 1946)
Glover, E. (1931). The therapeutic effect of inexact interpretation: A con-
    tribution to the theory of suggestion. *International Journal of Psycho-
    Analysis, 12*, 397–411.
Hilliard, R. B. (1993). Single-case methodology in psychotherapy process
    and outcome research. *Journal of Consulting and Clinical Psychology, 61*,
    373–380.
Holland, S. J. (1994). *Development and validation of a scale to assess patient
    progress in psychodynamic therapy.* Unpublished doctoral dissertation,
    Rutgers University, New Brunswick, NJ.
Holland, S. J., Roberts, N. E., & Messer, S. B. (1998). Reliability and validity
    of the Rutgers Psychotherapy Progress Scale. *Psychotherapy Research,
    8*, 104–110.
Horowitz, L. M., & Rosenberg, S. E. (1994). The consensual response psy-
    chodynamic formulation: 1. Method and research results. *Psychother-
    apy Research, 4*, 222–233.
Horowitz, M. J., & Eells, T. D. (1997). Configurational analysis: States of
    mind, person schemas, and the control of ideas and affect. In T. D.
    Eells (Ed.), *Handbook of psychotherapy case formulation* (pp. 166–191).
    New York: Guilford Press.
Howard, K. I., Kopta, S. M., Krause, M. S., & Orlinsky, D. E. (1986). The
    dose–effect relationship in psychotherapy. *American Psychologist, 41*,
    159–164.
Jones, E. E., & Windholz, M. (1990). The psychoanalytic case study: To-
    ward a method for systematic inquiry. *Journal of the American Psycho-
    analytic Association, 38*, 985–1015.
Klein, M. H., Mathieu-Coughlan, P., Gendlin, E. T., & Kiesler, D. J. (1986).
    The Experiencing Scales. In L. S. Greenberg & W. M. Pinsoff (Eds.),
    The psychotherapeutic process (pp. 21–71). New York: Guilford Press.
Koss, M. P., & Shiang, J. (1994). Research on brief psychotherapy. In A. E.
    Bergin & S. L. Garfield (Eds.), *Handbook of psychotherapy and behavior
    change* (4th ed., pp. 664–700). New York: Wiley.
Levenson, H., & Strupp, H. H. (1997). Cyclical maladaptive patterns: Case
    formulation in time-limited dynamic psychotherapy. In T. D. Eels
    (Ed.), *Handbook of psychotherapy case formulation* (pp. 84–115). New
    York: Guilford Press.
Luborsky, L. (1997). The Core Conflictual Relationship Theme: A basic case
    formulation method. In T. D. Eells (Ed.), *Handbook of psychotherapy case
    formulation* (pp. 58–83). New York: Guilford Press.
Luborsky, L., & Crits-Christoph, P. (1990). *Understanding transference: The
    CCRT method.* New York: Basic Books.
Mann, J. (1991). Time limited psychotherapy. In P. Crits-Christoph & J. P.

Barber (Eds.), *Handbook of short-term dynamic psychotherapy* (pp. 17–44). New York: Basic Books.

Marmar, C. R. (1990). Psychotherapy process research: Progress, dilemmas, and future directions. *Journal of Consulting and Clinical Psychology, 58*, 265–272.

Messer, S. B. (1991). The case formulation approach: Issues of reliability and validity. *American Psychologist, 46*, 1348–1350.

Messer, S. B., Sass, L. A., & Woolfolk, R. L. (Eds.). (1988). *Hermeneutics and psychological theory: Interpretive perspectives on personality, psychopathology, and psychotherapy.* New Brunswick, NJ: Rutgers University Press.

Messer, S. B., Tishby, O., & Spillman, A. (1992). Taking context seriously in psychotherapy research: Relating therapist interventions to patient progress in brief psychodynamic therapy. *Journal of Consulting and Clinical Psychology, 60*, 678–688.

Messer, S. B., & Warren, C. S. (1995). *Models of brief psychodynamic therapy: A comparative approach.* New York: Guilford Press.

Messer, S. B., & Wolitzky, D. L. (1997). The traditional psychoanalytic approach to case formulation. In T. D. Eells (Ed.), *Handbook of psychotherapy case formulation* (pp. 26–57). New York: Guilford Press.

O'Malley, S. S., Suh, C. S., & Strupp, H. H. (1983). The Vanderbilt Psychotherapy Process Scale: A report of the scale development and a process–outcome study. *Journal of Consulting and Clinical Psychology, 51*, 581–586.

Perry, J. C. (1997). The idiographic conflict formulation method. In T. D. Eells (Ed.), *Handbook of psychotherapy case formulation* (pp. 137–165). New York: Guilford Press.

Ricoeur, P. (1981). *Hermeneutics and the human sciences.* Cambridge, England: Cambridge University Press.

Roberts, N. E. (1994). *Reliability and factor analysis of the Rutgers Psychotherapy Progress Scale.* Unpublished doctoral dissertation, Rutgers University, New Brunswick, NJ.

Schacht, T. E., & Henry, W. P. (1994). Modeling recurrent patterns of interpersonal relationship with structural analysis of behavior. *Psychotherapy Research, 4*, 208–221.

Schafer, R. (1992). *Retelling a life: Narratives and dialogue in psychoanalysis.* New York: Basic Books.

Silberschatz, G., & Curtis, J. T. (1990, June). An empirical test of psychotherapy process predictions derived from alternate psychodynamic formulations. In J. T. Curtis (Chair), *Applications of a model for studying and comparing theories of psychotherapy.* Symposium conducted at the meeting of the Society for Psychotherapy Research, Wintergreen, VA.

Spence, D. P. (1982). *Narrative truth and historical truth.* New York: Norton.

Spence, D. P., Dahl, H., & Jones, E. E. (1993). Impact of interpretation on associative freedom. *Journal of Consulting and Clinical Psychology, 61*, 395–402.

Spillman, A. (1991). *The development of a scale for measuring patient progress and patient stagnation in psychodynamic psychotherapy.* Unpublished doctoral dissertation, Rutgers University, New Brunswick, NJ.

Suh, C. S., Strupp, H. H., & O'Malley, S. S. (1986). The Vanderbilt process measures: The Psychotherapy Process Scale (VPPS) and the Negative Indicators Scale (VNIS). In L. S. Greenberg & W. M. Pinsoff (Eds.), *The psychotherapeutic process* (pp. 285–323). New York: Guilford Press.

Tishby, O. (1991). *The effects of patient interventions on patient progress in brief psychodynamic therapy.* Unpublished doctoral dissertation, Rutgers University, New Brunswick, NJ.

Tishby, O., & Messer, S. B. (1995). The relationship between plan compatibility of therapist interventions and patient progress: A comparison of two plan formulations. *Psychotherapy Research, 5,* 76–88.

Weiss, J. (1990). Unconscious mental functioning. *Scientific American, 262,* 103–109.

Weiss, J., & Sampson, H. (1986). *The psychoanalytic process.* New York: Guilford Press.

Woolfolk, R. L., Sass, L. A., & Messer, S. B. (1988). Introduction to hermeneutics. In S. B. Messer, L. A. Sass, & R. L. Woolfolk (Eds.), *Hermeneutics and psychological theory: Interpretive perspectives on personality, psychopathology, and psychotherapy* (pp. 2–26). New Brunswick, NJ: Rutgers University Press.

Research on Unconscious Mental Functioning in Relationship to the Therapeutic Process

Suzanne M. Gassner and Marshall Bush

Terry Waite endured 1,763 days as a hostage held in captivity in Beirut, Lebanon. When Waite first was captured, he had a dream that he was utterly unable to recall throughout his long years of imprisonment. The dream was as follows:

> I am alone walking by the sea. It's dusk—I walk along the sand. The sea laps at my feet. Suddenly I am conscious of being alone. When I look up, I can no longer see land. The sea rolls in. I feel panic. I am going to be cut off. Unless I get off this beach quickly I will drown. Why can't I find my way? I see in the distance two figures coming towards me across the sand. I recognize two of my children. They take me by the hand as they would a blind man and guide me off the beach to the shelter of a familiar town. (Waite, 1993, p. 28)

During all the years that Waite was held in solitary confinement, his recall of this dream eluded him. It was only after Waite had safely returned to England and was reunited with his wife and two children that he was able to recall this dream of terror and rescue. Why should it be that a man who spends more than 4 years of his life in solitary confinement can remember only a dream such as this one once his ordeal has ended and he is returned safely to the family he loves? Weiss (1993; Weiss & Sampson, 1986) has proposed a theory, *control-mastery theory* (CMT), that helps to explain phenomena such as Waite's repression of his dream and the timing of its subsequent recovery. This theory has inspired the San Francisco Psychotherapy Research Group (formerly called the Mt. Zion Psychotherapy Research Group), under the leadership of Sampson and Weiss, to conduct a series of studies focused on unconscious mental functioning (Weiss, Sampson, & the Mt. Zion Psychotherapy Research Group, 1986).

Introduction to the Higher Mental Functioning Paradigm

The purpose of this chapter is to describe research about mental processes that operate outside of conscious awareness. There is a growing appreciation in both psychoanalysis and cognitive psychology of the unconscious mind's capacity always to be making appraisals. The research we describe is concerned with fundamental laws governing the unconscious mental functioning of the patient who is undergoing either psychoanalysis or psychoanalytically oriented psychotherapy. The unconscious mental functioning hypotheses tested were based on what Weiss et al. (1986) referred to as the "higher mental functioning paradigm" (HMFP).

The CMT of unconscious mental functioning is rooted in Freud's (1926/1964) seminal work, *Inhibitions, Symptoms and Anxiety*. In this account of unconscious mental functioning, people are understood to be capable of exercising unconscious control over their repressions. People typically maintain their repression of a mental content when they anticipate that experiencing the content would create a situation of emotional or interpersonal danger. People may lift their repressions and make the content conscious when they judge that they may experience it safely. This paradigm assumes that higher mental functions, such as unconscious thoughts, judgments, anticipations, decisions, and beliefs play a central role in the unconscious regulation of defenses and in pathogenesis. The HMFP has profound implications for how patients use treatment in terms of their unconscious appraisals of safety and danger, their beliefs, and their decisions and plans. CMT (Weiss, 1993; Weiss & Sampson, 1986) elaborated and expanded the HMFP, thereby offering a comprehensive theory of the therapeutic process.

The first series of studies we describe compared how well the HMFP accounted for the patient's behavior in psychoanalytic treatment when it was compared with an alternative set of hypotheses that Weiss et al. (1986) referred to as the "automatic functioning paradigm" (AFP), derived from Freud's early theory of how the unconscious mind functions. This is the theory of unconscious mental functioning developed before the ego psychology that Freud presented in *The Interpretation of Dreams* (Freud, 1900/1953a), the *Papers on Technique* (1911–1915/1953b), and the *Papers on Metapsychology* (Freud, 1914–1916/1953c). According to this view, much of people's unconscious behavior can be understood as an interplay of psychic forces that are either seeking or preventing discharge and that are governed by the pleasure principle. The dynamic interaction of these unconscious forces, namely the dynamic–economic interaction of impulses and defenses, determines behavior. According to this view, unconscious psychic forces are the basic causes of behavior, and thoughts and beliefs are merely epiphenomena derived from these unconscious forces.

Many contemporary psychoanalytic clinicians accept to some extent both the HMFP and the AFP and use their intuition to decide when each paradigm helps them to understand their patients better. Psychoanalysts may be placed on a spectrum on the basis of how much they rely on the AFP at one end and the HMFP on the other.

The research that we present involves a series of interrelated studies of a single patient. The data come from an audio-recorded psychoanalytic case and use both the verbatim transcripts of the treatment sessions and the detailed process notes made by the treating analyst, who summarized the content of each session.

The Case of Mrs. C.

We briefly describe Mrs. C., the patient who was studied. Mrs. C., a professional woman in her late 20s, had been married for several years at the time she entered analysis. She was the second of four children, with a sister 2 years older, a sister 3 years younger, and a brother 6 years younger. She came from a highly conservative Protestant New England family. Her mother, a social worker during the patient's childhood, later devoted herself to civic causes. Her father, like her husband, was a successful businessman. Mrs. C. grew up in a comfortable suburb, attended public schools through high school, and then went to a prominent women's college. She earned a master's degree in social work from a prominent Eastern university and had been employed for several years at a child guidance clinic at the time she sought treatment. During the intake interviews, the patient stated that she was seeking help primarily because her husband, who had been in analysis for 2 years, had strongly urged her to do so, and her husband's analyst had supported the idea.

Her major presenting problem was her inability to enjoy and reluctance to have sexual relations with her husband. In addition, Mrs. C. described a fear of simply being a nonentity, of existing as a maid to her husband, and of not occupying an equal position in the relationship. She also complained of feeling chronically tense, self-critical, overly anxious, and unable to relax and interact comfortably with others. At work she felt driven by a strong sense of obligation and duty. She also felt more distant from coworkers than she thought she should be.

In attempting to explain her sexual inhibitions to the intake worker, she mentioned that her family was controlled, unemotional, and unaffectionate. Mrs. C. felt she had deeply internalized her father's disapproval of sensuality. She characterized him as a stern, ascetic tyrant who rarely showed her any physical affection but who often punished her in violent outbursts of emotion.

The patient described herself to be much like her mother—efficient, overly organized, and afraid to show emotion. Like her mother, she felt unable to relax and enjoy herself. The patient expressed long-standing resentment toward her mother for not having protected her from her father's rage.

The patient remembered an incident from her childhood in which her older sister hit her in the stomach. She protested to her then-pregnant mother, who seemed uninterested. Mrs. C. reacted by punching her mother in the stomach even harder than her sister had hit her. Her mother, in a typical fashion, made no effort to defend herself or to discipline Mrs. C. Doubled over in pain, she simply went to her room to lie down. When her father came home, he had one of his characteristic anger outbursts. He beat Mrs. C. severely, making her feel that he might even want to kill her, and threw her into a closet and shut the door.

Mrs. C. believed her fear of sexual intercourse stemmed largely from an incident that occurred when she was 9 years old. She had been playing with her brother and accidentally fell on a long stick, sustaining an injury to her genital area that required stitches in the perineum. Many years later, during her first mother–daughter talk about sexuality, her mother warned her that, in addition to the danger of pregnancy, intercourse might be particularly painful because of the injury. Her mother told her that she might have been stitched up too tightly and therefore that an operation might be required before she could have intercourse. Although a doctor assured her after a premarital examination that this was not the case, the patient thought the effects of the injury were a major factor behind her fear of intercourse.

Mrs. C.'s childhood and adolescence were generally characterized as lonely years. Between the ages of 5 and 8, she knew that she had recurrent nightmares of something happening to her mother. Throughout her childhood she went to a friend's mother to confide her problems and receive affection. An early childhood memory of the patient was of using a wooden object in her play that represented a penis. Throughout childhood she wished she had a penis. During high school, Mrs. C. had one close female friend, but on the whole she considered her dates and friends to be uninteresting and inferior to those of her older sister. Mrs. C. always felt like an outsider to her family and currently lived some distance from them.

Mrs. C. had been diagnosed by the psychiatrist who referred her for analysis as a neurotic woman who was suffering from obsessive–compulsive difficulties. The analyst who treated Mrs. C. was highly experienced, was located in a distant city, and had no knowledge of our research group's hypotheses at the time that he conducted the analysis. With the consent of the patient, the entire analysis was tape-recorded for research purposes. In addition, the analyst wrote detailed process notes during the sessions. The first 100 hr of the analysis have been transcribed, and the studies we are presenting made use of both the verbatim transcripts and the process notes from this same period.

Two training analysts working independently from our research group read the first 100 hr of the process notes and described their observations. These analysts were not informed of our group's hypotheses. They concluded that there was clinical evidence of true improvement taking place during this period of treatment. They observed that Mrs. C. became considerably more relaxed, acquired an increased ability to enjoy her work and be effective at it, began to enjoy sex more, and was generally happier in her marriage. They also felt that she was bringing out important material on her own.

The HMFP and the AFP: Two Theories of Unconscious Mental Functioning

We now describe a network of research findings that may most easily be explained by the HMFP. This research demonstrates that patients keep mental contents warded off until they decide unconsciously that they may safely be experienced. Because patients may wait until they are no longer endangered by a particular content before bringing it forth, warded-off contents may emerge without anxiety or conflict and then be kept in consciousness without anxiety while being experienced vividly and used progressively. Moreover, patients may, while bringing forth warded-off contents, feel more, rather than less, in control of themselves.

By contrast, the AFP assumes that repressed mental contents are regulated in accordance with the pleasure principle (i.e., by indications of pleasure and pain). These unconscious processes are understood to operate beyond patients' ego control. Because patients have no control over these contents and are therefore unable to lift their defenses against them, the analyst's interpretations are believed to play the central role in making such contents conscious. According to this paradigm, if a repressed mental content is not interpreted, it ordinarily remains unexpressed or is expressed in disguised ways through symptoms and other compromise formations.

An unconscious content may become conscious during analysis because of a shift in the dynamic balance between the repressing and repressed forces in favor of the repressed. When a repressed content becomes intensified, it evokes intensified defensive efforts as it pushes toward consciousness. The repressed content, if powerful enough, may break through into consciousness in a relatively undisguised form. In this instance, patients are likely to be anxious when the content emerges and to continue to feel conflict about it. Because the content is still dangerous to patients, they are likely to attempt to repress it. More commonly, repressed contents spontaneously become conscious only in well-disguised compromise formations. In this circumstance, because the content is still being defended against, patients do not feel anxious about its emergence and do not come into intense conflict with it. Moreover, because the true import of the emerging content is disguised, patients do not understand its significance and cannot use insight into it to advance their therapy.

Research That Compares the HMFP and the AFP

In the first study we describe, Gassner, Sampson, Weiss, and Brumer (1982, 1986) investigated how well the AFP and the HMFP could each account for observations about how warded-off contents emerged in the course of the first 100 hr of Mrs. C.'s psychoanalysis. The two hypotheses may be compared empirically because they lead to different predictions. As noted above, the AFP assumes that mental contents are regulated automatically and that this regulation takes place in accordance with the criterion of pleasure–unpleasure. The HMFP assumes that repressed mental contents may be regulated by unconscious thoughts and decisions and that this regulation is based on appraisals of danger and safety. The HMFP suggests a combination of expected findings that the AFP cannot explain: that patients are able to bring forth previously warded-off contents without benefit of interpretations from the therapist; to report these contents without experiencing anxiety, coming into conflict with them, or trying to ward them off; and to maintain conscious control over them.

We describe this study in some detail to convey a sense of the methods that the Mt. Zion Psychotherapy Research Group used to study the two psychoanalytic hypotheses that we have described. To study the conditions under which warded-off contents emerge in analysis, we needed a method for identifying warded-off contents that would not use clues about whether their emergence was accompanied by conflict. To this end, we used a method for identifying previously warded-off contents that also met the psychoanalytic criterion that the contents had been previously unacceptable to the patient and consequently warded off by defenses.

Gassner et al. (1982) used a modified version of a novel method for identifying previously warded-off contents devised by Horowitz, Sampson, Siegelman, Wolfson, and Weiss (1975) in the case of Mrs. C. The major procedural steps were as follows: All new ideas that emerged in Hours 41–100 previously unexpressed in Hours 1–40 were identified by two judges who independently read through the process notes of the first 100 hr. More than 500 such statements were identified and were organized by their thematic content. One hundred of the 500 statements were randomly selected, with the constraint that the thematic contents of these statements had to be in direct proportion to the total number of statements found in each family of thematic contents.

The 100 selected statements, as well as the process notes of the first 10 treatment hours, were presented to 19, all highly experienced clinicians. Their instructions read as follows: "These statements come from hours 41–100; they appeared for the first time during those hours. Please read each statement. We want to know whether you think that the content had been warded-off earlier. Use your clinical intuition to make this judgment, applying whatever criteria would lead you to call a content warded-off. As one possible criterion, you might want to ask whether that content would have been acceptable to the patient during the first 10 hours of treatment. Other criteria may also occur to you. Feel free to apply whatever criteria seem pertinent."

Judges rated the 100 statements on a 5-point scale that indicated the degree of confidence they had that a content had been previously warded off. A rating of 5 indicated a strong belief that a content had been previously warded off; a rating of 1 indicated a strong belief that the content had not been previously warded off. The treating analyst also rated which of the 100 statements had been previously warded off, using all that he had learned about the patient in the course of the entire analysis, to make these judgments.

The split-half reliability coefficient for the 100 statements studied, calculated by correlating the mean values of one randomly selected group of 9 judges' ratings with those of another group of 10 judges, produced a correlation of .90, indicating that the clinical judges showed considerable agreement about which statements had been previously warded off.

These instructions encouraged judges to use the usual clinical method for making such judgments, but two stringent requirements were added that clinicians ordinarily do not have to meet: First, we established the reliability of our clinical judgments by demonstrating agreement among a group of judges. Second, we avoided basing the judgment about whether a particular content had been warded off by considering how the patient felt while it was emerging.

Many practicing clinicians who are influenced by the AFP make the post hoc assessment that if a content that would have been expected to have been repressed is calmly discussed, the content had never been repressed. We did not assume what the AFP predicts, namely that an uninterpreted content that emerges without anxiety could not have been previously warded off.

Thirteen of the 100 statements received a mean scale value of 4 or higher. These statements made up the items considered to be highly warded-off statements. Examples of statements that received a rating of 4 or higher are as follows: (a) She recalls wanting to kill her older brother. (b) She looked at her bowel movements with the urge to see what she had done. (c) She knew how to work her parents, their guilt, and their need to be absolutely fair. (d) She controls when her husband has an orgasm by whether she moves or not.

The set of contents judged previously warded off conformed to what psychoanalytically informed clinicians mean when they refer to *unconscious contents* or *warded-off contents*. Nonetheless, because we were aware that our measurement procedures might result in a distortion of the phenomenon under investigation, we sought additional evidence by other means that would enable us to assess further whether the contents that the judges identified as previously warded off were clinically significant. We looked for information from both the patient and the treating analyst as well as our own psychotherapy research group.

Of the 100 statements judged, 7 contained phrases that directly acknowledged the difficulty the patient had in facing the expressed content. Gassner et al. (1982) designated "cued as previously warded off," statements that contained phrases such as "I've never let myself think . . ."; "Suddenly I realize . . ."; "I can't believe I'm saying that . . ." and so on. To avoid giving the judges such cues, we omitted all phrases that expressed the patient's judgment that the idea had been previously warded off. For example, had the patient said, "I've never let myself face it that my brother is really condescending," the opening phrase "I've never let myself face it that" was eliminated from the information that the judges received.

The mean of the 7 cued as previously warded-off statements was 3.96, whereas the mean of the noncued statements was 2.86. This difference in the scale values for the two groups of statements was statistically significant at the .05 level. We concluded that the judges were fairly well able to identify as previously warded off the "cues-deleted statements."

The treating analyst rated 11 of the 13 statements as previously warded off. Moreover, the treating analyst considered the statements that our judges gave the highest ratings to be so revealing and powerful that he asked us to disguise their contents for purposes of any publications.

Working independently of the judges, our research group made its own case formulation. This formulation focused on the kinds of ideas, feelings, and memories that the patient would have to allow into consciousness for her analysis to progress well. Our group felt that the statements judged to have been previously warded off involved powerful impulses or significant painful childhood memories and ideas and that these contents were directly connected to our own case formulation. These three converging lines of evidence suggested that the statements judged to be warded off were indeed clinically meaningful.

Examples of statements judged to be highly warded off are as follows: (a) "She recalls wanting to kill her older brother." (b) "She thought how she and her husband had had intercourse and she had wanted it and enjoyed it." (c) "She looked at her bowel movements with the urge to see what she had done."

Two members of our research group, Marla Isaacs and Carol Drucker (Shilkret, Isaacs, Ducker, & Curtis, 1986), independently cataloged all of the analyst's interventions. Drawing on their work, we were able to look at each of the analyst's interventions to determine whether anything he had said before the hour in which this content emerged was related to the ideas expressed in the patient's previously warded-off contents. We found one such interpretation made by the analyst that related to one of the previously warded-off ideas the patient had subsequently expressed. Twelve of the 13 statements emerged without any previous interpretation by the analyst.

We then studied these 12 statements to assess whether there was an increase in anxiety when they emerged. Brumer (Gassner et al., 1986) applied three techniques for rating the patient's anxiety at any given moment in the treatment. The three techniques are Mahl's (1956) speech disturbance ratio, the Gottschalk–Gleser Content Analysis Scale (Gottschalk & Gleser, 1969), and clinical ratings.

Mahl's (1956) speech disturbance ratio measures momentary anxiety in patients by quantifying aspects of how they speak. Speech disturbances such as slips of the tongue, sentence changes, intruding incoherent sounds, stutters, repetitions, sentence incompletions, and omissions are identified. A speech disturbance ratio can be obtained for any segment of speech by compiling the ratio of speech disturbances to the total number of words spoken. Numerous studies have shown that the Mahl measure is an objective quantification of anxiety and a reliably discriminating measure (Mahl, 1956, 1959, 1961).

The Gottschalk–Gleser Content Analysis Scale assesses immediate anxiety by measuring manifest anxiety-related verbal content. Phrases that focus on any of the following six contents are assessed as evidence of the presence of anxiety in the speaker: death, mutilation, guilt, shame, separation, and nonspecific anxiety. In addition, defensive and adaptive manifestations of anxiety are inferred when the speaker (a) imputes anxiety or anxiety-motivated behavior to other people, animals, or inanimate objects; (b) repudiates or denies the affect of anxiety; or (c) reports the affect in any attenuated form. Numerous studies have demonstrated the reliability and the predictive validity of this measure and some evidence of its construct validity (Gottschalk, 1974a, 1974b; Gottschalk & Gleser, 1969).

The third method to determine the patient's anxiety involved clinical judgments of anxiety. Interrater reliability was high for all three anxiety measures. A .91 reliability coefficient was obtained by the two judges who applied Mahl's (1956) speech disturbance measure to 103 episodes in which the 12 warded-off statements and 91 randomly selected statements appeared. Four judges applied the Gottschalk–Gleser technique to the same 103 episodes with an interrater reliability coefficient of .80. An intraclass correlation coefficient of .74 was obtained for the average intercorrelation between pairs of six raters who judged the amount of anxiety the patient was expressing in episodes containing the 12 warded-off contents and episodes containing the 20 control statements. None of the three methods showed any evidence that the patient was any more anxious when previously warded-off contents were emerging, or during the 5 min that preceded their emergence, than at randomly selected times during the analysis or at times when non–warded-off contents were emerging. The analysis of data based on Mahl's speech disturbance technique showed that randomly selected patient statements were accompanied by considerably more anxiety than were previously warded-off statements. The difference was statistically significant at the .025 level.[1]

To determine whether the patient was defending against the significance of the previously warded-off contents, we applied the Experiencing Scale (Klein, Mathieu, Gendlin, & Kiesler, 1970) to warded-off statements as well as to randomly selected statements. The Experiencing Scale assesses the degree to which patients focus on their ongoing flow of changing feelings as they occur during psychotherapy and how they reflect on these feelings and use such observations for problem solving. The scale is useful for micro-

---

[1] All significance levels reported are for two-tailed tests unless otherwise noted.

scopic process studies because it has been found to be sensitive to shifts in patient involvement (Klein et al., 1970). Four trained judges applied the Experiencing Scale to the 12 warded-off statements and to 91 randomly selected statements. Their interrater reliability was .75.

Two kinds of scores can be obtained from the Experiencing Scale. One is the modal score, which characterizes the overall experiencing level of the therapy segment being studied. When the modal measure was used, Mrs. C. showed a significantly higher level of experiencing when warded-off contents were emerging than when randomly selected statements were being made ($p < .05$). The second Experiencing Scale measure is the peak score that describes the highest scale level reached in the segment being studied. When the peak measure was applied, a similar result was obtained, although the difference approached significance only at the .10 level. These data indicate that the patient was actually more involved with reflecting on the feelings associated with the warded-off contents than with the randomly selected contents chosen from her psychoanalysis. Our measures suggested that the patient was particularly involved in the analytic process at just those times when she was doing the progressive therapeutic work of allowing previously warded-off contents into consciousness.

We know of no way that the AFP can explain this combination of observations. These findings support the idea that the patient has the capacity to lift her defenses, consistent with the HMFP.

In a subsequent study, Shilkret et al. (1986) investigated the emergence of a particular set of warded-off ideas, those concerning Mrs. C.'s unconsciously held beliefs about her own omnipotence. On the basis of the process notes of the first 10 hr, our research group had concluded that Mrs. C. not only had considerable difficulty with fighting with others but also that, to make significant gains, she would need to understand the reasons that fighting, criticizing, blaming, and so forth were so troublesome. It was further hypothesized that her conflicts in this area resulted from her omnipotence fantasies about her power to hurt others. For these purposes, omnipotence is defined as the patient's anxiety about hurting others and her unrealistic appraisal of her power to push others around.

Shilkret et al. (1986) developed a case-specific omnipotence scale on the basis of a clinical inductive study of the process notes of the first 100 hr of the patient's analysis. Their approach was to identify all of Mrs. C.'s expressions of omnipotence and then to order them sequentially. On the basis of a thorough reading of these process notes, Shilkret et al. identified five different levels of the patient's insight into these problems.

At the lowest level of the omnipotence scale, the patient displays little or no recognition of either omnipotent fantasies or feelings or awareness that she is troubled by these issues. For instance, at Stage 1 the patient expresses the general idea that she is in some way bad, harmful, or unable to be good, without qualification. The patient also feels weak, helpless, and impotent and is unable to exert control in interpersonal situations, so that she cannot do things she wants to do or feels compelled to do things that she does not want to do. She does not consciously experience guilt because she does not feel responsible for, or in control of, her thoughts or actions.

At Stage 2, the patient still feels unable to exert control, but she recognizes a vague sense of guilt or responsibility for others (or both) that she cannot account for or knows is unreasonable. Her insight at this stage is that she feels guilty for "something," but she is unaware of the omnipotent thoughts that are causing the guilt.

At Stage 3, the patient makes her concerns explicit—that she feels responsible, guilty, or blameworthy because of her thoughts or actions. The patient now feels that she can control others and is bothered that she can harm others by this control. She now understands the cause of her feelings of excessive responsibility (i.e., her idea that she can control and thus harm people).

At Stage 4, the patient feels she can control others without being bothered by such feelings. She feels powerful without feeling guilty. She may even enjoy feeling powerful, strong, or controlling.

At Stage 5, the patient is engaged in an attempt to realistically assess the extent of her ability to control others. As part of this assessment, she may distinguish between her thoughts and her actions, or she may attempt to anticipate the realistic consequences of her actions, even if this assessment is difficult to make.

Once the scale was developed, six judges read through the 100 hr and selected items that unambiguously pertained to the scale.

Because the intent of the scale was to measure Mrs. C.'s insight into her omnipotence, the judges were instructed to identify any explicit, conscious thoughts she had about her irrational feelings of guilt, responsibility, and power to hurt others. After this selection of 144 items, two experienced clinicians read through the statements and determined that the 144 selected items represented all of the stages of the scale. Three judges then rated these items according to the stage level, producing an average interrater reliability of .72. Each item was given the rating that two or more judges agreed on. The mean ratings for the 10-hr blocks showed a statistically significant change in the predicted direction across the 100 hr, providing evidence for the patient's increasing insight into her problems of omnipotence. The results of this study suggest that increases in Mrs. C.'s capacity to blame, criticize, and fight with others was accompanied by her acquisition of genuine insights into her problems with omnipotence. Thus, Shilkret et al. (1986) were able to trace how Mrs. C. began to develop insight into a central unconscious conflict, namely her unconscious fears of hurting people and her conflicts about having power or strength of any kind.

Isaacs and Drucker (Shilkret et al., 1986), building on the Shilkret study, investigated whether Mrs. C. gained these insights into her conflicts because they were interpreted to her or whether they were acquired without interpretation. They adopted the five-stage omnipotence scale of Shilkret et al. to investigate the analyst's interpretations into this same area of conflict. Without describing the entire scale again, as applied to the analyst's interpretations, we define a few points to provide some indication about how the analyst's interpretations were catalogued.

At Stage 1, the analyst interpreted that the patient was feeling weak, helpless, or unable to exert control in interpersonal situations. He may have interpreted that she could not do things that she wanted to do or felt compelled to do things that she did not want to do relative to other people. At Stage 3, the analyst pointed to the patient's feeling that she could control others and that she felt bothered by that feeling. At Stage 5, the analyst pointed out the realistic extent of the patient's ability to control others.

In the first 100 hr of the analysis of Mrs. C., 153 of the analyst's interventions were found to be interpretations. The other interventions not included in this study included direct questions, one-word responses, business matters, and so on. Two judges familiar with the case read the 153 interventions with instructions to select any statements that in any way alluded to the patient's conflicts over omnipotence. A final sample of 21 analyst interventions was identified that were given ratings of 1–4. The overall interrater reliability was .82.

It was found that the patient reached each of the five levels of insight before the analyst's making an interpretation at that same level. There also was evidence that the analyst's interpretations at the same level as those of the patient facilitated and accelerated her progress, even though the interventions came after she had first reached that level of insight on her own (Shilkret et al., 1986).

The unconscious AFP and the unconscious HMFP would be likely to account for these findings in different ways. Because the patient's ideas about omnipotence emerged regularly without interpretation, the unconscious AFP would explain the patient's expressions of omnipotence as the result of the analyst's frustrating her wish to be all powerful and to push others around. The HMFP hypothesizes that the patient's ideas about omnipotence represented a pathogenic belief from which she wanted to free herself. As the patient learned that she was not hurting the analyst with her thoughts and actions, she became relieved and felt safe enough to lift her defenses against the expression of these ideas for purposes of mastery. Although we know her omnipotent ideas came forth regularly and without interpretation, to confirm that they represented a controlled emergence we needed to study how anxious she was while expressing these ideas.

Later we describe a study that examined Mrs. C.'s level of tension during these 100 hr. First, however, we describe the research of Horowitz (1979), who demonstrated Mrs. C.'s increasing capacity to fight and to be close during the first 100 treatment hours. These changes, too, like the increase in insight about omnipotence, could in and of themselves be accounted for by each of the two psychoanalytic paradigms we have described.

The AFP would explain these findings as a mobilization of conflict, stimulated by the analyst's interpretative work and the frustration of the patient's unconscious libidinal wishes. By contrast, the HMFP hypothesizes that these changes could be understood to follow from the patient's unconscious sense of increased safety with the analyst. In keeping with this explanation, because of the patient's increased sense of safety, she was able unconsciously to exercise greater control in how directly she could express fighting and closeness. Only after we consider this study in combination with our other studies can we distinguish how well the two paradigms accounted for the combination of observations.

Horowitz (1979) had three clinicians read the process notes of the first 100 hr and identify all instances of fighting behaviors (i.e., all instances in which the patient blamed, criticized, disagreed with, or opposed another person). One hundred ninety such instances were identified.

These 190 passages were presented in random order to a panel of four clinicians who had no other information about the case. The judges applied a 4-point rating scale to assess how directly the patient was able to blame, criticize, disagree, or oppose. If the blame or criticism was implied, the scale value was at 1; if the blame or criticism was expressed and then undone, the rating was 2; if the blame or criticism of one person was expressed directly to someone else, the rating was 3; and a direct confrontation of someone was rated 4. An additional 0.5 was added to the scale value if the event occurred in the present tense, and thus the range of possible ratings expanded from 1 to 4.5.

A comparable procedure was used to identify all passages describing behavior that expressed closeness or intimacy. There were 106 instances in which confiding, cooperating, and loving were expressed. A corresponding 4-point rating scale was devised for these closeness items.

Both sets of passages were reliably rated. The mean ratings for each 10-hr block were computed; for both the fighting and closeness measures, the change across hours revealed the type of growth usually associated with a learning curve. Note that there were 18 statements that directly referred to the patient's sexual behavior. These were studied separately because they referred to her presenting complaint of sexual frigidity. For this subcategory of closeness behaviors, there also was a statistically significant change in the patient's capacity to directly describe her experiences with sexual intercourse. For example, in Hour 33 the patient said that sometimes when she is trying to make herself have intercourse with Bill, she feels as though she wants to hurt him. She just does not understand it. She will go from feeling very warm to feeling nothing toward him suddenly. By contrast, in Hour 67 she said that this weekend she and Bill had intercourse, and she was thinking how different it can be when she is thinking about him and feeling close to him and not all wrapped up in herself.

To distinguish the AFP from the HMFP, Mayer (Curtis, Ranso-hoff, Sampson, Brumer, & Bronstein, 1986) investigated Mrs. C.'s level of tension during the course of the first 100 hr, while she was progressing in the ways that we have described so far. The Mayer et al. measure, the Freedom-Beleaguerment Scale, assessed the patient's level of relaxation over time. Curtis et al. (1986) found that the patient seemed to maintain a constant level of tension during the first 100 hr (Curtis et al., 1986).

Horowitz et al. (1975) studied changes in the patient's level of drive. They identified all instances in the process notes where Mrs. C. expressed compulsions or inhibitions regarding closeness and fighting. These complaints were typically expressed in terms such as "I have to" or "I can't." Two hundred forty-eight such complaints were identified, among which were 60 statements referring to fighting and 56 statements referring to closeness. The patient's difficulties with closeness were typically expressed in the form "I can't." Mrs. C.'s difficulties asserting herself or expressing her aggression sometimes took the form of her having difficulty restraining herself ("I have to") and other times took the form of her feeling unable to express what she wished to convey ("I can't"). In both these ways, she was describing the driven quality of her behavior and her corresponding difficulty with feeling in control of herself.

Horowitz et al. (1975) found a statistically significant decrease in the patient's expressions of driven behavior over the course of the first 100 hr. Francis Sampson verified this finding working from the transcripts (Curtis et al., 1986).

Based on the research that we have described heretofore, we arrived at the following conclusions. Our research demonstrated that (a) The patient became conscious of previously unconscious ideas often without increased anxiety or conflict and kept these ideas in consciousness, experiencing them emotionally and integrating them within her personality. (b) The patient developed insights, especially into previously omnipotent ideas, ideas that she could magically harm others by her thoughts and actions. (3) The patient became more direct in her expression of aggression and love and developed an increased ability to experience sexual pleasure. (d) All of these changes took place largely without interpretation. (e) While these changes were taking place, the patient was becoming less driven and was feeling more in control of her behavior.

The HMFP can readily account for this combination of findings. During the first 100 hr, the patient made some symptomatic improvements. She became able to express her ideas and feelings concerning fighting, blaming, criticizing, and opposing others more directly. Likewise, she became less obsessive about her wishes, feelings, and ideas about closeness in general, including sexual intercourse in particular. Warded-off contents were emerging during the course of these hours, and the patient was gaining some insight into her problems with omnipotent ideas. These changes occurred largely without the analyst's interpretations preceding either the emergence of warded-off contents or her insights into her omnipotent ideas. Finally, while these gains were being made, the patient was becoming less driven and more in control of herself. Whereas this combination of findings cannot be parsimoniously explained as the result of an interplay of instinctual and defensive forces that have been mobilized by the analytical process, these findings can be readily accounted for by the HMFP.

Research findings such as these should be viewed cautiously. Replication by other investigators is needed to demonstrate that our findings were not influenced by research bias, a fortuitously chosen case, or other errors.

Research That Demonstrates the Predictive and Explanatory Power of CMT

CMT places a major emphasis on the unconscious pathogenic beliefs that children develop in their efforts to adapt to traumatic situations (Weiss, 1997). The most consequential of these beliefs are those that lead to unconscious guilt, impaired self-esteem, distrust of others, despair about the future, and a renunciation of normal developmental strivings toward independence, intimacy, success, and self-fulfillment. Pathogenic beliefs typically arise in the context of the child's relationships with parents and siblings. Children are highly vulnerable to developing false theories about themselves and others because they have a limited understanding of accurate causal relationships and tend to blame themselves for anything traumatic that happens to them or other family members. A major tenet of CMT is that in a well-conducted treatment, patients overcome their convictions in their pathogenic beliefs through a process called *testing*.

Introduction of the Concept of Testing

Testing in therapy is an extension of normal reality testing in everyday life (Weiss, 1989; Weiss & Sampson, 1986). It is a patient-initiated activity that uses trial actions to test one's expectations of danger and to elicit needed corrective emotional experiences in the therapeutic relationship. The patient's testing is usually unconscious because it is connected to traumas, pathogenic beliefs, affects, and wishes that the patient cannot yet face.

Testing is a crucial part of the patient's efforts at adaptation (Weiss, 1990a). Patients test in accordance with a reasonable unconscious plan for mastery (Weiss, in press) that takes into account their therapeutic goals, their pathogenic beliefs, their view of their own and the therapist's strengths and weaknesses, and their assessment of the therapist's capacity to help them. The notion that patients develop a reasonable unconscious plan for mastery logically follows from Weiss's (1990b) view of the unconscious mind as containing adaptive goals and engaging in high-level problem-solving activities.

> The idea that people plan their behavior is considered common sense for most human activities. However, this common sense view is not extended to the behavior of the patient in therapy. The patient's behavior is thought to be governed to some extent by unplanned unconscious forces. The present paper challenges this view. It assumes that the primary motive of patients in psychotherapy, including psychoanalysis, is to solve their problems by disproving the pathogenic beliefs that underlie them, and it assumes, too, that patients make and carry out plans for solving their problems. The patients' plans are for testing their pathogenic beliefs with the therapist, in the hope that the therapist

will not react to their tests as their beliefs predict. In research studies carried out by the San Francisco Psychotherapy Research Group we demonstrated that we can reliably infer patients' plans from their behavior at the beginning of therapy, and that patients work consistently in accordance with these plans throughout the therapy. (Weiss, in press, p. 2)

The patient's testing is guided by considerations of safety and danger (Sampson, 1989; Weiss et al., 1986) and by the priority assigned to different problems the patient wishes to master. Within Weiss's (1989, 1993) theory, testing is considered to be the primary unconscious work patients engage in throughout therapy. Through their testing behavior, patients attempt to disprove their pathogenic beliefs, assess conditions of safety and danger in the therapeutic relationship, discern their therapists' conscious and unconscious intentions toward them, and create opportunities to identify with strengths in the therapist that they want to acquire.

Patients typically begin by testing cautiously and progress to testing more boldly. Because testing entails some degree of emotional risk, it tends to produce strain in the patient that is relieved if the therapist passes the test. Passed tests decrease, at least momentarily, the patient's unconscious sense of danger and therefore tend to be followed by decreased anxiety, lessened defensiveness, increased confidence in the therapist, and indications of therapeutic progress. Failed tests increase the patient's unconscious sense of danger and therefore tend to be followed by increased anxiety and defensiveness. Patients generally "coach" the therapist after failed tests and give the therapist other opportunities to pass their tests before giving up on an important goal. Repeatedly failed tests result in therapeutic retreats and negative therapeutic outcomes. Consistently passed tests result in positive therapeutic outcomes.

Any behavior can be used for testing purposes, including apparent instances of transference, resistance, and acting out, although certain behaviors stand out as particularly clear examples of testing. Actions that contrast sharply with a patient's usual behavior or that call for some response from the therapist are likely to have an important testing function. Tests vary considerably in their complexity, intensity, duration, and centrality to the patient's core pathogenic beliefs.

Patients unconsciously adjust their testing to accommodate to their perception of the therapist's strengths and weaknesses as well as to the length of time they expect to be in therapy. Just as patients may pose tests in numerous ways, therapists can pass or fail tests in a variety of ways. Whether the therapist is passing or failing a patient's tests can be gauged by the patient's reaction to the therapist's response. Therapists typically pass and fail tests without awareness that they are being tested.

Weiss (1993; Weiss et al., 1986) has described two basic forms of testing. In the form called *transferring*, patients repeat some past behavior that resulted in their being traumatized as a child. In the form called *passive into active*, patients take the role of the traumatizing parent and place the therapist in the position of the traumatized child. Transference tests are intended to prove that some feared consequence will not occur if the patient behaves a certain way. For example, a patient might pose a transference test to prove that the therapist will not withdraw if the patient expresses loving feelings. Passive-into-active tests are undertaken to give patients a chance to identify with the therapist's capacity to handle parental behaviors that patients found traumatizing as children. For example, patients who were traumatized by a parent's rejecting attitude may act rejecting toward the therapist in the hope of being able to learn how to deal with rejection. Many tests contain elements of both testing strategies. Patients typically use a variety of testing strategies to disconfirm a single prominent pathogenic belief.

Testing can best be studied on a case-specific basis. To understand a patient's tests accurately, one must have a comprehensive grasp of the patient's childhood traumas, pathogenic beliefs, and therapeutic goals. The patient's testing provides an unconscious lens through which a patient will attempt to decode the "true" meaning of the therapist's interventions. The San Francisco Psychotherapy Research Group has been able to successfully demonstrate the predictive power of the testing concept by studying conspicuous and pertinent examples of tests in the therapeutic process.

Research on Testing

The first empirical study of testing (Horowitz et al., 1975) was part of a wider investigation into the emergence of formerly warded-off contents in the first 100 hr of a recorded analysis (the case of Mr. B.). Using an innovative methodology, the investigators compared the six sessions containing the most highly warded-off contents (W hours) with the six sessions containing the least highly warded-off contents (N hours). Each session was divided into thematically distinct "episodes" of patient speech that were rated for anxiety using a modified version of Mahl's measure of speech disruptions (Kasl & Mahl, 1965). The anxiety measure (referred to as a "discomfort quotient"), which had an interjudge reliability of .97, gauged the effect of the analyst's passing and failing tests in the 12 W and N hours.

For purposes of this study, which took place at an early stage in Weiss's (1971) development of CMT, tests and the analyst's response to them were not defined in a case-specific way. Mr. B. was considered to be testing when he openly disagreed with the analyst, expressed anger at the analyst, or demanded something from the analyst. Passing a test was defined as the analyst's remaining "neutral." The analyst's remaining silent was always considered a passed test. Although some tests will be failed if the analyst remains neutral or silent, this study produced statistically significant findings because the generic way in which tests and the analyst's response to them were defined happened to fit Mr. B.'s psychology. In other cases, a test might be badly failed if the patient announced an intention to do something self-destructive and the therapist remained neutral or said nothing.

In the Horowitz et al. (1975) method, two psychologists independently read the transcripts of the 12 W and N hours and identified 23 tests with perfect agreement. Three other judges rank-ordered the analyst's responses (for the degree of neutrality) with a high level of agreement. The episodes in which passed and failed tests occurred were compared with the episodes that immediately followed. Several statistically significant findings emerged. The first was that passed tests were followed by a drop in anxiety, whereas failed tests gave rise to increased anxiety. Passed tests also were significantly more likely to be followed by the emergence of previously warded-off contents. The opposite was true for failed tests. The W hours contained more passed tests and the N hours more failed tests. There also was evidence for the proposition that patients become more anxious while testing and less anxious if

their test is passed. The patient's discomfort quotient during testing episodes was higher than the mean discomfort quotient for the
hour. The patient's discomfort quotient was also significantly more
likely to drop following passed tests and to rise following failed
tests.

Silberschatz (1978; Silberschatz, Fretter, & Curtis, 1986) carried
out the first empirical study of testing that used a case-specific
method for identifying significant tests and judging whether the
therapist had passed or failed them.[2] He examined the consequences of passed and failed "key tests" using the verbatim transcript of the first 100 hr of the case of Mrs. C. The treating analyst
was unfamiliar with CMT and had terminated Mrs. C.'s treatment
before the study was undertaken. Silberschatz tested the hypothesis that a patient will feel less anxious and become more productive following significant passed tests. Conversely, significant failed
tests should be followed by increased distress and signs of retreat.

Judges were given a control-mastery case formulation[3] that described Mrs. C.'s therapeutic goals, pathogenic beliefs, and likely
testing strategies. One group of three judges reviewed a sample of
87 potential tests and identified those examples of testing that reflected Mrs. C.'s working to disconfirm a central pathogenic belief.
A set of 46 patient–therapist interactions was selected by all three
judges as instances of a key test. A second group of judges used
the control-mastery case formulation to reliably determine the degree to which the analyst passed or failed each test. Other groups
of judges applied several different rating scales to measure changes
in patient behavior immediately after each key test. Those scales
were the Experiencing Scale (Klein, Mathieu, Gendlin, & Kiesler,
1970), the Boldness Scale (Caston, Goldman, & McClure, 1986), the
Relaxation Scale (Curtis et al., 1986), and an affect classification
system that measured the patient's level of fear, anxiety, love, and
satisfaction (Dahl, 1978). Silberschatz found that the patient became significantly more involved, productive, and relaxed when
the therapist passed a key test. Passed tests correlated positively

---

[2]Parts of Silberschatz's study are described in a chapter by Weiss and
Sampson (1986) that appears in Volume 2 of this series.

[3]Caston (1986) developed a new methodology for obtaining good rater
reliability in the preparation of control-mastery case formulations.

with increased experiencing ($r = .33$, $p < .05$), boldness ($r = .32$, $p < .05$), relaxation ($r = .35$, $p < .05$), and feelings of love ($r = .37$, $p < .05$) and satisfaction ($r = .15$, $p < .05$), and negatively with fear ($r = -.34$, $p < .05$) and anxiety ($r = -.29$, $p < .05$). The opposite was true for failed tests.

The following examples of passed and failed tests are taken from Silberschatz's (1978) study. In the passed test, the patient was attempting to disconfirm her pathogenic belief that she had to diminish herself to make the analyst (and others) feel superior to her. The analyst's response implied that he did not need her to belittle her ideas for him to maintain his sense of authority. In the failed test, the patient was attempting to find out whether the analyst could tolerate her being in control in the sessions. The analyst's response conveyed a demand that she submit to his authority.

Example of a passed test

Patient: (Silence) It's funny. I just, when I finished saying what I said about um, the way I'm emphasizing what, what the trouble is or what's important, last night when I was thinking about it, it just seemed such an important thing to have realized. And now today when I think about it, it, I just sort of feel, well, of course, there's no point in even saying it. Or perhaps I'm feeling that's what you're thinking.

Analyst: Ah (patient laughs) I was going to just say that here you are again sort of taking away from yourself, degrading it immediately. It can't be worth much if you thought it, that kind of feeling.

Example of a failed test

Patient: (Silence) Is it better to force yourself to say something that you feel sort of not ready to say?

Analyst: Well, what was the rule I told you? Or what did I say was your job?

Silberschatz and Curtis (1993) subsequently applied the foregoing repeated measures, single-case research design to the study of testing behavior in short-term therapy. Their participants, drawn from the Mt. Zion Brief Therapy Research Project, were self-referred and screened to ensure their suitability for brief treatment. Patients were seen by an independent evaluator for an initial intake interview and for follow-up interviews on completion of treatment, 6 months after termination, and 1 year after termination. The therapists, experienced clinical psychologists and psychiatrists who represented different schools of brief dynamic therapy, were unaware of the hypotheses being investigated. The research was conducted after the completion of treatment.

The two cases studied (Gary and Diane) were judged to be therapeutically successful by the patients themselves and by the therapists and the independent evaluators. Diane was seen for 16 sessions and Gary for 12. The following procedures were followed in both cases: (a) A control-mastery case formulation was prepared using a revised version of Caston's (1986) method for achieving interrater reliability (Curtis, Silberschatz, Sampson, & Weiss, 1994; Curtis, Silberschatz, Sampson, Weiss, & Rosenberg, 1988). The formulations included a description of the patient's problems and history, the patient's goals for therapy, the central pathogenic beliefs impeding the attainment of those goals, ways in which the patient was likely to test the therapist, and insights most likely to be helpful to the patient. (b) A two-step process was used to identify key tests. Five experienced clinicians read verbatim transcripts of each therapy session and identified all possible instances of testing. Each potential test was then excerpted from the transcript, randomized, and presented to a new group of four judges who used the case formulation to select the key tests (i.e., instances of the patient's testing a central pathogenic belief). Forty-five key tests were identified in the case of Gary and 69 in the case of Diane. (c) The same judges used a 7-point Likert scale to rate the degree to which the therapist passed or failed the patient's tests. (d) Three-minute segments of patient speech immediately before and after each test were excerpted from the transcript and presented in randomized order to three new groups of judges who rated the segments on the Experiencing Scale (Klein et al., 1970), the Boldness Scale (Caston et al., 1986), and the Relaxation Scale (Curtis et al., 1986). For both patients, test passing was significantly correlated with increased experiencing immediately following each test. The semipartial correlations between the mean test-passing scores and the mean residualized gain scores for experiencing were .35 ($p < .01$) for Diane and .40 ($p < .01$) for Gary. Only Diane, however, displayed significant positive correlations between test passing and increased boldness ($r = .45$, $p < .01$) and relaxation ($r = .37$, $p <$ .01). In addition to assessing the immediate impact of passed and failed tests, the investigators measured the cumulative impact of the therapist's passing or failing tests by averaging, for each hour, the therapist scores and the residualized shift scores for experiencing, boldness, and relaxation. The mean therapist scores for each hour were correlated with each of the mean patient shift scores for that hour. The same pattern of significant correlations emerged, indicating that sessions in which the therapist received higher test-passing scores were characterized by more indications of therapeutic progress. Thus, the therapist's reaction to tests has not only an immediate effect on the patient's functioning but a cumulative effect as well.

Three other testing studies were carried out on a 16-session short-term therapy that had an unsuccessful outcome (the case of Fran). Fifty-eight key tests were identified using the procedures described above. Bugas (1986) had three judges apply a measure of adaptive regression to the 5-min segments of patient speech that immediately preceded and followed each key test. Bugas adapted Holt's (1977) Adaptive Regression Scale (which was designed for measuring primary process manifestations and their control on the Rorschach test) for use with transcript material. Bugas found a significant positive correlation ($r = .54$, $p < .01$) between passed tests and adaptive regression, indicating that the patient had more controlled primary process material after passed tests. Kelly (1986) applied an electronic measure of anxiety, the long-term voice spectrum (LTVS), to the pre- and posttest audio segments of patient speech. The LTVS systematically analyzes acoustic components of speech that correlate highly with stress, emotion, and psychopathology. Kelly obtained a significant negative correlation ($r = -.62$, $p < .01$) between passed tests and the LTVS measure of anxiety, indicating that the patient's anxiety level immediately dropped after passed tests. Linsner (1987) developed a case-specific insight rating scale (the Plan Compatibility of Insight Rating Scale [PCIRS]) to measure the level of pro- and antiplan insight displayed in each of the pre- and posttest segments of patient speech. He obtained a significant positive correlation ($r = .52$, $p < .01$) between test passing and the PCIRS, indicating that the patient developed more useful insight immediately after a key test was passed. Linsner also found that proplan insights were associated with a higher level of ego control (over primary process material) and a lower level of anxiety. The PCIRS correlated positively with adaptive regression ($r = .58$, $p < .001$) and negatively with the LTVS ($r = -.28$, $p < .05$). These three studies demonstrate that even in an unsuccessful treatment (in which the therapist is failing the majority of the patient's tests), there is still a lawful relationship between passed and failed tests and immediate signs of patient progress or the lack thereof.

Linsner (1987) discussed the following example of a passed test:

> **Test segment.** (The patient, who recently separated from her husband shortly after having his child, has just visited his parents.)
>
> Patient: Yeah, yeah. I know they didn't know what to say (about their son's marital difficulties), but you still gotta try and talk about it since we were all thinking about it. So I was kind of depressed when I first went there, you know, because I had been there five other times before with Stan, but actually I had the best time that I ever had this time, you know. You know I decided I was going to have a good time too. I just feel like I'm really in touch now with the power to make things turn out good for myself you know. I mean at first it was sort of an effort to think positively but now it's really kind of easy. I almost feel guilt because I feel so good. And —you know things that go on around me, I mean I can sympathize with them but I don't—they don't bring me down, so—I just—
>
> Analyst: Why do you suppose you should feel guilty about feeling so good?
>
> Patient: Why should I feel guilty?
>
> Analyst: What's the crime?
>
> **Post-test segment**
>
> Patient: (Pause) I don't feel like there's a crime but it's just that I don't know. . . . I mean, I don't really feel guilty, but I feel like I should, you know what I mean? I just . . . I don't know. But everybody I talk to about how good I feel, they are real happy about it. They are real happy for me, and they are real supportive of it. Some people

might get down on it and think that I was just being egotistical or whatever, but the people that care about me are really glad to see it. And I feel real good because it's not something I'm faking, you know what I mean? I really feel that I have that strength inside, and I don't feel like . . . well, I tend to be a sort of moody person, so I was always afraid . . . well, I feel good now, but the next mood I'm going to crash you know, but I don't feel that way anyway. I just feel like I can do anything, you know, and I don't feel that other people can necessarily drag me down.

Commentary. The patient is posing a transference test that draws on past experiences with her mother. She is reporting an important accomplishment—that of overcoming her guilt at being better off than her husband—and is feeling proud of herself. She is testing to see if the therapist will support her attempts to master her guilt, or whether the therapist, like her mother, will be dour and pessimistic about her ability to succeed. Had the therapist remained silent, his intent would have appeared ambiguous and his support for her in question. Had he questioned the lifting of her depression and guilt, for example by interpreting along the lines that her feeling good was a defense against sadness at losing the relationship, he would have recapitulated her mother's lack of confidence in the patient's ability to advance, and confirmed associated beliefs that she must fail (i.e., remain depressed and helpless) in order to maintain the relationship with important parental figures (i.e., the therapist).[4]

Pro- and Antiplan Intervention Studies

Therapists not only help patients by passing their tests but they also facilitate the therapeutic process through their interventions. Interventions that help patients disconfirm their pathogenic beliefs and move toward their therapeutic goals are considered to be "proplan"; interventions that reinforce a patient's pathogenic beliefs and thereby impede therapeutic progress are considered to be "antiplan." Proplan interventions generally increase patients' feelings of safety in the therapeutic relationship and help them feel more entitled to pursue their goals. Antiplan interventions do the op-

---

[4]From Linsner (1987, pp. 168–169). Reprinted with permission of the author.

posite. For a full exposition of the various ways interventions can help or impede patients in their efforts to carry out their plans, see Weiss (1993).

The first empirical study that we know of of the immediate effect of pro- and antiplan interventions (Caston et al., 1986) was based on the first 100 hr of Mrs. C.'s analysis. Caston (1986) developed a procedure for diagnosing Mrs. C.'s unconscious plan with good rater agreement. The resulting plan formulation was used by four clinical judges to reliably assess the plan compatibility (how pro- or antiplan each intervention was) of 81 randomly selected analytical interventions. Another group of four judges reliably assessed the patient's level of insight and degree of boldness immediately before and after each intervention. Caston et al. tested the hypothesis that proplan interpretations would be followed by immediate increases in insight and boldness, whereas antiplan interventions would be followed by the opposite. Their results only partially supported their hypothesis. There were significant positive correlations between plan compatibility and boldness ($r = .37$, $p < .005$) as well as insight ($r = .47$, $p < .005$) across the range of proplan interventions, but there was no relationship between plan compatibility and insight or boldness across the range of antiplan interventions. These findings suggest that Mrs. C. was helped by proplan interventions but not measurably set back by antiplan interventions.

An intervention study by Bush and Gassner (1986), using the last 114 hr of Mrs. C.'s analysis, examined how the patient's resistance to termination was affected by the analyst's termination interventions. Their research used the analyst's detailed process notes because the latter part of the analysis had not yet been transcribed. They expected to find a lawful relationship between the plan compatibility of the analyst's termination interventions and the patient's feelings about termination because the interventions selected for study were all highly relevant to the patient's plan for termination and spanned a wide range of pro- and antiplan interventions. They also were interested in comparing the treating analyst's understanding and a control-mastery understanding of Mrs. C.'s resistance to termination. For the treating analyst, Mrs. C.'s resistance to termination was primarily a defense against loss and renunciation. The plan formulation prepared by the investigators considered Mrs. C.'s resistance to termination to be primarily a defensive reaction to her fear of hurting the analyst by wishing to leave him and establish her independence.

The following procedure was used to test the investigators' hypothesis. All interventions that bore on termination were included in the study. Four experienced therapists familiar with CMT were given a plan formulation for the last 14 sessions and asked to rate 112 termination interventions on a 7-point plan compatibility scale. Plan compatible interventions conveyed the idea that the analyst would not be hurt by the patient's leaving and no longer needing him. Two other judges applied a 5-point Attitude Toward Termination Scale to segments of patient speech before and after each termination intervention. This scale assessed the patient's feelings of readiness for, or opposition to, termination. Both sets of judges achieved good rater reliabilities (.80 and .83). The immediate effect of the analyst's termination interventions was measured by correlating the mean plan compatibility scores with the mean residualized Attitude Toward Termination scores. The obtained correlation ($r = .44$, $p < .0001$) strongly supported the hypothesis that Mrs. C. would feel more ready to terminate after proplan interventions and more resistant to termination following antiplan interventions.

To assess how the patient's attitude toward termination fluctuated with the plan compatibility of the analyst's termination interventions over longer time periods, we averaged patient and analyst scores over 19 blocks of six sessions each. The correlation between the pooled scores for the therapist's interventions and the pooled ratings of the patient's attitude toward termination for the 19 blocks of sessions was .66 ($p < .01$), indicating that the patient's resistance to termination fluctuated in tandem with the plan compatibility of the analyst's interventions. Over time, the analyst's interventions became progressively more proplan and the patient felt increasingly ready to terminate.

Bush and Gassner (1986) described two testing sequences from the last 100 hr that illustrate the patient's way of working on overcoming her resistance to termination:

> We will describe here two interrelated tests that Mrs. C. simultaneously and successfully carried out with the analyst over a block of 10 sessions (the first 10 of the last 100 hours of her

analysis). The first test involved an attempt to disconfirm her belief that the analyst desperately needed her to remain dependent upon him and involved with him. She carried out the test by claiming that she did not feel ready to terminate and by repeatedly asking if she could rescind the termination date or continue seeing the analyst after termination on a once-a-week basis. The second test involved a form of turning passive into active in an attempt to disconfirm her unconscious belief that she was cruelly rejecting and abandoning the therapist by terminating her analysis. She carried out this test by accusing the analyst of heartlessly rejecting and abandoning her. The ostensible rationale for this accusation was that if the analyst really cared about her, he would actively oppose her termination instead of agreeing to it.

The analyst passed both tests by acting perfectly comfortable with the patient's demands and accusations. In other words, he acted as though it was reasonable and appropriate for her termination to proceed as scheduled even though she was expressing painful feelings of rejection and requesting a postponement. He never responded to her questions about the possibility of changing the termination date or continuing to see him on a different basis after termination. Moreover, he told her that she was trying to manipulate him into letting her stay on by attempting to make him feel guilty and sorry for her.

Following this testing sequence the patient started to feel better, to express feelings of readiness for termination, and to become aware of thoughts about the analyst dying as a consequence of her leaving.[5]

Another series of studies demonstrated the ability of the plan concept to predict patients' immediate reactions to an important subclass of interventions, namely interpretations. Three brief audio-recorded therapy cases were randomly selected from the Mt. Zion Brief Therapy Research Project. The three patients were similar with respect to the severity and nature of their problems. They were each diagnosed as suffering from chronic neurotic depression and inhibitions. The therapists had specialized training in short-term dynamic therapy and held different psychoanalytic orientations. The patients selected for study represented a range of outcomes: excellent, good, and poor.

---

[5]From Bush and Gassner (1986, p. 404 [Appendix 26]). Reprinted with permission.

The initial study (Fretter, 1984; Silberschatz et al., 1986) examined whether the dimension of plan compatibility could predict a patient's immediate reaction to the therapist's interpretations (interpretations were considered to be interventions that attempt to convey insight). It also attempted to compare the predictive power of the plan compatibility concept with the predictive power of category of interpretation (transference vs. nontransference) using a typology devised by Malan (1963, 1976). For each case, four clinical judges read the entire verbatim transcript and categorized every therapist intervention (i.e., all therapist comments) as an interpretation or a noninterpretation, depending on whether it added an emotional content beyond what the patient had already said. Following Malan, all interpretations were then further categorized as transference or nontransference depending on whether they were directed at the patient's feelings about the therapist or the therapy.

To assess the plan compatibility of the therapists' interventions, it was necessary first to prepare reliable control-mastery case formulations (also referred to as "plan formulations") following the method described by Curtis et al. (1988, 1994). This type of case formulation specifies the patient's therapeutic goals, the pathogenic beliefs that inhibit the patient from pursuing those goals, tests that the patient is likely to pose, and insights that the patient may find useful. A team of five experienced clinicians prepared each case formulation on the basis of the intake interview and the first two therapy sessions. The average interjudge reliabilities for the components of the patients' plan formulations were .89 for goals, .90 for pathogenic beliefs, .82 for tests, and .86 for insights.

The procedure for assessing the plan compatibility of the therapists' interpretations entailed excerpting all interpretations from the verbatim transcripts and presenting them in random order to different groups of control-mastery judges (so that they would not be influenced by order effects or by the patient's subsequent reactions). For each case, four to six judges used the patient's plan formulation to assess the therapist's interpretations on the 7-point Plan Compatibility of Interventions Scale. Each judge worked independently. The reliability coefficients (coefficient alphas) of the mean plan compatibility ratings for the three cases ranged from .85 to .89.

The Experiencing Scale (Klein et al., 1970) was used to assess the patient's immediate response to the therapist's interpretations. Three- to 5-min speech segments immediately before and after each interpretation were excerpted from the transcripts and presented in randomized order to six raters trained in the use of the Experiencing Scale. The raters worked independently and did not know the therapist's interventions or the outcome of the treatments. The reliability coefficients of the mean experience ratings for the three cases ranged from .80 to .86. Residualized gain scores were used to measure shifts in experiencing following each interpretation.

The data analysis was conducted as follows: To assess the immediate effects of pro- and antiplan interpretations, we correlated plan compatibility ratings with residualized experiencing scores on a case-by-case basis. The resulting correlations were significant for all three cases (Case 1, $r = .54$, $p < .001$; Case 2, $r = .28$, $p < .01$; and Case 3, $r = .25$, $p < .05$). To gauge the cumulative impact of pro- and antiplan interpretations across sessions, we averaged the plan compatibility scores and residualized experiencing scores for each session (the number of sessions varied between 12 and 14). The correlations between those hourly mean scores also were significant (Case 1, $r = .78$, $p < .01$; Case 2, $r = .54$, $p < .05$; and Case 3, $r = .57$, $p < .05$).

These results clearly demonstrate that the plan compatibility of interpretations had both an immediate and a cumulative impact on patient progress in the manner prescribed by CMT. Proplan interpretations tended to be followed by increases in experiencing. Decreases in experiencing tended to follow antiplan interpretations. There also was suggestive evidence that therapeutic outcome was related to the overall level of plan compatibility of the therapist's interpretations. Among the three cases studied, the patient with the best outcome received the highest percentage (89%) of proplan interpretations, the patient with the second best outcome received the second highest percentage of proplan interpretations (80%), and the patient with the poorest outcome received the lowest percentage of proplan interpretations (50%).

The data concerning the differential therapeutic effectiveness of transference versus nontransference interpretations were analyzed in three ways. In the first analysis, t tests were used to compare shifts in experiencing after transference and nontransference interpretations. For two patients, there were no significant differences between the two types of interpretations on the residualized experiencing scores. For the third patient, there was significantly more experiencing after nontransference interpretations. In the second analysis, the proportion of transference interpretations per session was correlated with the mean-per-hour residualized experiencing scores. For two of the cases, there were no significant correlations between the proportion of transference interpretations and mean residualized experiencing. For the third case there was a high negative correlation ($r = -.81, p < .005$) between transference interpretations and residualized experiencing, indicating that for this patient transference interpretations were far more antiplan than nontransference interpretations. (If nontransference material is incorrectly interpreted to be a manifestation of unconscious transference feelings, the patient may feel that the therapist cannot tolerate being left out of the patient's emotional life.) In the third analysis, another series of t tests was performed using only proplan transference interpretations and proplan nontransference interpretations. Again, there were no significant differences in residualized experiencing after proplan transference and proplan nontransference interpretations. The investigators concluded that plan compatibility of interpretations has a predictable therapeutic effect but that the categorical distinction between transference and nontransference interpretations does not.

The preceding findings were reinforced by subsequent research (Fretter, Bucci, Broitman, Silberschatz, & Curtis, 1994) that added two additional measures of therapeutic progress to the study described earlier. Broitman (1985) had nine experienced clinicians apply the seven Morgan (1977) Patient Insight Scales and a Global Insight Scale (Broitman, 1985) to the same pre- and postintervention segments that had been previously rated for experiencing. The coefficient alpha rater reliabilities for the insight scales ranged from .81 to .95. Bucci (1987) had three judges apply the Referential Activity Scale to the same pre- and postintervention segments. The reliabilities of the judges' ratings ranged from .65 to .75. The Referential Activity Scale measures how well intellectual awareness is integrated with sensory and emotional experiences.

The previously described data analyses were repeated using the two new measures of patient progress (insight and referential activity). The results were essentially identical to those previously reported. The plan compatibility ratings of the therapists' interventions correlated significantly with residualized insight (Case 1, $r = .45$, $p < .01$; Case 2, $r = .32$, $p < .05$; and Case 3, $r = .35$, $p < .05$) and referential activity (Case 1, $r = .25$, $p < .05$; Case 2, $r = .32$, $p < .05$; and Case 3, $r = .34$, $p < .05$) for all three patients. The only significant differences in patient progress after transference versus nontransference interpretations were in the direction of patients' showing more signs of progress after nontransference interpretations. When plan-compatible transference interpretations were compared with plan-compatible nontransference interpretations (using t tests), there were no significant residualized differences in insight or referential activity. These findings lend further support to the explanatory and predictive power of the plan concept and challenge the special therapeutic importance that has often been assigned to transference interpretations in psychoanalytic therapy.

Evidence that the plan compatibility of the therapist's interventions affects outcome in short-term therapy was obtained by Norville, Sampson, and Weiss (1996). They used seven patients from the Mt. Zion Brief Psychotherapy Research Project for whom plan formulations had been prepared. Two judges independently identified all therapist statements that could be considered interpretations in Hours 1, 5, 8, 11, and 14. Interpretations were defined as interventions that were explanatory in nature, that suggested an emotional meaning beyond what the patient had said, or that were hypothetical constructions.

All interventions identified as interpretations by both judges (who had 90% agreement) were extracted from the verbatim transcripts and rated for plan compatibility by different sets of judges, each of whom worked independently. The reliability coefficients for the mean plan compatibility ratings for each case ranged from .83 to .92. Each patient also was evaluated on a patient-specific outcome measure called "Plan Attainment." The plan attainment measure was developed by Nathans (1988; Silberschatz, Curtis, & Nathans, 1989) to assess the degree to which patients achieve their goals for therapy. Groups of four experienced clinicians rated each patient for plan attainment at the conclusion of therapy and at the 6-month follow-up interview. Each judge read the patient's pretherapy interview, the patient's plan formulation, and the posttherapy interview. The interrater reliabilities averaged .73 for the plan attainment ratings at the end of therapy and at the 6-month follow-up.

The data were analyzed by correlating the mean plan compatibility ratings with the global plan attainment scores at termination and at the 6-month follow-up. For the sample of seven cases, both correlations were significant at the .05 probability level (one-tailed). Plan compatibility of the therapist's interpretations correlated .69 with plan attainment at termination and .70 with plan attainment 6 months after termination. These results strongly suggest that plan compatibility of therapeutic interpretations influences long-term as well as immediate therapeutic outcome in brief psychotherapy.

Conclusion

The studies we have described demonstrate the feasibility of conducting rigorous, quantitative research on the therapeutic process and scientifically testing fundamental assumptions about the nature of unconscious motivation and thinking. Our findings do not support Freud's early conception of an unconscious mind that is governed by the pleasure principle, operates in accordance with primary process modes of thinking, and is dominated by primitive instinctual impulses that continually seek discharge without regard to external reality. Our findings instead support a model of the unconscious that contains powerful adaptive motives and is governed by considerations of safety and danger (the reality principle).

Our research also supports the assumptions that psychopathology stems from trauma-born pathogenic beliefs and that patients unconsciously make plans for mastering their problems by testing the therapist to disconfirm their pathogenic beliefs. Patients' unconscious plans for mastery can be inferred from the initial sessions of a treatment and used as a guide for understanding their testing and formulating helpful interventions. Patients make progress in therapy to the extent that the therapist passes their tests and intervenes in proplan ways. Conversely, they are set back by antiplan interpretations and interventions that fail their tests. Unlike classical psychoanalysis, which leads one to focus on patients' resistances to treatment, our theory leads to a collaborative model of the therapeutic process in which the therapist works with patients to pass their tests and support their goals. Giving consideration to what patients are trying to accomplish leads to a different experience of the therapeutic relationship than focusing on what patients are trying to avoid. Our findings provide clear support for the hypotheses that patients are unconsciously motivated to lift their repressions, overcome their inhibitions, and acquire insight into their pathogenic beliefs. Moreover, they will strive to accomplish these things on their own (i.e., unaided by the therapist's interpretations, as long as the therapist passes their tests).

Control-mastery therapists follow their cases in a manner similar to the research designs we use to study the effects of passed and failed tests and pro- and antiplan interventions. We form hypotheses about our patients' therapeutic goals and the pathogenic beliefs that prevent their attainment. We then develop a therapeutic stance that will help disconfirm patients' pathogenic beliefs, and we use their responses to our interventions to gauge whether we are being pro- or antiplan and are passing or failing the patient's tests. In this manner, the theory helps us stay closely attuned to our patients, correct for our mistakes, and be maximally helpful. To date, CMT has been successfully applied to a wide range of patients and a variety of therapeutic modalities (long- and short-term therapy, individual and group therapy, and child and adult therapy).

CMT provides an integrated model of mind, personality development, psychopathology, and therapy (Weiss, 1971, 1990b, 1993; Weiss et al., 1986). The theory leads to testable predictions about the therapeutic process and has a growing empirical body of evidence to support it. We hope that the research that we have presented will be replicated by other investigations. Such replications would provide an additional basis for viewing our reported findings with confidence.

References

Broitman, J. (1985). Insight: The mind's eye—An exploration of three patients' processes of becoming insightful. *Dissertation Abstracts International, 46.* (University Microfilms No. 85-20425)

Bucci, W. (1987). *Instructions for scoring referential activity (RA) in transcripts of spoken narrative texts.* Unpublished manuscript, Derner Institute, Adelphi University, Philadelphia.

Bugas, J. S. (1986). *Adaptive regression and the therapeutic change process.* Unpublished doctoral dissertation, Pacific Graduate School of Psychology, Menlo Park, CA.

Bush, M., & Gassner, S. (1986). The immediate effect of the analyst's termination interventions on the patient's resistance to termination. In J. Weiss, H. Sampson, & the Mt. Zion Psychotherapy Research Group (Eds.), *The psychoanalytic process: Theory, clinical observation and empirical testing* (pp. 299–320). New York: Guilford Press.

Caston, J. (1986). The reliability of the diagnosis of the patient's unconscious plan. In J. Weiss, H. Sampson, & the Mt. Zion Psychotherapy Research Group (Eds.), *The psychoanalytic process: Theory, clinical observation and empirical testing* (pp. 241–255). New York: Guilford Press.

Caston, J., Goldman, R. K., & McClure, M. M. (1986). The immediate effects of psychoanalytic interventions. In J. Weiss, H. Sampson, & the Mt. Zion Psychotherapy Research Group (Eds.), *The psychoanalytic process: Theory, clinical observation and empirical testing* (pp. 278–298). New York: Guilford Press.

Curtis, J. T., Ransohoff, P., Sampson, F., Brumer, S., & Bronstein, A. (1986). Expressing warded-off contents in behavior. In J. Weiss, H. Sampson, & the Mt. Zion Psychotherapy Research Group (Eds.), *The psychoanalytic process: Theory, clinical observation and empirical testing* (pp. 187–205). New York: Guilford Press.

Curtis, J. T., Silberschatz, G., Sampson, H., & Weiss, J. (1994). The plan formulation method. *Psychotherapy Research, 4,* 197–207.

Curtis, J. T., Silberschatz, G., Sampson, H., Weiss, J., & Rosenberg, S. E. (1988). Developing reliable psychodynamic case formulations: An illustration of the plan diagnosis method. *Psychotherapy, 25,* 256–265.

Dahl, H. (1978). A new psychoanalytic model of motivation: Emotions as appetites and messages. *Psychoanalysis and Contemporary Thought, 1,* 373–408.

Fretter, P. B. (1984). The immediate effects of transference interpretations on patients' progress in brief psychodynamic psychotherapy. *Dissertation Abstracts International, 46.* (University Microfilms No. 85-12112)

Fretter, P., Bucci, W., Broitman, J., Silberschatz, G., & Curtis, J. (1994). How the patient's plan relates to the concept of transference. *Psychotherapy Research, 4,* 58–72.

Freud, S. (1953a). The interpretation of dreams. In J. Strachey (Ed. and Trans.), *The standard edition of the complete psychological works of Sigmund Freud* (Vol. 4, pp. 339–627). London: Hogarth Press. (Original work published 1900)

Freud, S. (1953b). Papers on technique. In J. Strachey (Ed. and Trans.), *The standard edition of the complete psychological works of Sigmund Freud* (Vol.

12, pp. 83–171). London: Hogarth Press. (Original work published 1911–1915)

Freud, S. (1953c). Papers on metapsychology. In J. Strachey (Ed. and Trans.), *The standard edition of the complete psychological works of Sigmund Freud* (Vol. 14, pp. 105–259). London: Hogarth Press. (Original work published 1914–1916)

Freud, S. (1964). Inhibitions, symptoms, and anxiety. In J. Strachey (Ed. and Trans.), *The standard edition of the complete psychological works of Sigmund Freud* (Vol. 20, pp. 257–269). London: Hogarth Press. (Original work published 1926)

Gassner, S., Sampson, H., Weiss, J., & Brumer, S. (1982). The emergence of warded-off contents. *Psychoanalysis and Contemporary Thought, 5,* 55–75.

Gassner, S., Sampson, H., Weiss, J., & Brumer, S. (1986). The emergence of warded-off contents. In J. Weiss, H. Sampson, & the Mt. Zion Psychotherapy Research Group (Eds.), *The psychoanalytic process: Theory, clinical observation and empirical testing* (pp. 171–186). New York: Guilford Press.

Gottschalk, L. A. (1974a). The application of a method of content analysis to psychotherapy research. *American Journal of Psychotherapy, 28,* 488–499.

Gottschalk, L. A. (1974b). Quantification and psychological indicators of emotions: The content analysis of speech and other objective measures of psychological states. *International Journal of Psychiatric Medicine, 5,* 587–610.

Gottschalk, L., & Gleser, G. (1969). *The measurement of psychological states through the content analysis of verbal behavior.* Berkeley: University of California Press.

Holt, R. R. (1977). A method for assessing primary process manifestations and their control in Rorschach responses. In M. A. Rickers-Ovsiankina (Ed.), *Rorschach Psychology* (pp. 263–315). New York: Krieger.

Horowitz, L. (1979). On the cognitive structure of interpersonal problems treated in psychotherapy. *Journal of Clinical and Consulting Psychology, 47,* 5–15.

Horowitz, L. M., Sampson, H., Siegelman, E. Y., Wolfson, A., & Weiss, J. (1975). On the identification of warded-off mental contents: An empirical methodological contribution. *Journal of Abnormal Social Psychology, 84,* 545–558.

Kasl, S. V., & Mahl, G. F. (1965). Disturbance and hesitation in speech. *Journal of Personality and Social Psychology, 1,* 425–433.

Kelly, T. (1986). *Voice stress measure and therapists' interventions.* Unpublished manuscript.

Klein, M. H., Mathieu, P. L., Gendlin, E. T., & Kiesler, D. J. (1970). *The experiencing scale: A research and training manual* (Vols. 1 and 2). Madison, WI: Psychiatric Institute, Bureau of Audio Visual Instruction.

Linsner, J. P. (1987). *Therapeutically effective and ineffective insight: The im-*

mediate effects of therapist behavior on a patient's insight during short-term dynamic therapy. Unpublished doctoral dissertation, City University of New York, New York, NY.

Mahl, G. F. (1956). Disturbances and silences in the patient's speech in psychotherapy. *Journal of Abnormal Social Psychology, 53,* 1–15.

Mahl, G. F. (1959). Measuring the patient's anxiety during interviews from "expressive" aspects of his speech. *Transaction of New York Academy of Science, 21,* 249–257.

Mahl, G. F. (1961). Measures of two expressive aspects of a patient's speech in two psychotherapeutic interviews. In L. Gottschalk (Ed.), *Comparative psycholinguistic analysis of two psychotherapeutic interviews* (pp. 91–114). New York: International Universities Press.

Malan, D. H. (1963). *A study of brief psychotherapy.* London: Tavistock.

Malan, D. H. (1976). *Toward the validation of dynamic psychotherapy: A replication.* New York: Plenum.

Morgan, R. W. (1977). *The relationships among therapeutic alliance, therapist facilitative behaviors, patient insight, patient resistance, and treatment outcome in psychoanalytically oriented psychotherapy.* Unpublished doctoral dissertation, University of Miami, FL.

Nathans, S. (1988). Plan attainment: An individualized measure for assessing outcome in psychodynamic psychotherapy (Doctoral dissertation, California School of Professional Psychology, 1988). *Dissertation Abstracts International, 49,* 08B.

Norville, R., Sampson, H., & Weiss, J. (1996). Accurate interpretations and brief psychotherapy outcome. *Psychotherapy Research, 6,* 16–29.

Sampson, H. (1989). How the patient's sense of danger and safety influence the analytic process. *Psychoanalytic Psychology, 7,* 115–124.

Shilkret, C., Isaacs, M., Drucker, C., & Curtis, J. T. (1986). The acquisition of insight. In Weiss, J., Sampson, H., & the Mt. Zion Psychotherapy Research Group (Eds.), *The psychoanalytic process: Theory, clinical observation and empirical testing* (pp. 206–217). New York: Guilford Press.

Silberschatz, G. (1978). Effects of the analyst's neutrality on the patient's feelings and behavior in the psychoanalytic situation (Doctoral dissertation, New York University, 1978). *Dissertation Abstracts International, 39,* 3007B.

Silberschatz, G., & Curtis, J. (1993). Measuring the therapist's impact on the patient's therapeutic progress. *Journal of Consulting and Clinical Psychology, 61,* 403–411.

Silberschatz, G., Curtis, J., & Nathans, S. (1989). Using the patient's plan to assess progress in psychotherapy. *Psychotherapy, 26,* 40–46.

Silberschatz, G., Fretter, P., & Curtis, J. (1986). How do interpretations influence the process of psychotherapy? *Journal of Consulting and Clinical Psychology, 54,* 646–652.

Waite, T. (1993). *Taken on trust.* San Diego, CA: Harcourt Brace Jovanovich.

Weiss, J. (1971). The emergence of new themes: A contribution to the psychoanalytic theory of therapy. *The International Journal of Psychoanalysis, 52,* 459–467.

Weiss, J. (1989). The nature of the patient's problems and how in psychoanalysis the individual works to solve them. *Psychoanalytic Psychology, 2,* 105–113.

Weiss, J. (1990a). The centrality of adaptation. *Contemporary Psychoanalysis, 26,* 660–676.

Weiss, J. (1990b, March). Unconscious mental functioning. *Scientific American,* 103–109.

Weiss, J. (1993). *How psychotherapy works: Process and technique.* New York: Guilford Press.

Weiss, J. (1997). The role of pathogenic beliefs in psychic reality. *Psychoanalytic Psychology, 14,* 427–434.

Weiss, J. (in press). The patient's unconscious plans for solving his problems. *Psychoanalytic Dialogue.*

Weiss, J., & Sampson, H. (1986). Testing alternative psychoanalytic explanations of the therapeutic process. In J. Masling (Ed.), *Empirical studies of psychoanalytic theories* (Vol. 2, pp. 1–26). New Jersey: The Analytic Press.

Weiss, J., Sampson, H., & the Mt. Zion Psychotherapy Research Group. (1986). *The psychoanalytic process: Theory, clinical observation and empirical testing.* New York: Guilford Press.

Author Index

Numbers in italics refer to listings in reference sections.

Subject Index

About the Editors

Robert F. Bornstein is Professor of Psychology at Gettysburg College. He received his PhD in clinical psychology from the State University of New York at Buffalo in 1986. Bornstein has written many articles on perception without awareness and has published extensively on the antecedents, correlates, and consequences of dependent personality traits. He coedited (with Thane Pittman) *Perception Without Awareness: Cognitive, Clinical and Social Perspectives* (1992); coedited (with Joseph M. Masling) *Psychoanalytic Perspectives on Psychopathology* (1993), *Empirical Perspectives on Object Relations Theory* (1994), *Psychoanalytic Perspectives on Developmental Psychology* (1996), and *Empirical Perspectives on the Psychoanalytic Unconscious* (1998); and is the author of *The Dependent Personality* (1993), a comprehensive review of the empirical literature on dependency.

Joseph M. Masling is Emeritus Professor of Psychology at the State University of New York (SUNY) at Buffalo. He received his PhD in clinical psychology from Ohio State University in 1952; he was director of clinical training at Syracuse University (1959–1964) and chairperson of the Department of Psychology at SUNY–Buffalo (1969–1972). Masling has written numerous articles on interpersonal and situational variables influencing projective tests and has published widely on the empirical study of psychoanalytic concepts. He edited the first three volumes of the series Empirical Studies of Psychoanalytic Theories (1983, 1986, 1990) and coedited (with Robert F. Bornstein) Volume 4, *Psychoanalytic Perspectives on Psychopathology* (1993); Volume 5, *Empirical Perspectives on Object Relations Theory* (1994); Volume 6, *Psychoanalytic Perspectives on Developmental Psychology* (1996); and Volume 7, *Empirical Perspectives on the Psychoanalytic Unconscious* (1998).